D1591101

POWER FAILURE

DIANA DILLAWAY

POWER FAILURE

Politics, Patronage, and the Economic Future of Buffalo, New York

59 John Glenn Drive
Amherst, New York 14228–2197

Published 2006 by Prometheus Books

Inquiries should be addressed to
Prometheus Books
59 John Glenn Drive
Amherst, New York 14228–2197
VOICE: 716–691–0133, ext. 207
FAX: 716–564–2711
WWW.PROMETHEUSBOOKS.COM

10 09 08 07 06   5 4 3 2 1

Library of Congress Cataloging-in-Publication Data

Dillaway, Diana.
    Power failure : politics, patronage, and the economic future of Buffalo, New York / Diana Dillaway.
        p. cm.
    Includes bibliographical references and index.
    ISBN 1–59102–400–5 (hardcover : alk. paper)
    1. Buffalo (N.Y.)—History. 2. Buffalo (N.Y.)—Politics and government.
3. Buffalo (N.Y.)—Economic conditions. I. Title.

F129.B857D55 2005
974.7'97—dc22

2005038058

Printed in the United States of America on acid-free paper

This book is dedicated with love

to David, always,

and

to Roger, Ted, Carolyn, Hana, and Lucy,

the future.

CONTENTS

ACKNOWLEDGMENTS   **11**

INTRODUCTION   **13**

How the Book Came About   17
Whom the Book Is For   18
Methodology   19
My Approach   20
The Book's Structure   22
Note   23

**CHAPTER 1. ECONOMIC
TRANSFORMATION**   **25**

Leadership That Counted   27
Interests of Capital   28
Five Factors of Decline   30
Notes   38

CHAPTER 2. CULTURE AND POWER   40

Neighborhood Culture and Political Power   43
Political Party as Power   45
Economic Power   47
Three Elites Who Figured Prominently in Events   49
Elite Business Organizations   50
On Opposite Sides of the Street   53
On Opposite Sides of the Issue   54
Notes   56

CHAPTER 3. ON THE EDGE: THE 1960S   58

Economic Story   59
    Passing of the Old Guard to the Younger Establishment   59
    Urban Renewal   64
    The Campus Location Debate   66
    The Rapid-Transit Initiative: Part One   73
    A Football Stadium and the Urban Development Corporation   77
Political Story   79
    The Mayors   79
    Federal Decertification and the Housing Code   83
    Disregard for Planning: Exceptions or the Rule?   85
Community Story   88
    Bringing Alinsky   88
    Model City Program   93
Conclusion   97
Notes   101

CHAPTER 4. CRISIS: THE 1970S   106

Economic Story   107

Decline in the Steel Industry 111
Cascading Closures 115
After the Fall: Labor's Cooperation 117
A Downtown Strategy 118
Manufacturing's Initiative: Striving for a Role 119
The Erie County Industrial Development Agency 121
A Step Toward Partnership 126
The Rapid-Transit Initiative: Part Two 129
Political Story 133
Cordial Relations, and Change 133
An Old-Style Mayor under Pressure 134
Restructuring Political Power 135
An Independent's Race for Mayor 138
The Politics of Planning, 1978 and Beyond 140
Community Story 142
Power and Legalities: School Integration 144
Other Cases 145
The BUILD Organization 148
Conclusion 151
Notes 154

CHAPTER 5. NEW LEADERS, OLD STRUCTURE: THE 1980S   **158**

Economic Story 159
A New Elite Leadership 161
New Strategies 163
Downtown 167
Labor's Initiatives 169
Behind the Scenes 170
The Horizon Waterfront Commission—The Late 1980s 172
The Rapid-Transit Initiative: Part Three—End of the Line 175
Political Story 177

Core Issue 178
Community Story 180
   Community Development Block Grant Funds 182
   Housing 183
Conclusion 184
Notes 191

CHAPTER 6. TOWARD REGIONALISM

Recap 195
Intimations of Regional Governance 197
Projects and Initiatives 201
   A Strategic Plan 202
   Waterfront 203
   Peace Bridge 203
Politics and Neighborhoods 205
   A Financial Control Board 208
   Pending Issues 210
Regional Consolidation and Buffalo's Future 211
   Regionalism: The Hopes and the Fears 214
Notes 218

ECONOMIC TABLES **221**

BIBLIOGRAPHY **229**

INDEX **249**

ACKNOWLEDGMENTS

I can begin only by thanking the people of Buffalo who gave me the opportunity to tape long interviews with them and, in some cases, keep up an extended dialogue, while others faithfully sent clippings and memos on events of particular interest. The first round of interviews took place in 1986–87, which meant I arrived in Buffalo at a time of high energy and development downtown led by the new leadership, the Group of Eighteen, and Mayor Jimmy Griffin. More than thirty members of the major business, political, nonprofit, and community leadership circles (both old guard and new) agreed to meet with me. This was a good time to begin because of the apparent excitement everyone displayed. In 1996 I began a new series of interviews, continuing up to the time of this writing.

Time offered perspective to a complex story, leading to many more questions and the need to substantiate stories through additional interviews, newspaper accountings, and studies. The input and encouragement of many people have helped me get to this point, the publishing of what I consider to be a serious effort to understand and write Buffalo's political-economic-urban story.

So it is with great appreciation I give special thanks for the expertise, advice, and, in some cases, the many perusals of manuscript to the following: my husband, David Olsen; Michael Teitz; G. William Domhoff; Manuel Castells; Carmen Concepcion; Peter Wiley; Alan Kellock; Mark Dowie; Richard Flacks; Edward Blakely; Elizabeth Mueller; Tim McKeown; Ted Putnam; the staff and researchers at the Buffalo and Erie County Public Library, special collection; Laura Schiefer at the Buffalo and Erie County Historical Society; Albert Riess at the Buffalo Courier-Express Collection, Buffalo State College Archives; and a friend who is dearly missed, the late Carol O. Hoyt. I feel fortunate to have worked with Bettina Nicely Johnson, my California editor, who is such a strong and intelligent editor.

Editor in chief Steven L. Mitchell at Prometheus Books challenged me to argue my case more fully and bring the research and story up to 2006, for which I am grateful. And everyone else at Prometheus with whom I have had contact has made this last stage a very positive experience. Thank you all.

For friendship and genuine caring about my progress over the years, my thanks go to cousins Wendy and Murray Warner; Emmajane Olsen; Alan Davis and Mary Lou D'Auray; Dean Anderson and Connie Michelson; Meg and Adam Gottstein; Natalie Shiras; Gail Putnam; Wendy Schwartz; Linda Salsedo; Lilly Medina and Juan Gonzales; and other friends in our Ventura community who, I'm sure, tired of asking how the book was coming along!

And to those I love most, thanks for sticking with me on this project: David, with whom all things are possible, and our immediate family—to whom the book is dedicated—as well as Dana, Don, Dillon, Erin, Ursula, Anya, Kylan, Deborah, Alan, Meira, Ben, Linda, and Panos.

INTRODUCTION

Holding economic or political power is no guarantee of providing leadership in the true sense of the word. Effective leaders bring people together around a common cause or problem, listen to opposing points of view, and seek consensus whenever possible. Leadership takes courage and a willingness to risk change. The city of Buffalo did not have such a leader among those who were in positions of great power when it faced its greatest challenges in the 1960s and 1970s.

In fact, Buffalo's business, political, and community leaders—with some rare but interesting exceptions—were zealous in their defense of the status quo in the face of an economic slowdown and, later, spiraling decline. This case study tells the story of the leadership failure that left Buffalo in the difficult situation it is in today. Moreover, the city planning that did occur, a pile of studies and excuses generated by leadership organizations, replaced what was really needed: namely, a progressive coalition of competing interests with a mandate to action.

But action was not to be, as even the elite could not coalesce around a plan. (Some attempts came close, but arguments regarding who participated or what got funded led to crippling divisions.)

Competing and selfish individual interests among Buffalo's most powerful business leaders subverted the planning process and the potentially transformative outcomes. Some interesting innovations in downtown revitalization were finally put together in the 1980s, but the polarized political process by which they were executed undermined development efforts.

In the 1950s, by contrast, a group of financial elites and manufacturers worked in proactive partnership with the mayor and city council. They researched the leadership efforts of other cities and founded a nonprofit organization to spearhead urban development. But by the mid-1960s, these men had either retired or moved away, and other bankers came to the fore.

Two of these bankers wielded tremendous political and economic power as members of the establishment and as governmental appointees to head state agencies in Buffalo and New York. These financial powerhouses, along with the owner of the city's major newspaper, used their exceptional power—as individuals or in combination—quietly in boardrooms, at their social clubs, and on the editorial page. Events over the course of nearly two decades support the proposition that underlying all discussions having to do with downtown development was an implicit demand that nothing change the elite way of life. It logically followed, then, that any plan proposing to bring tens of thousands of students and university personnel into the city's downtown to a new university campus—with its mix of people and progressive ideas, not to mention hundreds of acres of built infrastructure—would be opposed. The resistance to new infrastructure did not bode well for plans for a rapid transit system to connect the university campus with downtown. The entrenched opposition to change by wealthy Buffalonians lent legitimacy to statements by some who considered Buffalo's leadership to be radically conservative, perhaps even racist, at a time when cities around the country were building progressive urban development alliances.

When the city faced bankruptcy in 1975 and the regional

economy continued to worsen, outsiders seized opportunities to invest in downtown, with its low cost of land, its declining costs of labor, and the low cost of capital. These investors, allied with a new generation of local elite, maneuvered to assume control of key business organizations. With each success, this new leadership (the Group of Eighteen) initiated a national search for a seasoned professional to direct the organization. Unlike earlier times when outsiders were "welcomed but not accepted," these newcomers replaced former establishment leaders at the top of the power pyramid and were invited into elite social clubs as well. Several of Buffalo's younger generation of establishment families and a number of local entrepreneurs worked in proactive collaboration with these newcomers as they initiated development strategies.

Political leaders, for their part, continued to use the power of electoral politics as a kind of jobs program for their respective communities. Historically, the office of mayor brought patronage and jobs to his respective ethnic community. As a result, reelection was foremost in each sitting mayor's mind, making him a follower by nature and subservient to elite interests. Leaders of the Polish, Irish, and Italian communities took turns heading a powerful machine of party bosses and hundreds of elected block and zone leaders who, when their time came, delivered thousands of patronage jobs. Over the years, the machine saw to it that ethnic communities had their turn at running a mayoral candidate on the Democratic ticket. Life was circumscribed by the neighborhood parish, district schools, the machine, and work in the steel and flour mills and assorted heavy manufacturing.

Until the economic crisis forced them to do otherwise, Buffalo's leaders did what they could to protect the status quo. Political parties protected their "machines" of patronage and power. Economic leaders protected elite positions of social prestige and economic power and, at times, used their powerful positions as leverage in land-based and industrial attraction decisions. Labor's successful track record using militant power, especially in the steel and automotive industries, dissuaded them from seeking new and innovative approaches that might modernize production processes.

The African American community on the city's East Side (adjacent to the urban core), by contrast, demanded change. They overwhelmingly favored a downtown campus. They supported plans for a rapid transit system to link downtown with the university once it was determined that the campus would be built in the suburbs. They also hoped someday to have their mayor. But during urban renewal, black neighborhoods were ripped apart for clearance, forcing families from single-family and duplex dwellings into high-rise public housing projects. The construction of an expressway destroyed the East Side's most beautiful tree-lined avenue and cut the black community's most affluent middle-class neighborhood in two.

The city's racial divide left black professionals, entrepreneurs, and workers to fend for themselves. Politically, the African American community remained outside the patronage systems of the Italian, Irish, and Polish mayors. Other isolating factors included segregated schools and the inability to move into white neighborhoods. The black community was not on the elite leadership's radar screen, other than in its worries about riots. Not until the community hired Chicago-based Saul Alinsky to help organize Build United, Independence, Liberty and Dignity (BUILD), and the Model City Program got underway, did elite leaders briefly take note. A number of meetings occurred, but, overall, black professional leaders continued to be excluded from leadership organizations, and the planning processes remained unchanged. The story at this point sounds like that of most other cities. The difference lies in the details of the relations of power, attitudes of leadership, and the process of planning.

I have focused this study on four decades of massive change. Both the economic decline in the 1960s and the loss of the steel industry through the 1970s represent a crisis that brought unimaginable change to Buffalo. The irony here is readily apparent. Major change—the very thing Buffalo's leadership hoped to avoid—

came, in part, as a result of the leadership's unwillingness to risk change.

This, then, is a book about a city's structure of power and its diverse interests, planning processes, and initiatives. As a case study, it includes three perspectives: economic, political, and community. As a story, it is one told from the unique perspective of the major players and written by, perhaps, the only urbanist who could gain access to the information. Nearly seventy of Buffalo's most powerful leaders tell their story here.

HOW THE BOOK CAME ABOUT

I am a product of Buffalo, born in 1941. As a child, I spent summers at the family farm on the American shore of Lake Erie, some fifteen miles south of the city. From the beach, we could see the distant orange, fiery glow of molten slag pouring into the lake from steel mills at the eastern end of the lake. This scene provided us with a kind of beauty and filled us with awe. I loved the area's natural wonders, the industrial power, the tree-lined streets, and architecture of what is now my former home.

Unfortunately, I have seen Buffalo transformed from a steel city and bustling port—a nexus of processing and transshipment, transforming grains to flour and beer, animal hide to leather, timber to paper, iron ore to steel—to a city that lost just about everything, including its one-hundred-year-old steel industry, and had to start over. Most distressing was the city's inability to mobilize around a vision and a plan.

Decades after watching the steel mills' fiery displays, while my peers were enjoying three-martini lunches in the mahogany-paneled and wainscoted dining rooms of our social clubs, I began to question why my city continued to lose economic ground and why the city's leaders from different ethnic communities did not work more closely together. I became intrigued, as I had heard very little discussion on the pressing issues of the day. It was not until years later when I launched my research and began to interview these same establishment leaders—many of whom I had grown up knowing and later met at parties, black-tie dinners, and debutante balls—that I found my way into the political battles and community struggles of the day.

For more than eight years, I have interviewed, taped, and reinterviewed as questions loomed or needed illumination. My taped interviews probed for details of the city's most divisive debates. It became clear that the issues were complex but had three key elements:

- power, with its structure, vested interests, relations, and attitudes;
- planning, with its processes and ability to be inclusive or exclusive; and
- initiatives, which can be proactive, reactive, bold, or risk-averse.

Power should bestow the ability to cobble together alliances—overt and covert— and push initiatives through. Yet powerful individuals or organizations, as previously noted, do not always provide leadership. In fact, people with the greatest power often do not lead at all. Or, when they do lead, it may be in one of several ways: they may refuse to share power; they may "sell" it; or they may use it selfishly to benefit only themselves.

WHOM THE BOOK IS FOR

As a case study, the book is one of a kind, built on an insider's access to a city's economic and social establishment. It has many audiences. First, academics will find this book a comprehensive case study, based on information from previously unavailable sources. I have divided each chapter in a way that those interested in only economic issues (e.g., transportation and housing) or community development can readily find them. As a whole, the story is as much sociological and cultural as political and economic, extending beyond a presentation of quantifiable data. The story derives from the leaders themselves, providing "real-world" dimensions to the story of political, economic, and sociological change. As a result of this layered and diverse approach, the Buffalo story provides a richly complex case study for students studying urban affairs, city and regional planning, political economics, sociology, and community and economic development. Second, practitioners in city and regional government, economic development agencies, industrial development corporations, transportation departments, and community organizations all can take something important from the story. This book represents a call to cities and regions to reexamine their own issues of power and planning. Third, loyalists who have remained in Buffalo through the difficult years, or who have returned, can gain insight through a comprehensive historical perspective. It can close the door on past woes and generate new understandings for the future.

METHODOLOGY

My research methodology was inspired by the work of Manuel Castells, international sociologist and urban planner, with whom I studied at Berkeley. Some questions he asked are these: How do structurally defined actors produce and reproduce cities through their conflicts, domination, alliances, and compromises? How do spatial forms, economic functions, political institutions, and cultural meaning combine themselves in a process of urbanization that we view as the outcome of social struggles and bargaining? How do class, sex, race, ethnic origins, cultural tradition, and geographical location contribute to the formation of the social actors that intervene in the urban scene? How does such a pattern of relationships vary in different historical contexts? What is the role of urban movements within urban social change?

MY APPROACH

The Buffalo story is a study of form (the structure of power), function (the process of planning), and outcomes (initiatives). I interviewed in person and taped my first round of thirty-five of Buffalo's leaders in 1987, while at the University of California. In 1996 I resumed the process, traveling to Buffalo multiple times for additional interviews and research at the Erie County library. I conducted intervening interviews by phone, with permission to tape. While I guaranteed anonymity to those interviewed, I am listing their affiliations.

Business executives worked for American Steamship; Rich Products; Freezer Queen; Buffalo Forge; Computer Task Group; Rigidized Metals; M&T Bank; Marine Midland Bank; Buffalo Savings Bank; Goldome Bank; the *Buffalo Courier-Express*; the *Buffalo Evening News*; Roswell Park Medical Center; Robert Traynham Coles, Architects, P.C.; the Greater Buffalo Development Foundation; the Buffalo Chamber of Commerce; the Erie County Industrial Development Agency; the Amherst Industrial Development Agency; and the Buffalo Niagara Partnership; other interviewees include an AFL-CIO Council president, partners in two prestigious law firms, and three industrial and commercial real estate brokerages.

Political leaders were a sitting mayor; aides to Mayors Frank Sedita (first and second terms), Chester Kowal, Stanley Makowski, and James Griffin; a commissioner of urban renewal; a director of city planning; three commissioners of community development; an official of the New York State Urban Development Corporation; members of the Common Council, including a council president; consultants to the Niagara Frontier Transportation Authority; a city transit planner; New York State legislators (one for thirty years); a US Congressman; and Erie County legislators.

Community leaders came from the Clarkson Institute/Center, the State University of New York at Buffalo, Buffalo State College (a president), the Area Committee for Transit, the Mass Transit Advisory Committee, the Committee for an Urban University of Buffalo, the Model City Program, the Citizens Advisory Committee to Mayor Sedita, the NAACP, the East Side Community Organization, and BUILD; there were also some community activist leaders. (In some cases, these organizations no longer exist, but I was able to speak with former directors.)

I conducted twenty in-person leadership interviews in Pittsburgh, Pennsylvania, to form a basis of comparison with another city of similar size and industrial base. Interviews included the retired presidents of the University of Pittsburgh and Mellon Bank, industrial development investors, and black community leaders, among others.

I promised anonymity to all those interviewed despite the fact that anonymous sources pose problems—including problems of accountability and trustworthiness. To address these concerns, I cross-check material. I use newspaper articles, annual reports, and studies to establish the historical and chronological framework. I corroborate events through additional interviews and material in the press. If discrepancies remain, such as differing reports of conversations between two principals, I use material only when the described behavior fits an established pattern. I also consider the source itself. When I use hearsay, I call it what it is. Finally, I have written Buffalo's story with some restraint. It is not a tell-all book, but I do not shy away from events when they are unflattering if I feel they contribute to a deeper understanding.

Unique as Buffalo's story is, in many respects it is every city's story of powerful interests jockeying for position, with ill-defined planning processes and a power structure dominated by banking and land-based interests.[1] Yet every city's leadership faces a set of constraints arising from its unique history, attitudes, needs, and resources.

THE BOOK'S STRUCTURE

Organizing the book by decades means that stories about the economy, political regimes, and neighborhoods continue as one part of each chapter. This allows the reader to view these strands of the story concurrently—just as it happened. It is a bit more work for the reader, keeping the story's thread in mind between chapters. But it is possible to simply flip between the chapters to follow the economic, political, or community strands. Each chapter flows from economic considerations (affecting industry and downtown), to political actions (revolving around the mayor, the city council, and especially contentious political issues), to community involvement (with emphasis on inner-city neighborhoods).

The book's primary focus is on the first three decades (1960–1990) of political, economic, and social transformation. Chapter 1 provides the historical economic context so important to understanding any "rust belt city." Chapter 2 lays out Buffalo's cultural mind-set and dominant power players. Chapter 3 delineates events that foretold, and in some cases might have subverted, Buffalo's economic decline. Chapter 4 describes the loss of industry, the first steel closures, the impending bankruptcy, the new political leadership, and community programs. Chapter 5 centers on how the newcomers catalyzed change and worked with the mayor to develop new strategies for economic development and how the city council's role was nearly extinguished. The final chapter recaps the critical decisions taken in earlier decades with their sorry effects on the present circumstances, showing the trend toward regional consolidation. Eight economic tables at the end of the book provide industrial and economic statistical understanding.

NOTE

1. John Logan and Harvey Molotch, *Urban Fortunes: The Political Economy of Place* (Berkeley and Los Angeles: University of California Press, 1987).

Chapter One

ECONOMIC TRANSFORMATION

B uffalo's location had much to do with its rise as an economic power. The village was founded in 1803 at a place where Lake Erie, the Niagara River, and the Buffalo River converge, about thirty miles from Niagara Falls. The Great Lakes and rivers provided a massive water network for trade, and the Falls in later years provided the first large-scale hydroelectric power in the United States. In 1825 Buffalo became the western terminus of the newly dug Erie Canal, which opened a direct route from Buffalo to the Hudson River and down to New York City. Because travelers also used this route to travel west from New York City to Lake Erie, the canal stimulated interest in the recently opened Northwest Territories, bringing new settlers to the territories and into Buffalo on their way. But the important flow was from west to east: raw materials arrived in Buffalo to be processed or manufactured into products before being sent to markets on the eastern seaboard and beyond.

All sorts of agricultural produce, especially grain, traveled through Buffalo on its way to eastern, southern, and European markets. By 1910 Buffalo had become the greatest grain port in the world and a mill port second only to Minneapolis. With the rise of the railroads, Buffalo became the second-largest railroad terminus in the United States, with seven direct lines connecting Buffalo to six East Coast cities; with six direct lines west to Chicago, Kansas City, Omaha, St. Louis; and with two direct lines to Pittsburgh. By 1910 Buffalo had also become one of the country's great centers of transshipment. Massive iron ore deposits on the shores of Lake Superior began to be exploited; large freighters were being built; the Sault Ste. Marie Canal was enlarged. These advances led to the development of a more diverse economy, with a boom in steel-related manufacturing. The increase in iron ore shipped to Buffalo by the end of the 1880s put Buffalo into the steelmaking big league, rivaling Pittsburgh. In large part, Buffalo's great rise as an economic powerhouse was driven by the harnessing of power at Niagara Falls. In 1883 George Westinghouse created an illumination system for the city of Niagara Falls using AC current. When methods for transmission were figured out in 1896, Buffalo became part of the growing power grid from Niagara Falls and received the first long-distance transmission of electricity for commercial purposes in the United States.[1]

Despite ongoing cheap electricity and a high demand for steel products during World War I and World War II, economic indicators revealed a fundamental economic slowdown. Between 1960 and 1980, Buffalo's rate of growth in overall employment in the two-county area slowed to 1.3 percent—with a loss of 21 percent in manufacturing jobs, the area's dominant sector. (See table 6 in the appendix.) Many Buffalonians attributed manufacturing's decline primarily to two events—the opening of the St. Lawrence Seaway (1959) and the loss of the steel industry (1971–1983). Time provides a broader perspective, however, and I will argue that five factors contributed to Buffalo's economic decline. First, there were changes in the transportation routes for raw materials and goods. Second, the steel industry faced competition and technological change. Third, Buffalo lost home-owned industries and corporate headquarters. Fourth, the labor movement brought about militant labor demands and high wages. Fifth, Buffalo's political and economic organizations competed for power to the detriment of the city. These five factors set the stage for many, if not all, of the challenges facing Buffalo in the second half of the twentieth century.

LEADERSHIP THAT COUNTED

> We should be like Samuel Wilkinson in 1820 . . . a visionary (and councilman) who convinced the city fathers to spend $5,000 of the city's treasury to have the farmers bring boulders down to the foot of the Buffalo River to build the first breakwall . . . which took an extraordinary amount of courage and vision . . . [believing that] the Erie Canal should end here.
>
> —A local attorney and judge

Between 1860 and 1910, Buffalo's population grew more rapidly than that of almost any city in the United States. Nevertheless, area leaders worried that the local economy remained vulnerable, concentrated in commerce and in need of diversification to protect against economic downturns.[2] In an effort to diversify the economy, elite leaders emphasized production processes that used raw materials brought through the Great Lakes from Midwestern states, such as iron ore for steel, grain for flour milling, hides for tanning, and lumber for furniture and building. They also advocated "linkage" industries, that is, industries that further developed Buffalo's products. For example, manufacturers used steel produced in Buffalo to build the earliest automobiles (such as the 1901 Pierce Arrow), railroad cars and rails, and military equipment. By the century's end, Buffalo had become one of the ten largest cities in the country.

Buffalo's economic growth and diversification was because, in large part, of the vision of business and political leaders and the bold initiatives they enacted to retain and attract industry. Leaders collaborated to improve the waterfront for flour mills. They dredged the canal so it would be deep enough for railroad and iron foundry needs. They built a sewer line for one steel company, and,

in 1900, they gave three hundred acres to Bethlehem Steel to build
its plants outside the city's jurisdiction. And they granted rights of
way to nearly twenty railroad lines that covered over six hundred
miles of city streets and roads along the waterfront.[3] Before the turn
of the century, Buffalo prepared to challenge Pittsburgh as the iron
and steel capital of the country. In 1891 one daily paper wrote that
Pittsburgh "has had its day. Making iron is a matter of geography."[4]
By 1910, Buffalo had become the greatest grain port in the world.
Flour processing, lumber processing, the production of paper products, tanning, and brewing all played major roles in this commercial entrepôt.

INTERESTS OF CAPITAL

It is well documented that the capitalist leaders who controlled
banking and utilities in Buffalo began, as early as the 1920s, to
invest in New York City, Cleveland, and Minneapolis, among other
cities. This meant not only a significant exit of wealth out of local
industry but also a loss of influence; because these leaders did not
sit on local company boards, they could neither directly influence
the activities of these boards nor direct the boards' commitments to
the city. In addition, as in other parts of the country, a large number
of local corporations merged or were acquired by other firms.
Thirteen local banks participated in mergers in 1919; in 1927 six
additional banks merged. In 1922 Bethlehem Steel bought out
Lackawanna Steel.

The early stages of this economic transformation brought short-
term gains and long-term losses to the area. The buyouts produced
record profits and levels of production throughout the 1920s. Yet
slowing rates of population growth (from a 19 percent population
gain in the 1910s to only a 13 percent gain in the following decade)
indicated a weakening of the local economy. Cleveland and Detroit,
two great industrial rivals, surpassed Buffalo in size and industrial

output in the 1930s, indicating that Buffalo's economy was less competitive.[5]

By the 1930s, giant corporations owned the region's largest steel companies, and multinationals owned twelve automobile factories in the area. In addition, most of the lumber, tanning, soap, and brewing businesses that had at one time contributed to a diversified and stable economic base had all but disappeared. According to one study, "the growing level of regional dependency was not immediately apparent as the demands of the Second World War produced an unprecedented spurt in heavy industrial activity."[6] Buffalo's citizenry found it reassuring to focus on what remained there, which was still impressive: thirteen trunk-line railroads, an active port, and large corporations (each employing more than a thousand people in the two-county area), including American Machine and Foundry, Westinghouse, Twin Coach, Remington-Rand, Wurlitzer, Bethlehem Steel, Republic Steel, Colorado Fuel and Iron, American Standard, Allied Chemical and Dye, General Motors, Ford Assembly Plant, General Mills, Trico Products, Buffalo Forge, Dupont, Union Carbide, Bell Aircraft, and Hooker Chemical.

Change was gradual—imperceptible to those not wishing to see it. The two world wars and the Korean War provided local economic booms and obscured the underlying patterns of declining rates of growth. One critical piece of information was available to analysts, however. When the country was not in war production, Buffalo's local economy took significant dives, as in 1946, when eighty thousand people became unemployed almost overnight. The biggest single loss was when Curtiss-Wright closed its operation and moved to Columbus, Ohio, shutting forty thousand people out of their jobs. Over the next decade, Buffalo lost DuPont, Hooker Chemical, Allied Chemical and Dye, Spencer-Kellogg (the largest linseed oil product company in the United States), Bell Aircraft, and others.

The city's leadership apparently rationalized the economic downturns and the departures, denying any cause for concern. Rather than promote strategies for a peacetime economy, the elite leadership argued that cheap power, excellent waterways and transportation facilities, and large numbers of skilled and unskilled workers mitigated whatever problems existed. With the onset of the Korean War, one newspaper exclaimed, "Buffalo's industrial machine once again packs a mighty war punch."[7]

FIVE FACTORS OF DECLINE

1. Transportation

Buffalo's success as a city and region depended on its location. The Great Lakes offered nearly one thousand miles of seaway from the Midwestern heartland to Buffalo. In the other direction, the opening of the Erie Canal in 1825, followed by the railways, made it possible to ship directly from Buffalo to New York City and the eastern seaboard—affecting the flow of goods as well as capital between these two centers of commerce. Buffalo had access to every major port in an area constituting ninety-five thousand square miles. The canal's importance in accessing eastern markets lasted only forty years, but this mattered little as railroads quickly became the most efficient means of transport. Between 1864 and 1868, transportation on the canal declined by 75 percent as shippers of flour and grain turned to rail for delivery to mills and markets. Buffalo continued to flourish, with the latest in loading and unloading mechanisms for grain elevators and the latest processing operations. Industry took advantage of electricity generated at Niagara Falls, at that time the largest and cheapest power source in the world.

But clearly the commercial water routes were critical to Buffalo's economic health. With the opening of the Panama Canal in 1910, Buffalo's economy took its first major hit. Now a less expensive water route connected eastern and western markets, providing an alternative to the old centers of transshipment, such as Buffalo, with their rising transfer costs.[8] From that point onward, Buffalo's position as a center of commerce and transshipment began to slip, and Buffalo's rate of economic growth began its long decline. Even the twenty rail lines could not adequately compensate for the lost volume of shipping and the related commerce, a loss that undermined the regional industry.

Forty-five years later, in 1959, the St. Lawrence Seaway opened. Before reaching Buffalo, ships now headed north through the Welland Canal to Lake Ontario en route to the St. Lawrence Seaway and markets on the East Coast, as well as foreign markets. It was not long until the city's usefulness as a center of transshipment all but ended. Buffalo's flour industry—for over a century locally controlled—diminished. Then, in the 1970s, "the regional steel, auto and chemical industries, including such important firms as General Motors, Ford, Bethlehem, and Republic Steel, started a massive retreat resulting in the loss of more than 50 percent of the 49,000 jobs in these sectors."[9] For more than half a century, then, driven by transportation shifts, the area economy engaged in a fundamental restructuring. There was a shift in ownership (with outside interests taking control of manufacturing) and a shift in industrial mix (with the diverse economy giving way to a predominantly steel-related manufacturing base).

2. The Steel Industry

By the 1940s, Buffalo's concentration in steel and steel-related industries made the regional economy susceptible to changes in the steel industry itself. Aging plants and equipment undermined the industry in an increasingly competitive world economy that was driven by new technologies, affected by national subsidies, and subject to overcapacity. For Buffalo, the problems were exacerbated by the fact that management decisions on critical issues (such as labor disputes, investments, and tax strategies) were made at corporate headquarters that were located elsewhere.

According to the literature, both the supply of and demand for steel played a role in the decline of the domestic steel industry. When, following World War II, the US industry entered its "mature stage"—with its aging facilities and old production processes—the domestic supply of steel put onto the world market decreased markedly. In fact, the United States had become a net importer of steel by 1959.[10] This led to a consensus among US steelmakers that the domestic industry might not be able to meet international demands for steel. "Virtually everyone concerned with the steel-making industry is plagued by a single, overriding question: Where are we going to get the additional capacity to satisfy demand for steel by 1980?"[11] Such forecasts encouraged foreign countries to build "showcase" factories and spurred the domestic industry to increase capacity to meet projected demand. As foreign competitors entered the market, subsidized heavily by their governments, a new problem developed: worldwide excess capacity resulting both from the increased supply (as new plants came on line) and from the new materials (alternatives to steel) that began to erode demand for steel.

The oil crisis in 1973 became "a watershed for steel producers worldwide. By 1975 it was obvious that the world economy had a substantial excess steelmaking capacity. The steady growth and sustained profitability that had characterized steel production in the previous decade gave way to uncertainty about the prospects for a rebound and pessimistic forecasts of future demand."[12] To make matters worse, foreign competitors were able to offer cheaper and sometimes higher-quality steel. Europe and Japan (having had to rebuild after World War II) were making gains with a new technology called the Basic Oxygen Furnace (BOF) rather than the old, much less efficient large open-hearth furnaces. A few US steelmakers adopted this technology, but most were reluctant to invest given the worldwide overcapacity. Some argued that by the 1970s the domestic steel industry had entered the stage of obsolescence—and negative profits—having left behind the stage of oligopolization and barons. In order for domestic production to compete, US steelmakers had to promptly upgrade facilities and employ new technologies. This was the situation faced by Buffalo's steel producers and Buffalo's leaders.

The demise of steel in the Buffalo area occurred over a decade while leaders watched in disbelief. The first jolt took place in 1971 when Bethlehem Steel laid off nine thousand people, half of its entire workforce. In 1978 the company cut thirty-three hundred more workers, and in 1980 the Bethlehem Steel Foundry closed. The next year, they closed the twelve-inch bar mill and its lime plant. Republic Steel followed by closing its South Park plant, affecting twenty-five hundred jobs. The final blow came in 1983 when Bethlehem Steel closed its basic steelmaking operation, leaving a skeletal force of fifteen hundred workers at the bar and galvanizing mills and coke factory. In all, the Buffalo area lost nearly seventy thousand jobs in steel and linkage industries between 1970 and 1984.[13] By 1975 Buffalo was experiencing a full-blown economic crisis.

3. Absentee Management

The disappearance of locally owned industries and Buffalo's subsequent reliance on multinational corporations contributed to the city's economic decline. These multinational corporations became centers of concentrated capital, with the power to make decisions overriding local interests or even regional considerations. Studies indicate that corporate decisions to locate in one place or another, or to expand or contract, are based on strategic planning influenced by global political and economic concerns and not regional advantages.[14] Absentee ownership and the new global economy complicated the ability of local leaders to create or attract new firms and shape Buffalo's economic destiny.

By the 1970s, the majority of existing large firms had become branch operations. Along with having less corporate attention to local needs, the city suffered when leading corporate families were persuaded to move their investments, residences, and allegiances to more cosmopolitan centers, resulting in what could be called phil-anthropic disinvestment or, seen another way, a form of cultural redlining of lesser centers of business activity.[15] In addition, the strong, local companies that were bought out were often used by the parent company as "cash cows" to be milked for capital investment and expansion elsewhere. Studies have found that outside-owned firms often have fewer links with local businesses. And plant-closing studies in New York State showed that subsidiaries and local operations of larger corporations were far more likely to disinvest than firms that were independent and locally owned. Specific data on the Buffalo Two-County Area of Erie and Niagara between 1965 and 1980 revealed that companies with out-of-town headquarters were twice as likely to close as locally owned companies. Conversely, locally owned firms were more likely to expand.[16]

By 1986, outside forces controlled nearly three-quarters of Buffalo's local and regional economy. Among the largest firms of five hundred or more employees in the eight-county Buffalo region, 69.4 percent were either branches or subsidiaries of nonregional businesses. These branches and subsidiaries employed 77 percent of the region's workforce.

Executives of absentee-managed firms tend to be less engaged in local politics. For this reason, as well as because these local executives are not part of corporate top management, they often are not part of the city's leadership elite. This lack of involvement can be a particular problem in a city where a majority of businesses in the dominant industry have absentee owners, resulting in an under-representation of key interests within the local leadership structure. Economic power becomes severed from political power. Branch executives who do become politically active or part of the local elite often face an unsupportive pool of corporate executives in the national office.[17]

The centralized management structure used by many companies and by the steel industry allowed local managers little room for autonomous decision making. For example, Bethlehem Steel's form of management proved economically and politically ineffective because the top-level management in Pennsylvania remained oblivious to the needs of local managers and labor at the Lackawanna plants in the Buffalo area. During the 1970s, at any one time, six thousand to seven thousand union grievances were pending in Buffalo, and the Lackawanna plants were ranked high in terms of time lost because of strikes. When disputes reached the arbitration stage, according to one insider, corporate representatives "would simply fly in, sweep the local people aside, and decide what was to be done."[18] This out-of-touch style of management lit the fires of labor militance, leading to a combative atmosphere reinforced by the sheer number of workers at the Lackawanna plants.

4. Militant Labor and High Wages

The American steel industry is infamous for its adversarial labor relations. The carnage at the Homestead Works in Pittsburgh, when Henry Clay Frick unleashed his Pinkerton guards to attack striking workers in 1892, set the stage for labor-management struggles well into the next century. In terms of the modern history of the industry, the strike of 1959 represents a critical juncture. It was long and costly.[19]

During the prosperous 1960s, industry leaders avoided strikes by buying labor peace. For example, from 1967 to 1972, the wages of production workers in the Buffalo area increased by 17 percent. And from 1972 to 1977, they increased an incredible 46 percent.[20] By 1984 the Buffalo area's average manufacturing earnings were $11.38 per hour, as compared to New York at $8.08 and Boston at $8.16. Only Detroit beat Buffalo, with hourly wages of $12.53.[21]

Labor, on the other hand, felt the need to protect workers in dangerous industrial sites, the effects of which tended to lower productivity.

The union had fought hard to preserve jobs and protect its workers from arbitrary dismissal by establishing work rules that governed how specific jobs would be completed and by whom. Inherently dangerous work, restrictions of this sort are natural, indeed, necessary. But, whatever the need, it is widely acknowledged that these protections went badly awry—whether viewed from the perspective of management or labor. In far too many instances, productive time for workers in an eight-hour shift was minimal.[22]

Taken together, the high wages and low productivity must have been noted at management headquarters in Bethlehem. Because of the economic crisis, unions in the private sector (in steel and other manufacturing industries) lost much of their clout, and wages went down. Public employee unions, on the other hand, remained relatively unaffected and even grew stronger during this period. By the year 2000, union membership in the Buffalo area stood at 71 percent for government workers—not an insignificant figure.[23] The state's Taylor Law guaranteed powerful collective bargaining rights to government employees and education professionals in these public-sector unions, affording them great workplace power.

Finally, "past practice" standards in the public sector—which looked to precedent in the formulation of workplace policy—left local political leaders little room to make changes that would have enabled them to cut costs. For example, police officers invoked "past practice" standards for police patrols in Buffalo so that two police officers would continue to work together per patrol car, rather than one per car as in many other cities.

5. Competing Realms of Influence

Many different agencies held statutory authority to influence the city's infrastructure and development. In addition to these were the business elite's organizations, such as the Greater Buffalo Development Foundation and the Buffalo Area Chamber of Commerce. Competition, redundancy, and bitter fights between these entities wasted time and financial resources while undermining efforts to develop a coordinated economic development and industrial attraction agenda.

For example, a vision for developing the waterfront area eluded the city because too many discrete entities had partial jurisdiction or economic power over it. These included the City of Buffalo (the Department of Community Development and the Office of Planning), Erie County (the Erie County Industrial Development Corporation and other economic development committees), New York State (the Urban Development Corporation and the Niagara Frontier Transit Authority), the federal government (the Coast Guard), and the elite organizations (the Greater Buffalo Development Corporation and the Chamber of Commerce). According to one urban renewal commissioner I interviewed, the problem was complicated further when—at some point—the city handed over a deed to waterfront property to the Niagara Frontier Transportation Authority, where it was assumed to remain at the time of the interview.

Similarly, strategic planning in the eight-county western New York region proved difficult where roughly seventy-five to eighty public and quasi-public organizations worked on economic development from 1970 to 1985. These included different chambers of commerce, county and subcounty industrial development agencies (IDAs), job-training programs, and other nonprofit corporations with the task of supporting or energizing business. Important as these entities were, they were not as effective as hoped, owing to the lack of coordination. Regional leaders put no coordinating mechanism in place. Without a coordinated or a collaborative approach, turf battles commanded the scene.[24] One study found that the situation "resembles an 'entrepreneurial' economy, but with the public sector agencies playing the role of the entrepreneur and authorities competing to 'cut the best deal' with private sector firms."[25]

Governor Nelson Rockefeller, in the 1960s, tried to remedy this problem by founding the Urban Development Corporation, which could override local zoning and building codes and competing interests in order to move projects along. Yet problems persisted. According to an Urban Development Corporation official, "very powerful political and banking interests" dominated planning in Buffalo.

NOTES

1. Niagara Falls, "History of Power," http://www.niagarafrontier.com/power.html#Sch (accessed April 21, 2004).

2. Edgar Rust, *Metropolitan Areas without Growth* (Washington, DC: Institute for Child Health and Human Development, 1974), p. 40.

3. Mark Goldman, *High Hopes: The Rise and Decline of Buffalo, New York* (Albany: State University of New York Press, 1983), p. 131.

4. Ibid., pp. 127–29.

5. Ibid., p. 222.

6. David Perry and staff, "Ending Regional Economic Dependency: Economic Development Policy for Distressed Regions," rev. ed. (Buffalo: State University of New York, Department of Environmental Design and Planning, 1986), p. 5.

7. Goldman, *High Hopes,* pp. 267–68.

8. *Annual Report, 1929* (Buffalo, NY: Buffalo Chamber of Commerce, 1929), p. 14.

9. Perry and staff, "Ending Regional Economic Dependence," p. 6.

10. Steel Panel Committee on Technology and International Economic and Trade Issues of the Office of the Foreign Secretary, *The Competitive Status of the U.S. Steel Industry: A Study of the Influences of Technology in Determining International Industrial Competitive Advantage* (Washington, DC: National Academy Press, 1985), p. 17.

11. John Strohmeyer, *Crisis in Bethlehem* (Bethesda, MD: Adler & Adler, 1986), p. 100.

12. Roger Ahlbrandt, Roger Fruehan, and Frank Giarratani, *The Renaissance of American Steel: Lessons for Managers in Competitive Industries* (Oxford: Oxford University Press, 1996), p. 16.

13. Buffalo Area Chamber of Commerce, "Buffalo Metro Store/Office/Plant Listing," annual listings for 1981, 1982, 1983, 1984, 1985; Greater Buffalo Chamber of Commerce, "Buffalo Metro Store/Office/Plant Listing," annual listings for 1985, 1986, 1987.

14. David C. Perry and Alfred J. Watkins, "Uneven Development in the USA," in *City, Class, and Capital*, ed. Michael Harloe and Elizabeth Lebas (London: Edward Arnold, 1981), p. 118.

15. John Logan and Harvey Molotch, *Urban Fortunes: The Political Economy of Place* (Berkeley and Los Angeles: University of California Press, 1987), p. 205.

16. Perry and staff, "Ending Regional Economic Dependency," p. 12.

17. Roger Friedland, *Power and Crisis in the City* (New York: Schocken Books, 1983), pp. 34–36.

18. Interview no. 11.

19. Ahlbrandt, Freuhan, and Giarratani, *Renaissance of American Steel*, p. 19.

20. US Bureau of the Census, "Census of Manufacturers, 1967, 1972, 1977."

21. US Bureau of Labor Statistics, "Employment and Earnings" (Washington, DC: 1967, 1972, 1977, 1984).

22. Ahlbrandt, Freuhan, and Giarratani, *Renaissance of American Steel*, p. 20.

23. Fred O. Williams, "Union Town, USA," *Buffalo News*, May 29, 2000.

24. Interview no. 15.

25. Perry and staff, "Ending Regional Economic Dependence," p. 28.

Chapter Two

CULTURE AND POWER

In *Philadelphia Gentlemen: The Making of a National Upper Class*, published in 1958, . . . Baltzell gave us a city that was tightly under the control of a defined coterie whose members blended social and economic prestige with a ruthless efficiency that enabled them to engage in the "exercise of power over other men in making the decisions which shape the ends of a predominantly business-oriented social structure." In other words, Baltzell's people didn't just go to a lot of debutante parties; they also ran the place.

—Nicholas Lemann, "No Man's Town"
New Yorker, June 5, 2000

Digby Baltzell, in his appraisal of the role of Philadelphia's upper class in the 1950s, found that an elaborate social structure reinforced the power and controlling interest held by an economic elite. This was true for Buffalo as well.

Until the 1980s, Buffalo's economic elite was almost without exception white, Anglo-Saxon, and Protestant (WASP). These elites dominated the banking industry along with the businesses closely tied to land-based development, such as real estate, insurance, and law. They ran the major businesses and met together at businessmen's clubs and social clubs, along with family-oriented clubs for tennis, golf, swimming, riding, and even polo.

The ethnic communities had different lines to power. While the WASP elites wielded power by virtue of their control of business and financial institutions, the Irish, Polish, and Italian communities wielded their power through political patronage, especially when one of their own became mayor. The African American community also sought power through political representation, even though no black had been elected mayor. Instead, African Americans were elected to the city council in increasing numbers so that, with one or two white members, they could control the outcome of votes.

Throughout the twentieth century, Buffalo's social and economic leadership coalesced into what became known as "the establishment" or "old guard." As in many eastern industrial cities, where a socioeconomic class became entrenched over generations, establishment leaders continued to hold sway. In Buffalo, descendants of WASP families (some third and fourth generation) constituted the elite leadership. Not until the arrival of outside investors did this begin to change.

But one needed more than economic success to join the elite. It mattered that a person had the right credentials, that the person was white, Anglo-Saxon, and Protestant, sharing the characteristics of those leaders who founded many of Buffalo's earliest financial and commercial businesses. Despite waves of Catholic immigrants from central and eastern Europe and Ireland, it was difficult for non-WASP newcomers, even if successful in business, to join the ranks of elite leaders. This was true as well for Jews, and although an infinitesimal number of Jewish businessmen sat on elite boards, they were not considered part of the WASP establishment. Ethnic Germans were the exception. Many inventive and entrepreneurial Germans arriving in the second half of the nineteenth century, or coming out of the city's Protestant German enclave, were accepted. In fact, they could hardly be ignored. One, a tanner, for example, generated the country's first electricity at Niagara Falls, helping to drive Buffalo's great industrial growth. Others were leaders in manufacturing, brewing, and banking. Still, there were relative levels of acceptance. Nearly a century later, old WASP "bluebloods" could be heard quietly citing the fine distinction in social status between elites of German and Anglo heritage.

In their book *The WASP Mystique*, Richard Robertiello and Diana Hoguet argue that a person does not actually have to be a WASP to be accepted as one, but a person must adhere to WASP qualities and attitudes. One who aspired to join the ranks of the WASP elite had to conform in action and attitude to the prevailing social norm. For example, Buffalo's elites were predominantly conservative in nature, and they championed the status quo ante (believing that the turn of the century to the early 1920s marked the great old days). An individual from another culture or religious background might be accepted as a WASP if he adopted the values of social conservatism. According to *The WASP Mystique*, this was important because "a social conservative . . . feels challenged by progressive intellectual movements."[1] As a social class, this group of people is most concerned with retaining prestige and power. "Power is not something to be complacent about—once it's in place it must always be defended."[2] *The WASP Mystique* also notes that a person is more readily accepted as a WASP after changing the family name to one that sounds Anglo, changing church affiliation, or beginning to wear the appropriate clothes. Having the right qualities meant attending one of the city's prominent Protestant churches (Westminster or Trinity Episcopal). It meant sending children to one of the establishment schools (Nichols School for boys, Buffalo Seminary for girls in town, or one of the eastern boarding schools) and spending the summer on the Canadian or American shore or in horse country in surrounding areas. Men joined the Buffalo Club and Saturn Club; women, the Garret Club. WASP girls and boys went to one hall for ballroom dancing classes; Jewish boys and girls went to another. Daring Catholic boys crashed an occasional party. Wealthy young women became debutantes, while bachelors and families attended the swirl of parties and balls in the debutante's honor. Social prestige revolved around the arts and their boards of directors—the Buffalo Philharmonic Orchestra, the Albright-Knox Art Gallery—and the Buffalo General Hospital on the city's East Side, sponsor of the debutante ball. Such was the situation at the beginning of the 1960s.

NEIGHBORHOOD CULTURE AND POLITICAL POWER

The vitality of Buffalo's ethnic communities revealed itself in distinct neighborhoods. A visitor from California in the 1960s decided to stay in Buffalo based on what he saw.

> It was fascinating to drive through . . . a North Buffalo Jewish neighborhood, an Italian West Side neighborhood, a Polish East Side neighborhood, the German neighborhoods, the Irish South Buffalo neighborhoods . . . [all with their] restaurants and the bars. That was the fascinating part of the city. It gave the city great strengths. It also created a lot of ethnic and racial and political barriers. Back then it was still good and the barriers were manageable. But [with economic decline] what gave the city such strength and character contributed to its downfall. Most decisions today are either racial or ethnic based.[3]

The communities settled and shifted. Early settlement WASPs— led by an economic elite even then—pushed north from what is today the city's downtown, where Lake Erie and the Niagara River merge. They built both elegant and modest homes on large lots. Germans settled at first on the East Side but quickly began to disperse citywide. East European Jews, settling at first on the East Side, moved north beyond the WASPs, while prosperous German Jews tended to live on the West Side. The Irish expanded out from the First Ward—adjacent to downtown between the flour and tanning mills where they worked—south toward the steel mills, in what became known as South Buffalo. By 1900 Polish immigrants who had largely replaced Germans on the East Side, now teeming with manufacturing operations and railroads, continued to move eastward with their increasing numbers. African Americans, too, like so many others, initially settled on the Near-East Side, beginning with seven hundred or so runaway or freed slaves who found a welcoming community and remained. The Italians, arriving late in the nineteenth century, made the lower West Side their enclave. In 1960 census numbers for Erie and Niagara Counties revealed that 114,772 people were foreign-born, making foreign-born immigrants about 9 percent of the region's population. That same year, the black population weighed in at 6 percent (82,910 people) and rose to 10 percent (113,975 people) by 1980.[4]

Each community reflected the values and culture of the old country. A person could live happily in these neighborhoods speaking only his or her native tongue. The Catholics represented nearly 76 percent of Buffalo's total population in the 1980s.[5] Several generations of one family might live on the same street. Each enclave had its own neighborhood pastor, even when community populations overlapped. These enclaves were strong social units, with life revolving around the church, social and political clubs, newspapers and radio stations, and public neighborhood schools. Several generations of one family often worked in the same industry—steel, flour milling, automobile, aircraft, and other heavy manufacturing operations. Canisius College, founded in 1870 by Catholic settlers from Germany, provided a pathway into professional jobs for the sons of factory workers. Some ended up working in city government. These communities, like the WASP establishment, were defenders of the status quo—life as it existed.

In these neighborhoods, "community" and politics were one and the same. Ward committeemen (later district committeemen) were sprinkled throughout the neighborhoods. Political patronage connected whole families to City Hall, and everyone knew everyone. Everything depended on whom one knew and who was in office.

When someone had a problem, that person would meet with the committeeman in a local bar or shop to determine a solution. In the 1960s it was still accepted behavior for the Department of City Parks's employees to pick up paychecks at the neighborhood liquor store owned by the department head.[6] Ward representatives, political bosses, and patronage were the political party's—and each neighborhood's—lifeblood. One longtime West Side resident explained,

> On the West Side, it was [the party boss] and his family who ran the Democratic Club House here, forever. So, if your kid needed a job in the summer, like lifeguard . . . or Dad was out of work at the steel plant because he was on strike against Bethlehem Steel for the entire summer, you went over and he gave you a little chit to take over to the meat market to get some food. There was this little social network there.[7]

These communities were grounded in church and in Democratic Party politics just as the WASP community was grounded in business partnerships, social clubs, and church, though in this case church was simply one element of social cohesion. Rarely did these discrete communities intersect.

POLITICAL PARTY AS POWER

The power of the Republican Party declined in the city and, by the mid-fifties, essentially went to one-party rule. "The Republican Party for all intents and purposes disappeared in the city,"[8] while it strengthened in surrounding areas. As a result, Buffalo elected only one Republican mayor, because of a split among Democratic voters, in thirty years (1960–1990).

Patronage jobs and access to power provided the meat, potatoes, and relishes to the ethnic communities. The Democratic Party controlled the city and placed great importance on positions at all levels of the structure. For example, a candidate might spend thousands of dollars to be elected as a low-level, but powerful, Democratic zone chairperson in the city's neighborhoods. The "machine" was built from the bottom up. Neighborhoods—block by block— elected committeemen. Committeemen, in turn, elected the zone chairmen who represented each district. Zone chairmen, in turn, elected the party chairman. If any Democrat in the city wanted a job, he or she went to Democratic Party headquarters, not City Hall.

The party had many functions. It established positions on issues. Legislators could count on the party and its ranks of workers to shepherd legislation through, twist the appropriate arms, and do battle. The rules of the game were well known, and everyone played his role. Parties provided jobs to the rank and file, with the system acting as a form of job welfare. Politics was the business of communities, and contacts were important. The four legs of Buffalo's political stool were Italian, Irish, Polish, and, later, African American. In contrast, WASPs saw politics as a dirty business, although a number of elite were active in both parties. Until the late 1970s, with one or two exceptions (and probably for reasons of expediency), the WASP community was staunchly Republican.

Power was taken to new heights in 1966 under the leadership of Democratic County Chairman Joe Crangle, who came to power when a group overthrew the sitting chairman, Peter Crotty. According to a top Democratic official, this overthrow was a "truly Shakespearean thing because he was Peter Crotty's right-hand man." Chairman Crangle attracted a new kind of political animal into the party structure and remained in power well into the 1980s. An Irishman, he built a highly effective grassroots organization, at the time "unparalleled in the county." (He later headed the party statewide.) The chairman "used liberal doses of patronage to rebuild the machine in the city, rusty after four years under a Republican mayor. He gradually began replacing the cigar-smoking Polish, Italian, and Irish saloon-keepers and undertakers, who traditionally dominated Buffalo politics, with bright energetic and cocky young college and law school graduates."9

ECONOMIC POWER

Confessed one banker, "Buffalo's business elite has always been dominated by bankers and their lawyers."[10] In fact, as far back as the 1930s, "the lawyers came as close as any group . . . to constituting an aristocracy," which included young Millard Fillmore, among other Buffalo notables.[11] With the banks controlling mortgages, municipal bonds, and commercial lending, a banking coterie existed that went beyond the financial industry. Many professions and industries complementary to banking—in particular, the practice of law, real estate, and insurance—derive a percentage of their work from land-based development, as do banks. It therefore should not be surprising to find attorneys holding considerable power, along with real estate and insurance executives. One example of a banker-attorney partnership manifested in the politically powerful law firm of Diebold-Millonzi, founded by the head of Western Savings Bank and his attorney. One article in the *Buffalo Courier-Express* briefly referenced one of the many activities of the attorney in this partnership: "Buffalonian Robert I. Millonzi, a lawyer, and former State Supreme Court Justice William B. Lawless Jr. were named on Friday to a new Advisory Council to State Democrats."[12]

As law firms went, none was older or more a part of the old-guard establishment than the prestigious firm described in a document relating company history, "A Lawfirm and a City," by Bob Watson, which tells the story of Hodgson, Russ, Andrews, Woods and Goodyear, from 1817 to 1980. No one can doubt the historical role of attorneys among Buffalo's business elite. In their work, bankers, lawyers, insurers, and realtors were linked without seeming to be. Realtors (industrial, commercial, and residential) sold the land for development and the location of industry, which brought business to the banks in the form of commercial and industrial loans. Huge increases in suburban development likewise led to increases in the number of home mortgages and loans. The insurance industry played an integral role, too, insuring the new business operations and homes, as a result of this growth.

Interestingly, the manufacturing industry played a less significant role in Buffalo's leadership—despite the financial benefits it brought to the area and manufacturing's dominance in terms of the numbers of people employed. The "Census of Manufacturers" shows that in 1970 manufacturing employed 172,000 people, as compared with 20,500 in finance, insurance, and real estate (FIRE) combined.[13] In addition, in 1977 the value of output in manufacturing (nearly $10.4 billion, measured by shipments) exceeded that of all other sectors by far.[14]

Manufacturing leaders in general were peripheral to the power elite. To a large extent, the decision to focus on business was their own choice. However, one executive, who moved with a group that could always count on an audience with the shakers and movers when he wanted it, related: "Our fishing camp was a place where the ideas of several manufacturing leaders were developed informally, in a perfect environment. And all of the banking elite were there."[15] In social settings, old-guard manufacturing leaders were every bit a part of Buffalo's establishment and under such circumstances could make their ideas known.

But above all—and central to the story—is the fact that, as one establishment leader put it, Buffalo "was always the fiefdom of the individual elite." Individual interests trumped everything in a city where there were unclear lines of authority and an ad hoc planning process. The setting in which individual interests are able to prevail is best described by William Domhoff in his book *Who Rules America?: Power and Politics in the Year 2000*, where he discusses "social cohesion" as the only rule in the power game.

> The corporate rich are drawn together by bonds of social cohesion as well as their common economic interests. This social cohesion is based in the two types of relationships found in a membership network: common membership in specific social institutions and friendships based on social interactions within those institutions. . . . Social cohesion is greatest when (1) the social groups are seen to be exclusive and of high status, and (2) the interactions take place in relaxed and informal settings.[16]

THREE ELITES WHO
FIGURED PROMINENTLY IN EVENTS

Three individuals from Buffalo's wealthiest families were among those considered not to be "part of the team," according to a close associate of all three. They often acted independently of prominent business organizations, and, when interests converged, they joined in loose liaisons with others to effect designated outcomes. They interacted quietly (a WASP characteristic), using economic and social position in unexpected, and—in some cases—still-unexplained ways. I am not speaking of illegalities here, but of power and the ability to influence.

One banker, considered "an arts buff," was connected at the highest levels of state financial and political power in the 1960s. He sat as chairman of the board of the state's largest banking institution and its only statewide bank holding company. His holdings were less than 1.5 percent, yet "he still managed to control the place," maintained a colleague. He worked with Governor Nelson Rockefeller to form the New York State Council on the Arts and headed its first board. He had direct access to Rockefeller, which meant he had clout at Chase Manhattan. Back in Buffalo, "every lawyer in town [hoped] to get a piece of his estate business. Having zillions of dollars in management fees is a wonderful thing to dangle" when support for an issue was desired. Furthermore, he "held tremendous sway over the owner of the leading newspaper and she over him."[17]

A second important banker headed one of the city's major savings and loans, following his father, who had assumed control in earlier years. In the 1960s, he sat on a number of key commissions and boards, including the State University's board of trustees. He chaired the board of one of the commercial banks, was appointed by Rockefeller to be the first head of the Niagara Frontier Transportation Authority, and accepted the formation of a rapid transit committee for Buffalo. He made common cause with other elites on some of Buffalo's most divisive debates. A colorful figure, he was also considered an effective manipulator, which he would have likely considered a compliment. "Yes, I'm sure he was operating behind the scenes. . . . I've heard he could be a tough character," pointed out a former official of the Greater Buffalo Development Foundation. For years he maintained a close friendship with the financial editor of the *Buffalo Evening News*.

The third elite, the publisher and owner of the *Buffalo Evening News* (until its sale in the late 1970s), was the widow of the grandson of the paper's founder. She retained a somewhat rarefied position among the elite. From the days of President William McKinley on—when the president was to have dined at their residence on the day of his assassination—the family prominently supported the Republican Party.[18] As a woman—a grand one at that who resided a part of each year in Paris—she was unable to discuss issues with her male counterparts at the men-only business clubs. Instead, she worked with, and through, the paper's powerful editor in chief and the paper's editorial page. During the early 1960s, the editor in chief and owner were in close political alliance with the powerful Republican State Senator Walter Mahoney. Owning the largest daily between New York and Cleveland, as well as the majority of television stations in that market, put her in a position of enormous power. Throughout the years, the *News* chose its battles carefully, not wanting to be seen losing on critical issues.

ELITE BUSINESS ORGANIZATIONS: THE GREATER BUFFALO DEVELOPMENT FOUNDATION AND THE CHAMBER OF COMMERCE

Earlier in 1951, another three leaders—one manufacturer and two bankers—founded the forerunner to the Greater Buffalo Development Foundation (GBDF), the Buffalo Redevelopment Foundation.

They claimed to have "patterned" it after the Allegheny Conference on Community Development (ACCD), a nonprofit organization that led efforts for decades in the revitalization of Pittsburgh's Golden Triangle.[19] The CEO of National Gypsum, a man who had moved to Buffalo to head the company, spearheaded its creation with leading figures at the Manufacturers and Traders Trust and Marine Bank because together they were concerned about the city's economic health. The founding coincided with a new federal law that required channeling urban renewal funds through private-sector organizations.

These three leaders saw themselves as men of action who were not beholden to the Chamber of Commerce. Within a short while, the vehicle they had founded (the Greater Buffalo Development Foundation) came to be regarded as a positive counterpart to the Chamber of Commerce, with its much larger and unwieldy membership. "At the start and formation of GBDF, the founder's interest was improvement of Buffalo's housing conditions. [They] researched the potential for private housing rehabilitation, [they] publicized slum housing conditions, helped pass a strict housing code, and joined the City's Board of Redevelopment in initiating the Ellicott urban renewal project."[20]

The foundation's founding industrialist, a personable and hands-on leader, connected well with Buffalo's bankers. He enlisted fifty to seventy-five members, initially, from the financial and business community, raising funds by letter and in person from individuals. This inside group of men and their associates "structurally controlled" the Greater Buffalo Development Foundation through a rotating chairmanship of the board where each bank took its turn. The foundation depended on the financial institutions to raise much of the money, and it always chose bankers as its nominal head, "which made sense to them since bankers always took the lead."[21] They recruited active volunteers with connections to assist in fund-raising and project development.

In 1959 the foundation hired a well-connected but unseasoned executive director, a son of the founder of Buffalo's third commercial bank, Liberty Bank. He was eager to learn about business and development but readily admitted that his knowledge of urban renewal was limited to articles he had written as a newspaperman, his first job out of college. He allowed that it was hard to persuade anybody that he was a professional, but, according to one member of the foundation, what was important was that everyone knew him and his family. It is interesting to note that while Buffalo's leaders hired a known quantity (one of their own with no experience) as executive director, Pittsburgh's leaders hired a professional who was progressive and knowledgeable in the field for the same post there.

The Greater Buffalo Development Foundation focused its efforts on downtown, yet developing an industrial center outside the urban core became one of its first projects. And although action was the driving force in the beginning, research became a centerpiece of the foundation's activities when it merged with the Governmental Research Institute of Western New York in 1970.

The Chamber of Commerce and the foundation continually scrutinized their relations with each other. Foundation literature bent over backward to dispel notions that it might want to usurp power from the Chamber of Commerce: "Our relations with other nonprofit organizations have attempted to promote productive, complementary action rather than counter-productive, competitive effort. For example, we have deferred to the Chamber of Commerce on area-wide economic research and promotional programs to attract and expand industry."[22]

The Chamber of Commerce was always the attraction arm of Buffalo's industrial efforts.[23] The informal principle that "the business of business is business" guided the chamber's thinking. Members of the Chamber of Commerce from Erie and Niagara Counties saw their role as a form of customer relations. In keeping with that principle, they focused on solving business problems, providing group medical insurance for small start-up businesses, for example.[24] Among its charges, the chamber had oversight of the

Erie County Industrial Development Agency (ECIDA) until the late 1970s. During the 1960s, the Chamber of Commerce acted as liaison to the city administration on urban renewal. It gave outward support to foundation projects, despite the sometimes fierce rivalry, unless these projects were regional or overlapped too much with the chamber's turf.

Building relations with Buffalo's ethnic and black communities was not a priority for the Chamber of Commerce or for the foundation, which became a problem for the foundation as it became more involved in urban renewal and community development. One member recalls that "blacks were never brought into discussions. ... We didn't even know who the black leaders were until they started getting their names in the paper . . . [and those were] the ones leading the riots." In other words, none of the white elite leadership knew the professional and entrepreneurial leaders from Buffalo's large middle class in the African American community until forced to. So frustrated were black leaders by not being heard that, one Sunday morning, a contingent of activist leaders marched into Westminster Presbyterian Church during the service to face the foundation's chairman to demand a meeting. He got the meeting, but the chairman's retiring personality as well as the cultural differences "did nothing to inspire confidence between the two camps."[25]

ON OPPOSITE SIDES OF THE STREET

Buffalo's two major banks were rivals from the start. In 1925 Buffalo's Marine Bank made a move to monopolize banking in the state of New York by attempting to merge with the smaller Manufacturers and Traders Trust Company (M&T), another local bank. M&T's future (and longtime) chief executive officer, originally a New York banker familiar with Wall Street, mobilized the bank's defense and assembled the money to match Marine's offer but did not buy the bank. After taking over as its head, he engineered buyouts for M&T that enabled the bank to compete effectively with Marine and protect itself from future takeovers. He went on to become one of Buffalo's proactive leaders and, with others in the 1950s, founded the Greater Buffalo Development Foundation.

Competition between these two banks laid the groundwork for Buffalo's power dynamics among the elite. Although civil in tone, "from that time on, there was unhappiness between the camps. . . . You had competition that divided the city in half. If you wanted to get anything done, you had to unify the camps. If either of them disagreed, you had a sales job to do."[26] At times the banks worked cooperatively, as during the Depression when they provided loans on a daily basis that the smaller banks needed to survive. Over the decades, however, an uneasy civility prevailed, and Buffalo's major players aligned themselves with one or the other. Quite literally, the two banks were located on opposite sides of the street, as were their customers, metaphorically speaking.

Despite rivalries, during the 1950s and early 1960s, four men ran the city: the presidents of the city's three commercial banks, Liberty Bank being the third, and the editor in chief (aligned with the owner-publisher) of the *Buffalo Evening News*. According to one high-ranking bank official, "You needed those four men if a person wanted to accomplish anything or block anything." It was left to the paper's editorial page to argue positions. And when political initiatives were needed in the state legislature, Buffalo's powerful senator could be relied on to make the case. When these four leaders retired in the early and mid-1960s, others replaced them who seemed to care less about working cooperatively and proactively in the community.

ON OPPOSITE SIDES OF THE ISSUE

Rivalry between the two daily newspapers, the *Buffalo News* and the *Buffalo Courier-Express*, was cultural as well as political. The

Buffalo Evening News, the older paper and with the largest circulation, was conservative in outlook. Many agree that it had been very partisan Republican. Founded in 1880, it became the centerpiece of one family's influence in Buffalo's political economy until its sale in 1977. It had "always played an enormous role in politics and everybody was always very careful to pay deference to the *Buffalo News*."[27] Legend has it that the paper lost only two battles in the years covered by this book, the fights on the city's housing code and the stadium location issue—although the paper did get its wish to have the stadium located outside of downtown. On issues of urban development, says one newsman, the *News* "covered things like a blanket. They had a reporter who spent half of every day in the urban renewal office covering community development."[28]

After nearly one hundred years of local ownership, the paper was bought by Warren Buffett. While Buffett remained disengaged (in terms of both the paper and the city), the new publisher made alliances with several bankers along with the newly hired executive director of the Greater Buffalo Development Foundation and some of Buffalo's old-guard leaders. It took the unprecedented step of supporting the black candidate for mayor on the Democratic ticket in 1977, which engendered the ire of his opponent and winner, Jimmy Griffin. Editorially, the *Buffalo News* had shifted gears under its new ownership and introduced a liberal perspective on race issues.

Two papers merged to form the *Buffalo Courier-Express* in 1926. It, too, was identified with one family, and its appeal ran strongly among Buffalo's ethnic communities because of its Democratic, populist nature. It was perceived as a Catholic newspaper; in fact, under the first- and second-generation publishers, nearly every one of the journal's executives were Catholic. This changed somewhat in the early 1950s, but the paper continued to serve mainly Catholic community interests rather than those of the WASP establishment although it always had a strong society page.

The *Courier-Express* had a reputation for hard-hitting investigative reporting that took on both the political and economic establishments. Not only were political officials often put on the defensive, but also local polls disclosed that Buffalo's elites looked unfavorably upon certain investigations.

The newspapers arranged a number of agreements between them. One such understanding held that the *Buffalo Evening News* would not publish a Sunday paper—this being the province of the *Courier-Express*—an agreement that ended only with its sale. The two papers also had an understanding on advertising rates, where neither paper would undercut the other by offering lower rates than those published on their rate card. The *News* turned its back on this agreement in 1971 when a family publisher told his ad director to break rates and cut prices. With profits down, this helped put the *Courier-Express* into the red by 1973.[29] It was not long before the paper closed and Buffalo became a one-paper town, an absentee-owned daily at that.

NOTES

1. Richard C. Robertiello and Diana Hoguet, *The WASP Mystique* (New York: D. E. Fine, 1987), p. 198.

2. Ibid., p. 201.

3. Interview no. 62.

4. US Bureau of the Census, "Census of Population, General Population Characteristics," 1960, 1980.

5. Interview no. 5.

6. Interview no. 50.

7. Ibid.

8. Ibid.

9. Michael McKeating, "The Rise of Erie County's Warring Troika: Crangle, Regan and Slominski," *Empire State Report* (July 1976): 227.

10. Interview no. 37.

11. Richard C. Brown and Bob Watson. *Buffalo: Lake City in Niagara Land* (Woodland Hills, CA: Windsor Publications, 1981), p. 55.

12. "Albany Roundup," *Buffalo Courier-Express*, May 8, 1976.

13. US Bureau of the Census, "County Business Patterns, 1970, 1982, 1984" (Washington, DC: US Department of Commerce, Bureau of the Census).

14. US Bureau of the Census, "Census of Manufacturers 1967, 1972, 1977, 1982" (Washington, DC: US Department of Commerce, Bureau of the Census).

15. Interview no. 73.

16. William Domhoff, *Who Rules America*, 3rd ed. (Mountain View, CA: Mayfield Publishing, 1998), p. 72.

17. Interview no. 36.

18. Jan Cigliano and Sarah Bradford Landau, eds., *The Grand American Avenue, 1850–1920* (Rohnert Park, CA: Pomegranate Communications, in association with the Octagon Museum, 1994).

19. Greater Buffalo Chamber of Commerce, "Annual Report, 1975–76: Our 25th Year."

20. Greater Buffalo Development Foundation, "Annual Report, 1980–81: Thirty-Year Retrospective, 1951–1981."

21. Interview no. 44.

22. GBDF, "Annual Report, 1975," p. 4.

23. Interview no. 47.

24. Interview no. 44.

25. Interview no. 45.

26. Interview no. 37.

27. Interview no. 60.

28. Interview no. 44.

29. Interview no. 36.

Chapter Three

ON THE EDGE

The 1960s

In the 1960s, the signals of Buffalo's economic decline became pronounced, quite clear to a few but by no means clear to all. At the same time, development activity strengthened due to the state's funding of "monumental" public works—highway, transit, and development projects—and the federal government's War on Poverty and urban renewal. The convergence of economic decline and increased government funding for large projects could have worked to Buffalo's benefit. Unfortunately, the city's leadership let opportunities slip by. In fact, some of Buffalo's most powerful leaders fought them. No one doubts that Buffalo's elite, with their connections to the governor and to state legislators, could have forestalled Buffalo's decline, but it would have taken political will and action. This chapter on the 1960s begins the story. It is a scrutiny of events involving Buffalo's most powerful leaders, their initiatives, and the urban-planning process.

ECONOMIC STORY

Passing of the Old Guard to the Younger Establishment

As early as 1951, leaders were aware of a decaying downtown, and, according to business documents, they were worried about the spread of juvenile delinquency and tuberculosis.[1] In 1956 the board chairman of National Gypsum and the chairman of the reactivated Buffalo Redevelopment Committee, Inc., told the *Buffalo Evening News* that "the problems of re-development will grow as time passes. 'If we do not begin now to re-adjust our focus to take in the entire Niagara Frontier area, we will find that we are concentrating on one area while decay and deterioration eat away at another area.'"[2] The Redevelopment Committee, an early version of the Buffalo Urban Renewal Agency, pledged to the mayor and city council that it would help form an official slum clearance agency and assist in drafting legislation to spark neighborhood redevelopment. Aspects of their work resulted in the city's minimum standards ordinance governing health and safety.[3] The committee's initial program targeted the Ellicott District, mostly black neighborhoods adjacent to downtown, and was educational in its efforts. It encouraged homeowners to comply voluntarily with its new health and safety codes. The city's African American community did not fight these efforts; in fact, many placed trust in the procedures. The voluntary compliance effort was quite successful, and Buffalo's first houses were cleared away.

The committee's efforts became the frontline of the city's urban renewal in anticipation of new development, which, over the next two decades, according to a Greater Buffalo Development Foundation retrospective report, was "built slowly or not built at all."[4] Housing clearance in predominantly black neighborhoods got up steam. Two high-rise public housing complexes were built to replace the single-family and duplex homes.

It was during this period that a small number of forward-thinking executives from the business community founded the Buffalo Redevelopment Foundation (to become the Greater Buffalo Development Foundation in 1960). The presidents of regional savings and loans were among its first officers. These proactive business leaders had been aware of Pittsburgh's Allegheny Conference on Community Development. Although ACCD's board comprised city elites, its great success lay in the strong public-private partnerships it fostered and in the alliances of city, county, business, and community leaders it brought together to tackle problems. Pittsburgh's assets were (1) a strong and committed mayor; (2) elite leaders dedicated to the cause—and, in one case, willing to lose profits in order for development to move ahead; and (3) an extraordinary executive director who pushed elite leaders to engage in minority and worker issues across the board.[5] An article in the *Buffalo Evening News* underscored the need for "courageous and capable public administration" and the need to involve "citizens from all strata of community life." The article moved on to enlist the help of the city council, the county commissioners, and finally the state legislature in this process.[6]

The Greater Buffalo Development Foundation, modeled after the Allegheny Conference for Community Development, cooperated and succeeded on a few individual projects but did not attempt to put together a coalition, as leaders did in Pittsburgh. It may be that regional discord (reported continually in the press) made broad collaboration seem politically untenable. In terms of leadership, we shall see why there should be no doubt that Buffalo's leaders had the political clout to pull off a comprehensive strategy such as Pittsburgh's. It would have taken a concerted group of business leaders, with no end runs in pursuit of individual interests, to keep the process strong and on track.

Initially, the foundation did observe "a crying need" for new industry in the area. Foundation leaders brought a panel of experts to Buffalo from the Urban Land Institute in Washington, DC, to assist in planning the redevelopment effort. A task force of ten real estate and industrial executives from seven states worked alongside institute professionals as volunteers to research land availability for redevelopment.[7] They identified a vacant site on the East Side in the old railroad stockyards well suited for an industrial park. This project, at least, did become a collaborative effort: An East Side councilman sponsored the project; the foundation developed the concept; the Urban Land Institute prepared development recommendations to the city; and city planners created the plan and assembled the land with urban renewal funds. It was not long before the Thruway Industrial Park attracted six new businesses to its nearly seventy-five-acre site.

To lend legitimacy to their ideas, foundation leaders repeatedly hired outside consultants to prepare a study. Such was the case in December 1960, when foundation and business leaders turned to the Arthur D. Little consulting team. Its two-year study recommended developing the West Side of Main Street downtown.[8] It suggested that the foundation assume a broader role of policy adviser to regional affairs. It encouraged an awareness of "the need for broad participation and the use of the foundation as a vehicle to insure this participation" in order to avoid failures. The study also argued that the foundation could act as a liaison for the metropolitan area.[9] The foundation sponsored another report by the Architects' Redevelopment Collaborative, five firms that made recommendations for a downtown shopping and business center. Planners reminded the foundation that the downtown project was only a start and needed to be fitted into the city's master plan for renewal of the entire central city.[10]

While Buffalo's leadership talked over plans, Manufacturers and Traders Trust Company (M&T Bank) leaders declared their faith in the future of the city by secretly assembling purchase options on the entire block on the east side of Main Street, which resulted in the twenty-story M&T Bank Building, designed by American architect Minoru Yamasaki. M&T's proclamation "triggered announcements by Western Savings to build at Main and

Court, and by Erie County Savings Bank to demolish its gothic fortress in favor of a tower emerging from the proposed Main Place [Mall]."[11] The Marine Midland Trust Company announced its intentions to span the foot of Main Street with its new building —downtown's most expensive redevelopment plan to date. The Buffalo Urban Renewal Agency (1966), with its powers of condemnation and write-down of property (reassessed value of the condemned property) as part of the city's redevelopment plan, helped make the $50 million project possible.

In another effort that did succeed, the Greater Buffalo Development Foundation led a partnership team between businesses and the city to develop the Main Place Mall project. A small group of bankers, downtown businessmen, an attorney or two, and public officials created a public-private urban renewal partnership to help the city assemble the site. The city established a "nonassisted" urban renewal project, using state laws that allowed urban renewal development for a project. Private interests formed their own downtown development corporation for assembly that acquired the land directly, rather than the project acquiring the land. The city closed area streets and improved them. One of Buffalo's locally owned department stores, Adam, Meldrum and Anderson, made the site available when it moved across Main Street. In 1968 the Main Place Mall, with its twenty-six-story office building and three floors of underground parking, opened. Financing came from local banks and a New York developer. Concurrently, a group of lawyers and other business leaders established a quasi-private agency, Buffalo Civic Auto Ramps Inc., set up under city auspices to acquire properties through city authorities and then turn them over to lease to the group. City bond issues funded the public-private venture, all guaranteed by a firm set up in the business community. "I saw some of the agreements during that time and I got to know some of the older guys; there were some really good movers and shakers. They had like a handshake deal with the party and with Mayor [Frank] Sedita, and things were moving along."[12]

By the middle of the decade, this core group of proactive leaders—from M&T and Marine Midland Banks and National Gypsum—retired or began to move away. They had collaborated informally with the mayor and other political officials, which helped bridge differences. Although they appeared socially stuffy to some, their modus operandi was informal. Plans often moved ahead on a handshake (political leaders specifically remembered this when interviewed), as politicians and businessmen formed their public-private partnerships.

With the older generation of leaders all but gone by the second half of the decade, Buffalo's business leadership became amorphous, although no one doubted that the banks were still in charge any more than anyone thought the *Buffalo Evening News* had become less conservative. What changed was that the elite leadership became less proactive for a little more than a decade. One former foundation member remembers that people simply sat on its board of directors because they had been named to it, and it was an honor, "and that was the end of it."[13] Rather than taking the lead in any public planning process, the foundation seemed more inclined to hand-holding. "We have in the past and will continue to operate at a low profile without a great deal of public fanfare. This does not mean that we have any desire to be clandestine. . . . It does mean, however, that we prefer to be judged by our results and not our rhetoric."[14]

Even before merging with the Governmental Research Institute, the foundation in 1967 embarked on five years of research on economic development in cooperation with Erie County and the Chamber of Commerce.[15] The results of this five-year study appeared in the 1972 eight-report series titled, "A Growth Strategy for the Erie-Niagara Area in Conjunction with the 'Profit Opportunity Series'" for specialized investment opportunities. The specific recommendations of this study will follow in the chapter on the 1970s, when the study was released and debated.

Urban Renewal

Eight federally subsidized low-income housing developments had been built by the city in the 1950s to house people displaced by urban renewal clearance. Now the city set about renovating Dante Place, one such integrated public housing high-rise on the waterfront, turning it into middle- and lower-middle-income apartments, whose residents were all white ($25 million).[16] Further, as part of its urban renewal efforts, the city oversaw the completion of the Waterfront School ($10 million) and the Erie Basin Marina ($5 million).[17]

In 1966 Buffalo hired its first commissioner of urban renewal— the son of one of Buffalo's establishment banking families who had previously been the sole employee of the Greater Buffalo Development Foundation. Despite his inexperience, he gained a reputation for dedication to the task. Urban renewal planners agreed that comprehensive waterfront development was an urban renewal priority, but the commissioner was unable to bring the forces together to move ahead. There was much speculation at the time that the owner of the *Buffalo Evening News* wanted the land near the newspaper's new office building left undeveloped. Whether or not this was the case, the waterfront land— considered highly desirable in any other city— was left vacant. Former leaders are quick to point out that a psychological barrier existed for developing this land—land cut off by a skyway bridge and an expressway built by the state in the 1950s. Any development along the downtown waterfront had to factor these obstacles into its plan, surely not an insurmountable task.

To complicate matters, the Niagara Frontier Transportation Authority (NFTA) controlled the land on which waterfront development would occur, thus adding to the number of players and agendas. This agency, whose members were appointed by the governor, had its own power base and its own plan. One public leader states flatly that "the NFTA did a good job of gobbling up land on the waterfront and around the airport."[18] When it came to development, whoever controlled the land had a leg up on everyone else. It would have taken a coordinated and strategic effort by others, perhaps involving the state legislature and governor, to override reticent players in a useful planning process.

Although a convention center was not envisioned as part of a larger plan, it became an ad hoc attempt at urban renewal, to be paid for with city funds. For the public, the overriding issue in the convention center debate became cost and priorities, and many community groups opposed it, hoping to see funding used for other projects in the neighborhoods. An initiative appeared on the ballot that a divided city voted down in a referendum. With its defeat, the Erie County executive stepped in, offering to make the convention center a county project, whereupon the great debate then shifted to where the convention center should be located. The choices were (1) on the waterfront, where land had been cleared for urban renewal (with the potential for hotels, additional developments, and lakeside parks), or (2) downtown near the city's one and only major hotel (with no additional land for development).

The owner of this hotel, the Statler, promoted the idea that he would turn his hotel, situated on Niagara Square opposite city hall, into a world-class hotel space—with walkways between hotel and convention center—if the city would build it on a site downtown that was contiguous to his building. The proposed location was a small, rather undesirable, triangle of land lying behind another building on Niagara Square. The convention center would block a street radiating out from the vehicular circle in front of city hall.

Using his connections as bank director to lobby the county, and his friendship with the Democratic Party chairman to lobby the city, the hotel owner made his case. He argued that the convention center would need a hotel in proximity for business. Central to his offer was a plan to refurbish the hotel. After much debate, the county committed the convention center to the space sandwiched behind buildings downtown—and across the street from the hotel— thus meeting the hotel owner's demands. But things did not turn out as agreed upon. When the hotel owner reopened the space, it had been refurbished as an office building, not a hotel. In some quarters, there was outrage; others simply shrugged their shoulders. A few years later, the owner, who had won the battle to get the convention center sited next to his hotel, in a less than desirable space, sold his building to Kuwaiti interests.[19]

Because of this gentleman's agreement, an understanding between elite business leaders and the city, Buffalo was left without a single major hotel to support a convention center that was to be built. Development for the convention center went slowly and was not completed until 1978. Plans for a first hotel progressed at an even slower pace, as can be seen in the next chapter.

The Campus Location Debate

> Downtown interests turned their back on the university. . . .
> [T]hey fought Rockefeller. And partly they resisted because they
> saw it as a threat. If there's two or three billion dollars of stuff
> going on [either downtown or out there]—if it had been done the
> way it was intended to be—it was going to become *the* power
> center, and it was going to bring in new people and new money,
> and overwhelm them. . . . But local leaders could have made it;
> they could have been the lead of it.
>
> —Interview no. 72

In 1962 Governor Nelson Rockefeller announced that the State University of New York (SUNY) planned to acquire the University of Buffalo, a private university, and intended to build a second, much larger campus. A top official at the Urban Development Corporation (UDC) maintains today that this was to be Nelson Rockefeller's memorial. The idea of a downtown campus took Buffalo's leadership by surprise, and soon the campus location became a hot topic for discussion. It was astounding that neither the Chamber of Commerce nor the Greater Buffalo Development Foundation took formal positions on the issue, considering the possibilities of such a seminal project for downtown development. Small-business owners were solidly behind a downtown campus, as was the black community, taking into consideration what it would mean in terms of urban core development and jobs. Early on, however, it became clear that several individuals from the business elite opposed the downtown campus.

Five campus sites were suggested, but two quickly dominated the debate. The first site was located on the waterfront adjacent to the downtown business district. The other was in the suburban town of Amherst, twelve miles to the north of the central business district. Both sites offered approximately the same amount of space for learning facilities. Land mass favored a suburban campus, with three times the number of acres available as downtown for dormitory and learning facilities. The downtown waterfront location would depend more on local residential housing to fill student demand. While the suburban site offered space, the downtown site offered city-center cultural and professional resources. "Placing the university in the center of the urban complex will not do violence to its scholarly tradition. Such placement might, however, add a dimension of relevance and pertinency to the university's role and function" as well as provide "the challenge to use its traditions of learning, scholarship and research in fresh ways to deal with problems unique to an urbanized, technological society."[20] For four years, proponents of the two sites battled. Throughout, the Greater Buffalo Development Foundation and Chamber of Commerce took no formal position.

From the city's standpoint, a downtown campus offered a multitude of bonuses. It promised an infusion of jobs and cash into downtown, resulting from the influx of ten thousand students and the additional two thousand university-related jobs. In turn, this could revitalize the troubled retail merchants. And it would greatly expand the city's service sector not only with its myriad support services for the university community but also with the increased demand for entertainment, hotels, and medical and health services for students, faculty, and visitors. A downtown campus offered an incredible opportunity to ensure diversification from a concentration in manufacturing (especially in the steel industry). In addition, the city could utilize the university's resources and marketability in business attraction strategies and for industry itself. The local revenue base would increase dramatically. A committee in favor of a downtown campus estimated that "the credits obtained from a mammoth project of university construction would pay the cost of the city's total urban renewal program for decades."[21] Moreover, the economic activity, acting as a magnet, would attract capital investment into the urban core, investment funds that, in time, might spill over into other parts of the city as a healthy business district flourished.

Those who argued the above, that economic and social considerations were of primary importance, backed the downtown location. By contrast, those who argued that education mattered most fought for a suburban site. The argument boiled down to one's definition of education. The outgoing university president favored a suburban campus, believing that a university should have a sprawling campus separate from the bustle of the city with space for research and development.[22] But urbanists like Martin Meyerson (the incoming university chancellor) and Governor Rockefeller usually factored in elements such as urban economics, the urban environment and its architecture, public transportation, as well as the potential for the shared use of resources and collaboration between university and city.

Still, some establishment elite feared the changes that an urban campus might bring to downtown and to the city as a whole. They argued that along with the thousands of students would come a variety of political points of view, perhaps even some radicals. An influx of students would upset the city's racial and ethnic balance. Already the white community had responded to the growth of the black population with "fear and anxiety" during the 1950s, at which time nearly eighty thousand people (20 percent of the city's 1950 population) fled to the suburbs.[23]

During the increasingly rancorous debate, a banker, who also chaired the Albright-Knox Art Gallery board, blocked the display of a model of the proposed downtown university at the gallery. It was displayed instead at the Buffalo Public Library at the base of the main stairwell. "As a consequence, the rest of the political and social establishment was cowed into silence. . . . The unanswered insult sent a strong message to anyone who might harbor modern ideas for Buffalo."[24] Another banker made his feelings known informally to anyone who would listen, but most especially among the social networks of the establishment: "We don't want all those [New York radicals and people of color] running around downtown."[25]As fate would have it, both leaders sat on the University's Board of Trustees—one headed the board and the other chaired the Construction Fund.

What Happened

About the time that the State University of New York announced plans to buy the University of Buffalo, it bought two hundred acres of land in Amherst "as an insurance policy against future expansion."[26] No plans had been made for this swampy land, at least to the public's knowledge, despite the fact that student enrollment had increased from 12,633 to almost 18,000 between the years of 1955 and 1964. When the deal was completed in 1963, the State University quietly commissioned Vincent Moore (formerly a Buffalo planning aide and at the time a consultant for the State Budget Division in Albany) to evaluate and report on five potential sites for the new campus. They were Grand Island, Amherst, Elma, Cheektowaga, and Buffalo's downtown waterfront.

Moore, again quietly, submitted the report without recommendation. But this was odd because, according to some who had seen it, the early drafts had contained "a glowing recommendation for the downtown waterfront." But apparently Moore's *"superiors* removed this recommendation before submission [emphasis added]."[27] According to the chairman of the Buffalo Planning

Board, it was clear that the study "definitely favored" the water-front site.[28] And student leaders favored downtown.

Nevertheless, the University Council (an advisory group that included business leaders, state officials, and Chancellor Clifford Furnas—before the arrival of a new chancellor) preferred the suburban location. By April 1964, the report had passed through the State University Construction Fund and went on to the SUNY executive vice president (a member of the Central Staff) with no recommendation, and finally to the Central Staff. At a June 11 meeting, the Central Staff recommended to the Board of Trustees that the Amherst site be chosen. The trustees acted unanimously on that recommendation.[29] Incredibly, given the magnitude of the state's investment—which was to become $650 million—the council unanimously accepted the Central Staff report in one formal meeting.

Minutes of the meeting indicate there was little, if any, discussion concerning alternative sites prior to a vote. And the trustees made their decision without any direct input from government leaders in either Amherst or Buffalo. One Amherst assemblyman acknowledged that the decision came as a complete surprise to Town of Amherst officials, speculating that the trustees intended to limit conflict among western New York's communities. Approximately one year elapsed before representatives of the university met with Town of Amherst officials on the subject.[30]

At this point, the debate began to get interesting. Proponents of the urban site did not realize immediately that an alternative site study, the Moore report, existed. When they became aware of it, they began to organize. The first to organize were Amherst citizens themselves. Then, on July 4, 1966, a black architect called a meeting at a sympathetic university professor's home. This gathering included a number of bankers (who were not afraid to buck the establishment tide), a university dean, and several businessmen, who together began formulating arguments in opposition to the suburban site. This group laid the framework for what was to become the Committee for an Urban University of Buffalo (CURB). Once organizing began, CURB grew quickly and attracted members from the university, urban communities, and even the business establishment. Many activists working for an urban university belonged to the East Side Community Organization (ESCO) and Build Unity, Independence, Liberty and Dignity (BUILD), two black organizations. Others belonged to the Coalition for Action, Unity and Social Equity (CAUSE) and Independent Catholics Act Now (ICAN). These groups, often opposed to one another on other issues, coalesced around the drive to locate the campus downtown.

The committee contacted Governor Rockefeller, who told committee members that the strongest opposition to the downtown location came from the city's bankers on the Board of Trustees. In response to the committee's request for help, the governor offered, "Oh, I can take care of them."[31] It did not happen, however, perhaps because it was an election year.

In 1966 Martin Meyerson, a noted urbanist and planner, was appointed the university's new chancellor. The Committee for an Urban University felt certain he would advocate for a downtown campus, and, when committee leaders contacted him before his arrival, he asked to read its study. Upon completion, he told them, "Just keep developing your position."[32] Everyone waited to hear what this renowned urbanist had to say. But when he assumed his position as chancellor, he put forth no public opinions.

With pressure mounting from all quarters, on August 11, 1966, Governor Rockefeller announced that he had decided to have the state conduct another investigation of alternative sites.[33] In his letter, the governor claimed that the basis for his request was "the importance of this proposal to the program of revitalization of the heart of Buffalo."[34] Two months later, the governor appointed the president of Rutgers University, Dr. Mason Gross, to conduct a restudy, who, in turn, retained the services of Robert Heller and Associates of Cleveland. Seven criteria would focus the study: (1) area, (2) accessibility, (3) beauty and climate, (4) supporting facilities, (5) soil and drainage, (6) land availability, and (7) community integration. Excluded as criteria were the social, economic, and political issues concerning Buffalo's urban core. (The study included not only the proposed downtown and suburban sites but also the idea of expanding the present university's Main Street campus.) In response to Dr. Gross of Rutgers, the new chancellor himself formed the Ad Hoc Committee of Campus Site Restudy. And on July 29, 1966, the *Courier-Express* published an article based on research prepared by the Buffalo Planning Division that included a map of the waterfront site demonstrating that 423 acres were available for development—more acreage than six other major urban university campuses in the United States.

At last on February 6, 1967, the governor's restudy was ready. Mason Gross joined with his Heller Associates colleagues in recommending the Amherst site to the university trustees, declaring that the "desirability of site is the key." Economic and social factors had been excluded in study considerations.[35] The next day, the university council gave the report its unanimous support. And on February 10, the trustees reaffirmed their 1964 decision to locate the campus at the suburban Amherst site ten miles from Buffalo's downtown.

Who Stood Where

Momentum built over time as increasing numbers of people spoke out in favor of a downtown campus. The Greater Buffalo Development Foundation and the Chamber of Commerce continued to be notable exceptions. By 1967, when the final decision was made to put the university in Amherst, the city's retail merchants and businessmen—with the exception of the Black Rock Manufacturers Association—stood solidly behind the waterfront site. These included the Retail Merchants Association, the Broadway-Fillmore Merchants Association, the Main Street Association (representing three hundred downtown merchants), the Walden-Bailey Businessmen's Association, the Buffalo Junior Chamber of Commerce, and the Buffalo-Niagara Frontier Federation.[36]

Mayor Chester Kowal, a Republican, went from no comment to supporting the downtown effort in a low-key way. Two important state assemblymen signed on. The city's planning board chairman and its director argued that the downtown site provided urban conveniences, which was why most universities tended to locate in urban areas. Meanwhile, the *Buffalo Evening News* played down the campus issue. The *Buffalo Courier-Express* covered the various dimensions of the issue and helped build partisan support for downtown but did not back either site. Still, the Greater Buffalo Development Foundation and Chamber of Commerce said little despite all the opposition.

Attempts to determine Governor Rockefeller's true position on the campus issue have been unsuccessful. Knowledgeable people believe Rockefeller's restudy was his attempt to get elite leaders to reconsider their opposition to a downtown campus. Others have said that they considered this to be vintage Rockefeller, wanting to build the biggest university in the country, and in this case the appeal of more land outside the city would be compelling. Nevertheless, the Committee for an Urban University remained convinced that Rockefeller favored a downtown university.

Meyerson, who was about to become chancellor, was a different case. Proponents of an urban campus believed he initially wanted to voice an opinion but felt unable to, waiting until he had taken his post at the university. Upon arriving in Buffalo as chancellor, and taking his place on the board of directors of a leading bank (one whose chairman headed the university's board of trustees), he demurred from taking any position.

The Rapid-Transit Initiative: Part One

Buffalo is the only city in the US to build a transit system with no local funds for construction. The state met the local fund requirement.
—A Niagara Frontier Transportation Authority consultant

Background

Leadership requires the commitment to see a project through. Local commitment may be measured, at least in part, by how much money local governments and local private investors are willing to put up to accomplish a job. In Buffalo's case, zero dollars were put up for the construction of a rapid transit system.

Two years or so before the campus location decision, three western New York citizens envisioned a restoration of rail service to an area south of the city. In part, they wanted to promote service to the growing ski developments in this snowbelt area. Concurrently, the decision to build the university campus to the north of the city made it "instantly obvious to all those looking ahead that a rail connection with downtown Buffalo would be indispensable if the new campus was to fulfill its potential. All the University of Buffalo and state officials and advisors realized good 'transit' would be needed, but to them it just meant adequate bus service."[37]

In 1967 New York State announced the creation of the Niagara Frontier Transportation Authority for the area. Congruently, the New York State Department of Transportation had been mandated to develop a statewide master plan for transportation. Governor Rockefeller appointed a banker, one who had just participated in the campus decision, to become the first chairman of NFTA, which, it was hoped, would achieve a "balanced transportation system for the region." At this time, the city hired its first staff person concerned with transportation.[38] Over the decades, the Transportation Authority would operate the area's bus system, light rail, two airports, and a small boat harbor; in 1974 it would create a wholly owned subsidiary to provide mass-transportation services, the Niagara Frontier Transit Authority.[39]

Governor Rockefeller took it upon himself to write to the newly formed Transportation Authority to remind it that it was supposed to provide transportation between the suburban campus, now in the developmental stage, and downtown. His admonition fit with the

Transportation Authority's mandate to establish a unified mass transportation policy for the region, with a transit center built downtown as its regional hub. The governor's call transpired at a time when Buffalo's leaders continued to seek strategies to revitalize downtown—obviously not with an urban university—and, at the same time, the federal government was making available massive amounts of funding for rapid transit systems to catalyze economic revitalization in urban areas throughout the nation. A small group of people (a few business leaders, professionals, and transit experts) took it upon themselves to champion a light-rail rapid-transit system, but it never caught fire with Buffalo's business or political leaders. And while linkage between the suburbs and the urban core held benefits for citizens who worked downtown, Amherst's leaders did not much care for the idea either. Some feared the consequences of moving people around quite so easily— bringing students downtown and the urban poor into the suburbs.

Despite fears, a small group of civic leaders recognized rapid transit for what it was: a tool for economic development. Historically, this was a difficult time for such a debate as cars were the vehicle of choice over public transportation. For example, the New York State Department of Transportation preferred highways over rail, and so did the federal government, having just built much of the US highway system in the 1950s. This propensity for automobiles was magnified in Buffalo with all of its steel- and auto-related industries.

In the first year of the authority's life, a variety of transit concepts were floated, and considered, despite the board's overriding interest in the airport rather than surface transportation. Buffalo's planning board, in its "Community Summaries," proposed two rapid transit lines (June 1967). Two months later, M&T Bank and the Office of Urban Affairs at the State University of New York co-sponsored a meeting of community, business, and government leaders on regional transportation needs. This meeting had its roots in weekly or biweekly breakfast meetings at the newly constructed bank and were organized by its community representative. This loosely knit assemblage grew to a core of regulars who worked together over many years. They included professional planners from both the city and county, the Chamber of Commerce, the NFTA (intermittently), an NFTA consultant—who became the professional backbone of the group—and a representative from the Greater Buffalo Development Foundation. These individuals were joined later by an environmentalist and a soils engineer from the university. Over the years, the group changed somewhat but always had the same mission. The group became known as the Area Committee for Transit, and later, the Citizens Rapid Transit Committee.

Other plans appeared, most important of which were those studying a "Buffalo-Amherst Corridor," which will be discussed in the next chapter. The Town of Amherst's development plan included rapid transit along the Buffalo-Amherst corridor, linking the campus to downtown (1968). Erie County's Department of Planning developed a plan delineating four rapid-transit lines radiating from Buffalo's urban core (October 1968). The New York State Office of Planning Coordination completed the Buffalo-Amherst Urban Impact Study, which recommended investigating the feasibility of a rapid-transit line to serve as the spine for the Buffalo-Amherst corridor (March 1969). Four months later, the Erie and Niagara Counties Regional Planning Board recommended a Cheektowaga Rapid Transit Line as part of its regional planning document, suggesting that the line receive early attention (July 1969).[40]

Throughout 1968 the NFTA set policies for metropolitan transportation improvements statewide. Then in 1969, with all this activity, the Transit Authority filed an application with the federal government (UMTA) for a technical grant to advance and implement a transit development program for Erie and Niagara Counties; the authority hired a consulting firm to investigate transit alternatives and recommend a transportation center site in downtown Buffalo.

The future held promise when, in January 1970, the federal government announced a $524,000 grant to the NFTA for a mass transit study. The state announced a $196,500 matching grant. And the Transit Authority, along with other "local contributions," supported the study, for a total of $65,000 in funds. Plans were moving ahead and would continue to progress into the mid-1980s, until this saga ran its course. Meanwhile, other battles were afoot in the 1960s.

A Football Stadium and the
Urban Development Corporation

In an ardent football town such as Buffalo, the issue of where to locate a new stadium tended to raise the collective temperature of its residents. At the same time, for cities needing to revitalize their downtowns, building a new football stadium in the city's urban core had grown in popularity. Yet there were always those who wanted to put a stadium elsewhere. In 1964 Buffalo joined in this debate with talk of replacing War Memorial Stadium, located in a black neighborhood on the city's East Side. The issue was whether to renovate and enlarge the old stadium or build a new stadium someplace else. The Arthur D. Little report agreed with Buffalo's Planning Department and most others that a location close to the central business district would be optimal in order to get "maximum utility from stadium-associated enterprises." Plus, its proximity to downtown would make it possible for commuters and shoppers to visit some of the city's biggest taxpayers: retail stores, restaurants, and hotels. Acquisition of the land in this area (called the Crossroads) conceivably could be underwritten by a federally assisted program. Also acting in its favor, this site had good access to the New York State Thruway and other major traffic arteries.[41]

Three years later, the Buffalo Area Chamber of Commerce, through its stadium committee, refuted this conclusion. According to *Buffalo Magazine*, the Chamber of Commerce had "unprecedented, spontaneous and enthusiastic tribute" for its decision in favor of a two-stadium complex *outside* the city in the Town of Amherst.[42] In this decision, the chamber's board of directors had ignored all professional advice and chosen a suburb over downtown, unanimously—despite the fact that five separate sites were under consideration. Nevertheless, moving ahead, the Chamber of Commerce announced its implementation committee, which consisted of four attorneys, two bankers, two builders, three industrial executives, education administrators, sports team owners, and others.

The first proposal had been to build a stadium at the foot of Main Street, downtown. But when it became public knowledge that plans existed for a new stadium to be built outside city limits, the battle began in earnest. Prominent positions were taken: the *Buffalo Evening News* hated the downtown idea because the stadium would be built near its new office building and plant. (That it opposed the downtown stadium is historical fact, but some debate remains regarding the nuances of its reasoning.) While the *News* argued for the suburbs in its editorials, the *Courier-Express* championed downtown, and the dispute grew bitter. The Erie County Legislature deadlocked. Two bankers who had voted for a suburban university two years earlier again championed a suburban site. One of Buffalo's most prestigious law firms displayed a model of the rural domed stadium in its reception room, while the city's two major banks stood on opposite sides of the issue.

But things got worse. When another plan for a site in rural Lancaster surfaced in 1968, the story goes that a rump group of financiers at one bank and an executive (a son-in-law) at the *Buffalo Evening News* rebelled. Breaking ranks with other elite leaders, they argued that a domed stadium should be built downtown after all—at which time ferocious pressures were brought to bear on these breakaways. Later, when one bank executive looked like he might agree that a stadium should be built downtown, "he went into his board meeting, and came out a changed man," and was not heard to assert himself on the stadium issue again.[43] Implicit among the business leadership was the understanding that "if you [want to] build it downtown, you will be destroyed," according to one longtime political insider.[44] "The battle raged from the summer of '68 over plans to build a domed stadium in Lancaster, New York. The proposal fell apart in 1970. . . . [It was] a massive, searing debate involving every major power figure in Buffalo ranging from the owner of the dominant newspaper, bankers, local governments, politicians, editors, law firms. . . . Two people died of heart attacks, politicians quit, two went to prison. The proposal fell apart in 1970."[45]

The issue remained unresolved for another year, drawing into 1971. Finally, at a meeting of Buffalo's business, county, and state leaders, an agreement was reached—that they could not come to a consensus. Upon this realization, they took the unusual step of asking the New York State Urban Development Corporation to decide the stadium issue for them. In this unprecedented move, warring factions conceded they were unable to make a decision and agreed to support the Urban Development Corporation's choice, given a reasonable price, and move on. Interestingly, the UDC chose yet another location, Orchard Park, south of the city. The cost came in under $40 million; the county negotiated a lease with the Buffalo Bills's owner; and just about everyone was relieved that this chapter in the city's history was over.

Ten years after the battle over the stadium site ended, the State Supreme Court declared Erie County in breach of contract. It seems that the county had signed an agreement in which it was to acquire two hundred acres of land in the Town of Lancaster for a domed stadium, which Dome Stadium, Inc., would operate for forty years. By 1981 the county owed over $400,000 in attorney fees, of which it had paid $21,842.[46]

POLITICAL STORY

The Mayors

In 1954 Democrat Steve Pankow, a Ukrainian but recognized as Polish, became mayor. As a politician, he was on the scene in the city's neighborhoods; during his tenure, urban renewal picked up steam. Italian Frank Sedita followed as mayor (1958–1962) in what was the first of three terms in office—with a one-term Republican mayor intervening. He worked well with the old-guard business leadership where, according to a community development director, "he pleasantly presided over the city"—so much so that when it came time for reelection he could think of nothing to boast about except a little work on a park "casino" along Delaware Lake.

Two Democrats split the ticket in the 1961 election, which enabled the Republican Polish candidate Chester Kowal to become mayor. The split ticket came about when candidate Victor Manz challenged Mayor Sedita in the primary. Manz had Polish backing from the Democratic Party. Consensus among party loyalists had been that the Italians (through Sedita) had had their day, and it was now another ethnic group's turn to run the city. Sedita was defeated in the primary, after which he decided to run for mayor as an independent. The election's three-way race made a Republican victory possible with only 35 percent to 36 percent of the vote. Sedita's ability to run for a second term resulted from changes to the city charter—where Democrats (under party chairman Peter Crotty) made it possible for mayors and city council members to succeed themselves, with no limits on the number of terms. This backfired for Democrats later when Jimmy Griffin was reelected three times, for a full sixteen years in office.

Mayor Kowal (1962–1966) became the instrument of the Republican power structure, as Republicans were elated to be in power in the city's Democratic enclave. State Senator Walter Mahoney, a Republican, stayed in close touch with Kowal, but especially with elite leaders at the *Buffalo Evening News*. According to some who worked there, the editor in chief and publisher were only a phone call away from the senator. The mayor's relationship with the city council was more challenging, and, after two years, relations between the mayor and the city council of eleven Democrats and four Republicans began to deteriorate.

It is important to take note of an exceptional time when the two political parties collaborated effectively. In 1964 city and county officials agreed that additional revenues needed to be raised. Mayor Kowal and the county executive met to discuss increasing the county sales tax from 2 to 3 percent, with revenues to be split equally between the two governments. Both elected officials agreed to put aside notions of political gain in order to garner the twenty-eight votes in the county legislature. They knew that passing this tax in a heavily Republican county legislature would not be easy. To their credit, both sides agreed to approach the debate as a community issue, not a political vehicle for shoring up power.[47]

Halfway through Kowal's term, the Republican Party split seriously over the control of power, between the camps of the mayor of Buffalo and the state senator. The *Buffalo Evening News* aligned itself with Senator Mahoney, the Republican Party Chairman with Mayor Kowal; by the next election, the senator was weakened in such a way that he was defeated. This affected Buffalo financially, as Senator Mahoney had seniority and was effective in bringing money to the Buffalo region.[48] At the end of his term, Mayor Kowal left office under a cloud of political innuendo, with the Civic Auto Ramps Program the only plan to really take shape during his tenure. He died several months later.

After being out of office during four years of disarray, Frank Sedita made a comeback and was elected twice, until he resigned for health reasons just one year short of completing his last term (1966–1973). A political diplomat, Sedita felt at home in the neighborhoods. He spoke four languages, which helped with ethnic rivalries, and had excellent business contacts. He was unusual too because he maintained close alliances in the black community. The mayor organized a "kitchen cabinet" that included the commissioner of community development, the city planner, and others in the administration who met weekly with a small group of business leaders in the late afternoon when city hall cleared out.

By the late 1960s, with the retirement of old-guard elite leaders, planning shifted from the private sector to the Sedita administration, or to political appointees such as the Niagara Frontier Transportation Authority. But what was really needed was a strong partnership of committed leaders from both sectors. The politicians "were doing their best, but there was such a limited input to them from the business community," declared a ranking member of the Greater Buffalo Development Foundation.

The mayor attracted the same bright college graduates to him that the new Democratic party chairman recruited to the party machine. This positive circumstance was diminished by the fact that he also surrounded himself with old-line ethnic pols (mainly from the Italian community) who operated the patronage-laden departments at city hall. The city streets' department, for example, was headed by a man who treated the department as his private fiefdom, putting sons or nephews of cronies on the trucks as "temporary" workers. For a while, this proved successful in circumventing civil service requirements, until discovered. In another incident in 1974, he was indicted for using streets' employees to work on his West Side properties.[49] One scandal under this commissioner finally touched Sedita, at which point the mayor fired him as well as others. As it happened, approximately fifty "phantom" people turned up on the city payroll as per diem garbage collectors, people who did not work there but received paychecks every two weeks. Although Sedita's own people brought the problem to light, history has not resolved how much the mayor may have known about this clearly illegal activity. This latest incident also came on the heels of the discovery that some refuse workers were not working full eight-hour days. For these workers it was an issue of tradition. "Some of Buffalo's Sanitation Department crews, working five, six and fewer hours per day, pick up refuse between beer and coffee breaks . . . (although this does not meet the city ordinance requirement which holds that the work day shall be eight hours). 'It does not, however, conflict with custom,' according to . . . an administrative assistant in the Street Sanitation Department."[50]

Although he was a popular mayor, eventually it became clear that Sedita did not accommodate change well: "The future was something he just didn't understand."[51] When Sedita became ill and retired in 1973, the Democratic party chairman appointed Stanley Makowski interim mayor.

Federal Decertification and the Housing Code

In the spring of 1965, the *Courier-Express* wrote that "Buffalo has been under a federal-aid interdict since last August 30 because of the city's record of sluggishness on urban renewal and anti-blight programs—and because of the absence of an omnibus enforcement code."[52] Under Mayor Kowal, Buffalo lost its federal certification because of its inability to revise and enforce its multiple dwelling laws and move its programs along. For the city to requalify, it needed to update its property law, as well as submit "A Workable Program for Community Development." In this case, the federal government mandated that the program be based on, and include, results from neighborhood surveys. However, Buffalo never did the surveys. Further, the city skipped submission of the report altogether since it could not resolve a number of disagreements within the department. The possibility of decertification created a problem for Buffalo because it entailed losing large federal grants for urban renewal and community development projects.[53]

Decertification held up the Thruway Industrial Park project and the Masten General Neighborhood Renewal Program. The *Buffalo Evening News* reported that "the housing code is a pertinent issue because, without revision and enforcement, the annual federal recertification for urban renewal funds will be withheld."[54] Worse yet, the next day, it was reported that the city's chances of getting a $2.5 million state educational facility, the centerpiece of a massive new East Side renewal project, were (at least temporarily) lost.[55]

Mayor Kowal installed a North Buffalo party leader as head of inspections and licenses of real property, who soon noted corruption in that department and among real estate owners and developers. Arguing that Buffalo's law was outdated, complex, and incomprehensible—in addition to being unsuited to the needs and physical realities of Buffalo since the city had adopted New York City's Multiple Dwelling Law—he asked the mayor to appoint a citizens committee, the Special Technical Review Committee, to modernize the Housing and Property Code. The committee comprised twenty-nine business and political leaders considered trustworthy. The choice to head the committee was a well-known Republican elite, a community banker, later an outspoken proponent of the rapid transit.

Swirling around the issue of conversion of single-unit houses to multidwelling houses was an undercurrent of questionable involvement by public officials. "Under the state law covering Buffalo since 1949, conversion has been sometimes with public enforcement officials looking the other way. In some instances, public officials have falsely certified that frame buildings converted since 1949 were legally converted prior to 1949." In addition, "A great amount of rental housing is being operated outside the law. The hypocrisy attending the frame multiple dwelling conversion question . . . has been a major contributor to slum conditions in neighborhoods throughout the city."[56]

The committee labored for three months to write a new code to supersede the state code. It would be simpler, address Buffalo's specific needs, fit the city's type of housing (not steel high-rise buildings), and, they hoped, would be less easy to bend or circumvent. Delay tactics ensued with opponents locked in turf fights and jealousies. The building inspectors desired less stringent codes. The slumlords desired not to be identified or required to register by name through an attorney. Others were simply opposed to change. The African American community, in contrast, viewed the proposed changes positively, and, while the political fight raged on, the citizens spoke out: "This housing code is important to all citizens of Buffalo, but it will be of particular advantage to those who are now being exploited because of their race."[57] They argued that "the proposed code represents such a major step forward that its enactment cannot be delayed without adversely affecting the citizens of our community."[58]

The Greater Buffalo Development Foundation declined to be heard on the issue, nor did it endorse, encourage, or cajole the Special Technical Review Committee, headed by one of its own elite colleagues. The *Buffalo Evening News* remained hostile throughout. The *Courier-Express* stuck to the issues. The committee took the heat while the fight raged.

When a draft law went into review, the real estate and building industries went into an uproar that the city council could not easily ignore. In the final days of the vote, an assemblyman appended an amendment that let slumlords off the hook. When confronted, the responsible councilman said he had "not intended . . . to exempt 'slum lords' from registering with the city or from providing names of local responsible agents!"[59] In response, the council vetoed the amendment that exempted slumlords, the law passed, and the federal government recertified the city. The so-called Harriman Code cleaned up some corruption, made landlords publicly accountable, and cleared the city to once again receive urban renewal funds.

Disregard for Planning: Exceptions or the Rule?

Note: These two examples are purposefully obscure. Nowhere does raw power show itself more clearly than in these two brief instances. One cannot be sure if these were the exception or the rule in Buffalo's urban-planning process. But if left unchecked in any city, they will probably not lead to optimal outcomes for the city and its community.

A Story

With rapid-transit planning in full swing, a planner set about the task of hiring consultants to develop a site study for a transit center downtown. The committee chairman recommended consultants in Albany, whom he knew. Others on the committee had no problem with his choice. According to two separate accounts, the procedure was such that "before anything went to the committee, the planner first sat down privately with the chairman—and whoever the chairman might have gathered from the commission—so that when one went before the board everything was pre-agreed to."[60]

In this case, the city needed to agree to the recommendations and specifics of land acquisition. Planners and consultants prepared to make a formal presentation with slides and accompanying papers to the committee chairman, the mayor, and relevant city officials. Before the presentation, one elite business leader confronted the planners: "We don't care what you or your consultants want, we [already] got together with the mayor and decided where we want to put the transportation center." Since the consultants had planned to propose a site different from the one the business leader proposed, they told him so. The elite responded that that was all right since the chairman had said he'd abide by the mayor's decision, and it sounded like the mayor had already made up his mind.

As the meeting got underway, the consulting planner slipped a note to the chairman. In return he got a wink of the eye, and the chairman told the consultants not to make any recommendation. The consultants' presentation proceeded—and they made no recommendation as the chairman had requested.

Upon the presentation's completion, the chairman stood up "and made a very loud speech" that suggested his preferred site (not the one the consultants would have recommended after much study and research). He made it clear that anyone who wanted anything different was crazy and just didn't understand the needs of the city. He then sat down and turned to mayor: "Mayor, what do you think?" The mayor responded, "Mr. [Chairman], I think you hit the nail on the head. It's the site I've wanted all along."

After the meeting, a small group walked out with the chairman. At that point, the planner turned to the chairman: "Wow, that was quite the performance. How do you do things like that?" He replied, "My weapon is the . . . bank, which is at the top of a pyramid of banks. I control more than 60 percent of the mortgages in this city. Everybody knows it; I don't need to tell them that I can foreclose on the mortgage any time I want." Surprised, the planner said he thought a bank could only foreclose on a mortgage for failure to pay, and got the response: "Young man, go home and read your mortgage; a bank can foreclose a mortgage anytime it wants."

A Second Story

At another point in the design process, a number of elites turned their attention to the rapid-transit designs for the downtown transit center. Neither they nor the mayor were happy with the drawings. A group visited the governor, following which the consultants to the Niagara Frontier Transportation Authority were fired. The Transit Authority, along with their planners, were admonished to back off and were told that they would have nothing to do with transit center and mall designs for downtown in the future. The new group, in effect, became "a committee of one," with controlling authority over the transit center and mall design. The professionals were alarmed to think what this turn of events would mean in costly delays. Equally critical, the consultants were concerned about technical problems that would have to be solved, such as designing for wind, engineering to address heavy snowfalls, and locating stations to optimize service to riders, retailers, and pedestrians.

With the above scene unfolding, the lead transportation planner felt compelled to remind the committee and its chairman that the consultants' selection process had to meet federal guidelines, since federal dollars were involved in the project.

In time a compromise was reached between the group and the Transit Authority, and the transportation planners returned to the process. The consultants then were asked to rank the original list of five design consultants. Upon presentation they were told, "Boy, are you stupid. You've handed [us] this paper upside down." One committee member proceeded to turn the paper 180 degrees, declaring number five in ranking in fact to be number one. And the redesign began.

COMMUNITY STORY

The city's African American community, at the time a world apart from the debates of elite and political leaders, had different matters on its mind. Here the concept of black power, fueled by more than fifteen years of civil rights struggle, was on the rise among an African American population that had reached nearly 109,000 by 1970 (with total population at 1.3 million) in Erie and Niagara Counties—with large numbers concentrated on Buffalo's East Side.[61] The new drive to power, in combination with the black community's unique Buffalo experience, made for huge disruptions and challenges in this urban core community. According to one study, the population change, by race, for census tracts containing the waterfront urban renewal project and the city of Buffalo from 1950 to 1960 was 6,832.[62] During Republican Mayor Kowal's years, one African American sat on a council of fifteen members. In 1966 three black councilmen were elected along with Mayor Sedita for his second term. But despite gains, the African American community still did not have a place in the city's power structure.

Bringing Alinsky

> Cities were exploding to the east and west of us. We felt we ought to do something to see if we could alleviate the pressures over here, and we looked at Saul Alinsky as the possible person to be able to do that.
>
> —A local African American leader

Black leaders were as concerned as any whites that riots might hit Buffalo as they had in Watts, California; Detroit, Michigan; Newark, New Jersey; and nearby Rochester. Discussions took on an urgency among black community leaders at the time of the riots to determine their course of action. This resulted in the founding of the East Side Community Organization, which would lead the effort to bring Saul Alinsky's organization to Buffalo to "organize the East Side."[63]

ESCO became the funding vehicle for bringing Alinsky and for forming an action organization, later known as BUILD. Fundraising took three years, at the end of which ESCO reached its goal of $150,000. A series of news articles on Alinsky and his Chicago-based organization, Industrial Areas Foundation, left the white community feeling unsure and threatened. "This first year of [ESCO] has been a challenge of development and progress. ESCO was born in the midst of controversy, faced with opposition, prejudiced press coverage, and misunderstanding by the community at large. It began with five persons known to each other by name and reputation only; they have become personal friends respecting the unique talents, individual differences and personal contributions of each to the realization of our goals."[64]

Blacks felt that white fears had been aggravated by press coverage of Alinsky. They considered press coverage by the *Buffalo Evening News* to be distorted, especially its description of ESCO as highly secretive in its efforts to bring a "subversive" to town. Buffalo's conservative Catholic Diocese declined to fund ESCO's efforts, which came as a surprise given the strong Catholic support in Chicago for Alinsky's work. Suspicions rose on the community's part when the nonprofit corporation's tax-exempt status took longer to receive than usual, and an infrequently used city ordinance challenged ESCO's legal authority to solicit funds in the City of Buffalo. Nonetheless, things came together in what some called a Protestant movement, where the Council of Churches of Buffalo, Erie County, and North Tonawanda, along with more than a few local churches, put the fund drive over the top.[65] The East Side Community Organization went to work through its action organization, BUILD, but not without some legal battles and dissension between a number of churches and their parishioners.

In May 1966 the ESCO board of black and white leaders met with Alinsky for contract negotiations and to formulate the scope of future organizing efforts and responsibilities.[66] Work began in November. Alinsky's point of view was that "the only way you are going to get equality is by taking it." He accused unions, particularly building-trades unions, of discriminating and maintained that organizing in the interest of attaining power meant getting complete equality in everything, including housing and job opportunities.[67] However, he was impressed with the community's middle-class leadership, which he expressed in a letter: "I keep sort of rubbing my eyes from time to time. Buffalo is about the only community in America in which I have seen a certain number of middle-class professional Negroes committed to their people."[68]

Alinsky's strategy of excluding politicians from his organization—arguing that they had different agendas and needs—did not sit well with the powerful state assemblyman, Arthur Eve, who was unhappy at the thought of an eroding power base. To shore up his own support, while providing job skills training with state funds coming into the Buffalo area, Eve formed the Minority Coalition. Now the African American community had two competing seats of political power (and two competing strategies); people living on the East Side had to choose between the two.

Eve and a small group of black leaders/clergy went on a weekend retreat and returned to announce that they had formed the Minority Coalition and suggested that BUILD join it. BUILD responded that it was a federation of over a hundred black organizations and suggested that the coalition join BUILD. William Gaiter, BUILD's leader, observed: "Why should we join a group of twenty people? We're talking about power; what are you talking about?"[69]

BUILD's founding convention in April 1967 drew delegates from more than 130 community groups—churches, block clubs, business organizations, social clubs, youth groups, labor organizations, and more. An education committee presented the "BUILD Black Paper Number One on the Buffalo Public Schools," which became a "major turnaround in attitude for the black community," according to the new executive director.[70] For the first time, people in the black community articulated simmering concerns: that teachers in the public schools did not understand blacks or their culture, were afraid of them, and were not responsible to them. This laid the groundwork for one of BUILD's major projects and accomplishments in education.

Two months later, in the summer of 1967, riots around the country exploded. Violence broke out in Buffalo, although not with the vehemence of race riots in other cities. Windows were smashed, buses stoned, and forty-some people treated for injuries. Mayor Sedita and his police commissioner blamed outside agitators, while civil rights leaders blamed Buffalo's broken promises. In early July, Mayor Sedita reported: "On behalf of all our citizens, I am most appreciative of the offers of help we have received from the public and private sector. The State of New York, for example, has offered specific financial assistance to help us deal with this tragic problem of the thousands of unemployed and restless youths who . . . sparked the violence. . . . We have upwards of 2000 job opportunities for young people in our community . . . [and we] also discussed the question of additional recreational facilities."[71]

Six months later, the question of race arose in a civil suit filed by a US attorney in Buffalo against Bethlehem Steel under the Civil Rights Act of 1964. The basis of the suit included the preferential hiring of whites, especially for skilled jobs; the assignment of blacks to hot and dirty jobs in the coke ovens and blast furnaces; and the lack of opportunity for advancement for blacks.

BUILD took action on other issues of concern as well. The organization established committees on slum housing, merchants, and poverty. It proffered names for consideration for vacancies on the school board and established a campaign to register voters. Other proposals included the investigation of inspectors and public officials working with slumlords, the demand for street cleaning and trash removal, and the formation of a nonprofit housing corporation with a church group or foundation. BUILD also requested that the federal government investigate segregation in the public school system, asking that funds be withheld if sufficient evidence of segregation was found. Finally, to get the public's attention, BUILD hung white sheets on vacant houses left to rot or gutted by fire, demanding that the Building Division see to their proper repair or demolition. "This building has been standing vacant and open for almost two years. . . . BUILD said that the building is owned by a Hamburg man, and the mortgage is held by a realty firm in Rochester."[72]

In the quest for jobs for blacks, BUILD and the Retail Merchants Association reached an agreement in 1967 in which eight downtown stores agreed to hire three hundred African Americans for the Christmas season. After the 1968 boycott of Jones Rich Dairy Company, BUILD and the company signed a groundbreaking pact that gave priority to job applicants screened by the organization to increase minority employees. (Thirty to forty openings were created in the first year.) BUILD established a skills assessment center to evaluate people in the community.

By insisting that city and state officials meet together to resolve relocation issues, BUILD helped create a new division of relocation within the Department of Urban Renewal. Likewise, BUILD fought the county's decision to relocate its county hospital outside the city in Amherst—where the campus had been located. This is "'a disaster for 43,000 Negro patients a year,' BUILD declared."[73] "In 1967–68, BUILD became involved in the morass that passed for urban renewal in the Ellicott District. It took the position that there must be no more demolition until new housing was constructed for moderate and lower income persons."[74] BUILD's negotiations with leaders throughout the city led to informing

Roswell Park, the highly respected cancer center in the Ellicott District, that it could "expect no more land beyond the early acquisition . . . until a relocation plan and new housing . . . were underway."[75]

The most lasting, and arguably most significant, project of all commenced in 1969 with the founding of the BUILD Academy in partnership with Buffalo State University and the Board of Education. The community-based school opened in an old school building on Clinton Street (kindergarten through fourth grade) and became Buffalo's first magnet school and later a model for magnet schools nationwide. A verifiable community partnership, the academy's board included one representative each from the African American community, Buffalo State College, and the Board of Education, and it served children from the black community in ways that met their needs and reinforced values.[76]

Model City Program

> [When implementing the Model City Program, one] consideration is the effect which the emergence of a new economic system in the Model City neighborhood would have on Buffalo's existing business [power] structure. Regardless of how much lip service . . . business leaders may give to efforts at neighborhood self-determination, it is widely understood that they may be reluctant to act when it is discovered that self-determination in a Model City neighborhood might diminish the influence, income and prestige of the so-called "establishment."[77]

The federal government chose Buffalo as a demonstration city for its new Model City Program. This was a big deal. Senator Robert Kennedy, speaker at the program's inaugural conference in January 1967, put forth the challenge to Buffalo's community to take action: "This is vitally important. Title I of the Demonstration Cities Act provides a new framework for getting Federal money to the city—to you—in a coordinated way. . . . But it is no more than a framework—

a skeleton which will rattle in the closet of its creator unless local imagination and action gives it flesh and sinew and life."[78]

The Model City Program, as a vehicle, offered city leaders a chance to build trust and begin to engage, for the first time, in a community-planning process that would bring disparate interests together in a relatively conventional approach to planning (compared with the confrontational strategies of BUILD). BUILD developed an uneasy relationship with the Model City organization, as BUILD found the mayor's expanded steering committee to be top heavy with individuals from Buffalo's establishment, by a margin of two to one.[79] But despite the unease, the relationship was decidedly cordial.

Lyndon Johnson's War on Poverty through the Office of Economic Opportunity (OEO) had as one of its early objectives, maximum feasible participation. By the late 1960s, in a change of heart, the federal government (HUD) determined this community participation to be so disruptive that it coined a new phrase, "maximum widespread citizen participation," intending to involve citizens more broadly and, thereby, dissipating the black community's control. Local politicians were concerned that this meant the federal government was attempting to undermine and redistribute power.[80]

Buffalo's business leadership and community development officials at city hall saw the Model City Program, with its goals of building social and economic self-reliance, as a social welfare program. This work, they argued, should be left to social welfare agencies, and the Model City Program should focus its efforts on physical community development. Through the yearlong community process of weekly Sunday meetings, Model City participants concluded that their objectives were to obtain (1) access to jobs and capital so that they could support themselves and develop their community, (2) quality education, and (3) transportation to get to their jobs. These were hardly social welfare issues.

Local government officials continued to have other ideas, telling the Model City director that he had to understand that the

Model City Program was a physical program. He responded that it was more than an infrastructure program, it was also social and economic, and not limited to housing, space renovation, or redesign of neighborhoods. Because the program chair had credentials—he was a professor of sociology at Canisius College and assisted the mayor as part of his "kitchen cabinet"—officials finally allowed him to move ahead with his agenda. Although the Model City director won approval from the mayor to remove the program from political control, one council member warned him (as if speaking for the group), "You've got a second thought coming if you think you can take power from a councilman."[81]

The director proceeded with his action plan, based on the premise that citizens would bring specific expertise to a community process if a forum could be provided. He believed that citizens could become developers, for example. They needed only to build confidence in their ability to make pragmatic decisions and to seek professional advice along the way. Upon completion of his action plan, the director accompanied city officials from the department of community development and the mayor's office to Washington, DC, for a meeting at HUD with other Model City administrators.

The morning of the DC meeting, two city officials in community development who had accompanied the Model City director to Washington abruptly left him for an undisclosed meeting (as it turned out) with program administrators. This outraged the director, who believed that the city officials went ahead to lay out the program's position without him. "According to someone who was there, when the director arrived at HUD, he faced a

> huge football-sized table of regional heads of Model Cities, and . . . saw [the community development official], who says, "Here's your seat . . . everything's OK."
>
> [Director:] "What do you mean, everything's OK?"
>
> [City Official:] "We took care of everything. . . . [T]he two of us had a talk here, and we're satisfied that everything is going to be OK."

[Director:] "Well, I thought I was supposed to make a presentation. "

[City Official:] "Don't worry about it.'"[82]

The meeting carried on. When it was over, the director asked HUD
officials to see the planning document prepared by the city's community development officials. Upon learning of its contents, he stated
firmly, "No, we're not going to do that. There's a little disconnect
here, and I will talk to them about that when I get back to Buffalo,"
upon which he laid out the community's plans. HUD accepted. And it
was agreed between the parties that further communications would go
through the mayor and not community development officials.[83]

Back in Buffalo, the community process deepened. Because
many residents in the black community did not own cars, one innovative project that came out of the weekly Sunday meetings
addressed a real transportation need: a jitney transport service to
operate where no bus lines existed or where transportation was
inefficient. This was met with a small group's hostile opposition,
led by city councilwoman Alfreda Slominski, who vehemently
opposed the jitney and argued that it would compete with the
existing transit system. In addition, the drivers would be untrained.
But mostly, she did not want to see them "running all over the
city."[84] Noting bitter opposition, the director prepared a budget for
the jitney service program asking for $5,000 to $6,000 more than
the service needed to get on the road—exactly the amount by which
the city council ended up cutting the budget—which allowed the
project to go ahead: "Buffalo's jitney service will offer to many
elderly inner-city residents 'a small measure of dignity and convenience for the first time in their lives,' the president of BUILD said
. . . in defending the Model Cities program." He also said that "the
success of the program will not 'be due to the good intent of the
federal government nor the cooperation of the city fathers,' but to
the tireless and dedicated efforts and long hours and endless frus-
tration given the Model Cities' . . . director."[85] Successful as the

jitney project was, in time, the city chose to abandon funding it rather than build on what had successfully begun. Nearly three decades later, Erie County initiated another jitney program along these same lines, only countywide.

CONCLUSION

Events unfolded in such a way that, had the opportunities been seized, Buffalo's leaders could have slowed or reversed the city's economic decline. There are three reasons for this. First, during this period, urban renewal was ascendant. In Buffalo, federal and state funds were earmarked for clearance for an urban renewal project downtown. What was needed was a comprehensive plan and for leaders to see this plan through. The planning experience was available, and state officials and others were willing to help in the process. The New York State Urban Development Corporation, for example, represented a powerful vehicle that could, sometimes, override local obstacles or mediate arguments to see projects through.

Second, Governor Rockefeller was prepared to spend $100 million to develop a new State University campus at Buffalo—where an additional ten thousand students were to be educated within the decade, thus expanding the university's enrollment to 27,500 by 1971 and possibly to 40,000 students sometime later. Having such a university on the waterfront downtown would have provided enormous benefits to downtown's economy, culture, and neighborhoods.

Third, massive federal and state funds became available for urban transit systems and regional transportation projects to aid development efforts. Governor Rockefeller mandated the Niagara Frontier Transportation Authority to plan a transit line that would connect the suburban campus with downtown. It should have transpired, as all of the makings were there: money, political and personal links to the governor, and commitment at the top of the state apparatus. Everything, that is, except for committed local leadership.

But why would Buffalo's leadership prefer the suburbs? At times selfish interests were at play. In the development of open land in the suburbs, benefits accrued to the banking and associated land-based industries, which may have tilted their support toward the suburbs. Equally to the point, the WASP elite needed to defend its culture, which, with its economic power, lay at the center of its identity. A downtown university, for example, meant that thousands of students would bring their progressive politics and ideas into the heart of the city. It would also bring into the city a more progressive political constituency and electorate. Better, some mused, that these potentially powerful forces remain on Buffalo's doorstep, the suburbs. Remember, to the WASP elite, power was not something to be complacent about.

The plethora of development outside city limits led some to seriously consider remarks like the following from an African American:

> Some very powerful people apparently want Buffalo to die. The university goes out to a flood plain. The medical school follows, breaking its promises. The Chamber of Commerce wants to run the stadium out of the city. And now the state and county want to strip a badly needed hospital from us. Apparently some men are willing to decimate Buffalo, and declare [suburban] Amherst the center of a new city.[86]

Urban renewal funds went for land clearance, but little development followed. For example, federal and state funds for a waterfront urban renewal project went for clearance and business relocation, but the city's leadership had not come up with a vision or prepared a plan to move ahead. To make matters worse, Buffalo lost federal funding because of a housing code dispute, which may or may not have contributed to the lack of follow-through. Upon compliance, some federal funds were no longer available, resulting in time and money lost. What could have been done?

Collaboration between local resources and outside experts could have helped with urban renewal development, similar to when elite leaders and city officials worked collaboratively with the Urban Institute from DC to create the Thruway Industrial Park (a project begun in 1959). In this successful case, an East Side councilman sponsored the project, the Greater Buffalo Development Foundation developed the concept, the Urban Land Institute prepared recommendations, city planners created the plan and assembled the land. Unfortunately, nothing like this happened again in the development arena until the 1980s, and by this time the city had hit bottom.

An open and legitimate planning process could have led to a different outcome in the case of the proposed convention center. Instead, city leaders based their decision on the promises of a local hotel owner to refurbish his hotel as a ploy to build the convention center in proximity, thus enhancing the value of the owner's investment. Because there was nothing to make him comply to his offer, the city took a risk in locating the convention center in a less-than-desirable space, especially when other excellent options existed. Instead of a systematic planning process, the procedures catered to an influential developer, an elite himself, with all the right social and political contacts. When his promises went unfulfilled—and he refurbished the hotel as an office building—the city was severely compromised.

In the case of the football stadium, business leaders waged their battles in bank boardrooms and law offices rather than in public forums. The notion that a downtown stadium would bring people downtown was the loser in these discussions. The fact that the board of directors of the Chamber of Commerce unanimously chose the suburbs over downtown, despite the possibility of five separate urban sites, is difficult to comprehend—unless one considers that the "implementation committee" had four attorneys, two bankers, and two builders at its core.

Losing the university to the suburbs was Buffalo's greatest loss, as the university could have become the city's anchor tenant and its professional adviser—on everything from urban design to engineering, from investment to planning, from jurisprudence to business. And it could have provided jobs in a service sector specifically geared, in conjunction with training programs, to inner-city needs and resources.

For independent elites who refused to support the establishment position on the campus debate, a price was extracted. Two individuals who were active as proponents of an urban campus did so at great cost to themselves. According to a number of elite leaders, one prominent banker was fired from his job, and the other, a manufacturer, was unable to obtain bank loans for his business, which may (it is presumed) have prompted his move to Canada.

Some speculation has been accepted as fact, and perhaps includes some truths, although no firm evidence exists. Some Buffalonians claimed that suburban landowners were influential in Albany and pushed for the suburban campus location in order to increase their land values. Others claimed that land speculators who were privy to inside information bought the land after huge sums of money were loaned to them. And a third line of thought held that it was a case of financial institutions interested in low-risk loans favoring suburban development. Perhaps it was some of all three of these, converging in the logic of land-based economics and interests.

In the African American neighborhoods, problematic as housing was, the community's biggest needs were investments in business and education. Part of the problem was that black leaders had no point of entry into Buffalo's power structure, where trust and partnerships could be naturally built. Black middle-class leadership (which had so impressed Alinsky) could have benefited from collaboration with their counterparts among the white leadership, and the white community would have learned much in return. The city as a whole would have benefited, too, in that the political standoff to come in the 1980s between downtown and neighborhood interests would have been less likely. Many of the black community's accomplishments, small as they might have seemed to the establishment, occurred in a vacuum, but they succeeded. Unfortunately, as a Model City Program leader explained, politicians and business leaders alike "were not too comfortable about getting involved in what we were trying to do."[87]

The decade ended with the "Report on Metals and Related Industries," which stated that the growth prospects for the area were good.[88] Despite growing signs of decline around them, Buffalo's leaders across the spectrum, for the most part, agreed. People found it inconceivable that the region's steel-related industrial base could be at risk. And here was another study to prove it.

NOTES

1. Greater Buffalo Development Foundation, "Annual Report, 1980–81: A Retrospective of Thirty Years: 1951–1981."

2. "Mel Baker Asks Re-development," *Buffalo Evening News*, May 17, 1956.

3. City of Buffalo, "Workable Program for Slum Prevention and Elimination" (Buffalo, NY: Board of Redevelopment and City Planning Commission, December 1957).

4. Greater Buffalo Development Foundation, "Annual Report, 1980–81."

5. "Buffalo's Development Retarded by Political Discord," *Buffalo Evening News*, January 19, 1952.

6. "Community Conference Is Solving Pittsburgh's Suburban Problems," *Buffalo Evening News*, January 26, 1951.

7. "Team to Study Buffalo Area for Redevelopment Potential," *Buffalo Evening News*, September 14, 1959.

8. Greater Buffalo Development Foundation, "Annual Report, 1975–76."

9. "Expanded Role Envisaged for Development Foundation," *Buffalo Evening News*, December 8, 1960.

10. Greater Buffalo Development Foundation, "Downtown Buffalo Shopping and Business Center," prepared by the Architect's Redevelopment Collaborative, 1962.

11. GBDF, "Annual Report, 1980–81."

12. Interview no. 50.

13. Interview no. 52.

14. GBDF, "Annual Report, 1980–81."

15. Ibid.

16. Neil Kraus, *Race, Neighborhoods, and Community Power*, (Albany: State University of New York Press, 2000), p. 104.

17. Greater Buffalo Development Foundation, "Annual Reports."

18. Interview no. 44.

19. Interview no. 36.

20. Daniel McDonald, "Waterfront vs. Amherst: A Study of the Campus Site Controversy at the SUNY at Buffalo," unpublished paper (1971), p. 23.

21. Ibid., p. 24.

22. Roberta Roth, "The Amherst Campus," unpublished paper (1972), p. 3.

23. Mark Goldman, *High Hopes: The Rise and Decline of Buffalo, New York* (Albany: State University of New York Press, 1983), p. 285.

24. Douglas L. Turner, "For the Record," *Western New York Heritage* (Spring 2002).

25. Interview no. 36.

26. Roth, "Amherst Campus," p. 1.

27. Ibid., p. 3.

28. "Comment," *Spectrum* (September 7, 1966).

29. Michael D'Amico, "Urban Campus Committee Report Comment," *Spectrum* (September 7, 1966).

30. Roth, "Amherst Campus," p. 4.

31. Interview no. 34.

32. Interviews nos. 1 and 34.

33. David Richman, "The University Relocation Controversy," unpublished paper (1975), p. 5.

34. Roth, "Amherst Campus," p. 10.

35. Richman, "University Relocation," p. 15.

36. McDonald, "Waterfront vs. Amherst," p. 16.

37. Interview no. 37.

38. Gordon Thompson, "A Chronology of Transportation Development on Niagara Frontier," unpublished paper, Buffalo, NY, July 1975.

39. Niagara Frontier Transportation Authority, http://www.fta.dot.gov/library/reference/iad/NFTA.HTM.

40. Thompson, "Chronology of Transportation."

41. George Rasmussen, "The Stadium in Perspective," *Buffalo Magazine* (February 1964).

42. William L. Martin, "A New Stadium for Metropolitan Buffalo," *Buffalo Magazine* (June 1967).

43. Interview no. 37.

44. Interview no. 60.

45. Interview no. 36.

46. Richard J. Ruth, "County Has Rung Up $400,000 So Far for Outside Legal Fees in Stadium Suit," *Buffalo Courier-Express*, November 17, 1981.

47. Interview no. 67.

48. Interview no. 63.

49. Interview no. 44.

50. "City Sanitation Men Have Lots of Letdowns between Their Pickups" (first of a series), *Buffalo Evening News*, May 12, 1966.

51. Interview no. 60.

52. "Code to Enforce Standards for Housing Board," *Buffalo Courier-Express*, April 24, 1965.

53. Interview no. 44.

54. Frank Buell, "U.S. 'Reluctant' to Go Further Until City Shows Renewal Gains," *Buffalo Evening News*, March 23, 1965.

55. "Delays Cost City Renewal Program," *Buffalo Evening News*, March 24, 1965.

56. Douglas Turner, "Code to Enforce Standards For Housing Bared," *Buffalo Courier-Express*, April 24, 1965.

57. Housing Opportunities Made Equal (HOME).

58. Quote from Citizens Community Interest (a Masten district group) in "Harriman Reveals HHFA Approval," *Buffalo Courier-Express,* June 27, 1965.

59. "Hasty Tampering with Housing Code," editorial, *Buffalo Courier-Express,* October 1, 1965.

60. Interview no. 40.

61. US Bureau of the Census, "1970 Census of Population: General and Social and Economic Characteristics: New York," General Popula-

tion Characteristics (Washington, DC: US Department of Commerce, Bureau of the Census, 1972).

62. Eldor Miller, "Forced Relocation in Urban Renewal: A Sociological Analysis," PhD diss., 1970, p. 49, table III-1.

63. Preston Smith, "Lutherans Remain Divided on Support for Alinsky," *Buffalo Evening News*, February 2, 1966.

64. "President's Report," East Side Community Organization, Inc., newsletter (March 1966).

65. Interview no. 42.

66. East Side Community Organization, newsletter (April–May 1966).

67. Jim McAvey, "Alinsky Says IAF against Violence," *Buffalo Courier-Express*, May 14, 1966.

68. Letter from Alinsky to the ESCO leadership, BUILD Press Archives: 1964–74.

69. Debbie Dahlberg, "Alinsky in Buffalo: The BUILD Organization," unpublished paper, 1985, p. 36.

70. Ibid., p. 31.

71. "Sedita Reports Progress in Jobs Recreation," *Challenger* (July 6, 1967).

72. "100 Stage 'Sheet Hanging' to Publicize 'Fire Trap,'" *Buffalo Courier-Express*, no date, BUILD Press Archives, p. 157.

73. "BUILD Pledges to Oppose Moving Meyer Memorial," BUILD Press Archives, p. 164.

74. Dahlberg, "Alinsky in Buffalo," p. 33.

75. Ibid.

76. "School Board Accepts Plan to Set Up 'Ghetto Academy,'" BUILD Press Archives, p. 171.

77. Richard E. Baldwin, "Grass Roots Issue Snags Model City," *Buffalo Courier-Express*, in BUILD Archives, p. 216.

78. Senator Robert Kennedy, transcript, The Buffalo Model City Conference (sponsored by the Cooperative Urban Extension Center), January 19–20, 1967.

79. East Side Community Organization, newsletter (Winter Quarter 1967).

80. Interview no. 41.

81. Interview no. 44.

82. Interview no. 41.

83. Interview no. 44.

84. Interview no. 41.

85. "BUILD Head Endorses Jitney Plan," *Buffalo Courier-Express*, January 12, 1971.

86. "BUILD to Request Support of Medics," *Buffalo Courier-Express*, in BUILD Press Archives, p. 195.

87. Interview no. 41.

88. Greater Buffalo Development Foundation, "Report on Metals and Related Industries," 1969.

Chapter Four

CRISIS

The 1970s

A crisis of epic proportions unfolded when Bethlehem Steel announced its first layoffs. These losses continued with the closures of steel mills and other industrial operations, culminating in a loss of seventy thousand manufacturing jobs between 1970 and 1985 in the Buffalo area. Buffalo's economic decline, however, cannot be blamed exclusively on the loss of steel mills. There are many examples where the city's leadership did little to heed the warnings of industrial decline, with production output in 1972 dropping to .05 percent, compared with the national average of 3 percent.[1] Many proposed solutions went ignored or, when adopted, were too late to ward off spiraling decline. Significantly, the two elite nonprofit organizations, to whom everyone looked for leadership, expended time and energy in turf battles for control, rather than focusing single-mindedly—and collaboratively—on revitalization efforts.

Proposed solutions included a proactive agenda for diversifying the economy's industrial base. Such proactive behavior began in 1977, two years *after* Buffalo faced bankruptcy, and only owing to the efforts of a small group who temporarily assumed elite leadership. A long-awaited study admonished establishment businessmen to lead expansion of the service sector with a less "cavalier" attitude. The study also advised broadening the spectrum of interests in the planning process by including the region's diverse professional and entrepreneurial base, in particular the black community and the Model City Program.

In other words, the area's industrial losses were severe, but a crisis of leadership also played a central role in Buffalo's spiraling decline. Establishment leaders sought the status quo and did not use their powerful platform to lead or seek mitigating policies in state or local legislatures. In addition, they did not work to create community partnerships or an ongoing planning process that incorporated opposing interests and points of view. And they had already turned away from pro-growth strategies, such as a downtown university on the waterfront, an urban football stadium, and a transit system linking the suburbs and the university with downtown.

As the economy plummeted and the city faced bankruptcy, new political and economic forces emerged—driven by the arrival of outside investors and the election of neighborhood activists to the city council—which meant that Buffalo faced a radical reconstitution (though not a restructuring, since power continued to lie with the bankers and related interests) of its elite leadership.

On the political side, economic events set the stage for the election of Jimmy Griffin, an independent mayor, a former Democrat, who changed the rules of the city's planning and budgeting process—and thus the structure of power within the public sector. A great divide between the Office of the Mayor and the Common Council transpired and ensued for the sixteen years of Griffin's tenure, making inclusive urban planning for downtown, city neighborhoods, and the waterfront impossible.

ECONOMIC STORY

The business leadership did not watch what was happening. They did not argue and fight about the issues. For most of the 1970s,

Buffalonians blamed problems on other things: the oil embargo
of 1973; the cost of energy; then in 1979, the second oil shock;
and beyond that Buffalo lost its automobile production and went
out of the steel business.

—A business leader

The Greater Buffalo Development Foundation, the business elite's
prestigious nonprofit organization, took heart from one of its
studies released in 1969. Despite forecasts of decline in the "Report
on Metals and Related Industries" (1972), elite leaders focused on
the notion that "growth prospects for the Erie-Niagara area . . . are
good." Although local leaders wanted to enhance the area's
prospects, they could not agree on a regional vision.

County Executive Edward Regan expressed interest in the
foundation's work, which up to that point had been privately
funded, and found a way to commit county funds to underwrite
economic development research. This fit with his 1971 campaign
pledge to make county government a unifying regional force.[2] The
county agreed to pay the salary of the foundation's research
director. More important, Erie County agreed to fund a comprehensive analysis of Buffalo's economy by developing a mathemat-
ical model of its industrial base. By constructing an input-output
table using data from over two hundred local business operations,
the study would be able to identify industries—and strategies—
with the greatest growth impact for the future.

The study conducted in 1972, "A Growth Strategy for the Erie-
Niagara Area, No. 8: The Buffalo Area's Economic Prospects,"
underscored the industrial interdependence in the Buffalo two-
county area: the output of one industry is often the input of another.
For example, a 25 percent reduction of output in transportation
equipment led to reductions in total output by other industries. The
table below shows how a range of industries were affected when
the output of transportation equipment was reduced.

Reduced Outputs in Other Industries*
Based on a 25% Reduction in Transportation Equipment Output

construction=3%;   chemicals=2%;   petroleum=11%;
iron and steel=4%;   fabricated metals=25%; machinery=12%;
transportation=15%;   financial/insurance/real estate=9%.

*Percentages represent reduced dollar-value of production outputs. Source: "Buffalo Area's Industries Depend on Each Other, Too," *Courier-Express*, August 20, 1975.

The "Growth Strategy" study was unique not only for its basic economic analysis but also for its presentation of findings and recommendations. The study included statistical data from comparable cities and references to the national economy, analyzing Buffalo's past trends and predicted growth. The results were shocking. Buffalo's growth rate in production output had slowed to .05 percent, compared with the national average in 1972 of 3 percent. Combined with 9 percent unemployment for the same period, these figures highlighted the poor economic growth in the Buffalo area. Furthermore, the report continued, "trends over time and comparisons with other metropolitan areas emphasize the mediocre performance of industry and services in this area, both in terms of growth and level of income. . . . It can be stated unequivocally that another decade of decline can establish an irreversible downward spiral for Buffalo, Erie and Niagara Counties, as well as the outlying area."

The study's authors stressed the crucial role of the nonmanufacturing sector in jump-starting the economy. Recommendations for immediate action included the need to:

- Establish an "Existing Industry Program" to help retain jobs in manufacturing by vigorously addressing issues regarding taxes, manpower, productivity, land availability, community relations, trade regulation, and transportation.
- Organize a series of *productivity seminars* in order to increase productivity per unit cost of labor. Along these lines, the

study urged the area to join in the management-labor council network being encouraged by President Richard Nixon's Commerce Department by starting its own local council.

- Create a *Buffalo-Canada trade program* that the Development Foundation might head. It was thought that trade could double to a billion dollars, as only 5 percent of area businesses then traded with Canada.
- Make the *service sector* a priority to ensure further development and growth. The study said that until recently a "cavalier attitude" predominated, with little or no real understanding of what was needed to assure healthy growth in services and employment.
- Establish a *technical advisory board* and science council in order to strengthen high-tech programs.
- Create a *financial development corporation* to provide high-risk capital.
- Promote "area commitment by private and public leadership to strengthen and *extend economic development of the Greater Buffalo Area* through programs financed jointly by the public and private sectors" (a new concept in those days) in order to recapture the competitive edge.
- Consider and include *social objectives* in economic development goals with "strong participation by business leaders in the model cities effort, the Black Development Foundation."
- Consider creating programs to *clean up the air and water*.
- Seek facts and the latest data so that the business leadership might "assess problems intelligently and build programs that have a high probability of success." In other words, avoid crisis management.[3]

This was not what foundation leaders wanted to hear.[4] The study's analysis challenged the elite's accepted views of the local economy and its strategies. The study revealed the city not only as uncompetitive but in decline. It criticized the elite's "cavalier attitudes" and "reactive" style of management. And it suggested that elite leaders collaborate with the Black Development Foundation. A few individuals in places of power spoke out about the decline, such as Mayor Stanley Makowski's attorney. "The message was pretty unpopular, but [he] was really one of the first people to get [others] to pay attention."[5]

The foundation's research director and staff came under fire as a result of this much disparaged report. Rather than working feverishly to enact new strategies to address the report's findings, the business leadership argued that given strong national growth and the huge local workforce in steel the predictions of spiraling decline were unfounded. According to a number of business leaders active at the time, the foundation's board thought that the recommendations were an "overreaction" to a study that was really "not very good."[6]

Decline in the Steel Industry

> In the early 1970s, Bethlehem Steel's management began meeting quietly with political and business leaders about the cascading industrial decline around them. It was at this time that the company's chairman told Governor Rockefeller that he had just about given up on Buffalo.
>
> —Interview no. 1

The 1970s brought another rash of departures. Houdaille and National Gypsum moved south; Carborundum and Western Electric, all big players in Buffalo's economy, moved to the Midwest. Beyond the loss of industry, problems existed on many fronts: the decaying downtown, the inadequate transportation infrastructure, the flow of middle-class whites leaving for the suburbs, the ethnic tensions in the neighborhoods and segregation in the schools, and the growing divisions in city government. But with time, nothing matched the growing concern of city leaders about the "steel problem" facing Buffalo and the future of that industry's regional operations. For one hundred years, steel had been the great center-piece of the regional economy and Buffalo's cultural identity. Closures were one thing. But it was asking a lot of Buffalo's citizens or leaders to believe that its basic steel-making operation might ever leave in its entirety. Now mixed signals began to come from industry players.

In 1971 Bethlehem Steel expressed optimism about the industry's future. At the same time, the company laid off nine thousand of its eighteen thousand Lackawanna workers. Bethlehem's chairman cited "oppressive taxes," "unrealistic environmental control laws," and "an uncooperative labor force" as reasons for the cutbacks in the early 1970s.[7] To some, these excuses seemed self-serving: the steel plants had grown obsolete, and management knew this years before it closed them. The charge of "oppressive" taxes was more plausible. It was known that the City of Lackawanna kept the assessed valuation of Bethlehem Steel Company "written in pencil" to be changed easily. Bethlehem's real estate taxes fluctuated each year, often paralleling Lackawanna's income needs. These taxes represented up to 60 percent of Lackawanna's tax base. The *Courier-Express*, on November 15, 1971, quoted a company representative who recounted that "in comparison with one of the other six Bethlehem Steel plants, taxes per ton of steel were seven times greater at the Lackawanna plant."[8]

Tax relief became the steel company's preoccupation. Company executives met with the business elite and government leaders to argue in its favor. They made urgent appeals to the Republican Party chairman (who from all accounts did not intervene with the City of Lackawanna about Bethlehem's city taxes) as well as to the county executive, state legislators, and the governor. Bethlehem Steel supported County Executive Regan's sales-tax plan rather than a plan to raise property taxes. "One purpose of the tax plan was to avoid increasing property taxes which fall heavily on large corporations such as Bethlehem," stated the Lackawanna city council president.[9]

Still, Bethlehem's intentions were difficult to read. Meetings between executives and public officials became ongoing. In one all-day meeting with business leaders, editorial writers, and politicians, Bethlehem Steel's top management outlined its regional problems—which included being pawns in political maneuvers and facing ever-increasing tax assessments. Bethlehem's officials complained that they were always being "shaken down."

At stake was a state-of-the-art bar mill to be built by the steel company. Following pledges of cooperation, Bethlehem Steel decided to build the proposed mill. It also helped that a number of investigative pieces were written by the *Courier-Express* that exposed Bethlehem Steel's own maneuvers. In addition to the confrontations between the paper's reporter and Lackawanna officials, Governor Rockefeller put pressure on the appropriate politicians with threats of investigations. The plant was completed in 1975.

The chairman of Bethlehem Steel, at the dedication party for its $138 million bar mill, made a forceful speech about Buffalo's problems and the need for regional government—or at least a collaborative regional structure. He warned that, unless Buffalo's leaders took this step, the county was headed toward irrelevance ("the ash can of history"), and he argued that companies were getting picked apart by local entities. He won the county executive over to his way of thinking.

Despite the steel industry's remonstrations about taxes, it turned out that regional leaders did *not* lobby the state's capital for lower taxes. In 1976 the state legislature signed a *tax increase* into law, and Bethlehem's taxes increased 29 percent.[10] Caught between the needs of government and industry, Erie County's chief executive supported the tax increase.

This turn of events was not inevitable. Buffalo's leadership might have effected a different outcome had it made taxes a priority issue through a coordinated effort. Custom in Albany dictated that when local politicians strenuously objected to a bill, the state legislators would sit on it indefinitely. But this did not happen because strenuous objections were not lodged. Upon passage of the tax bill, one top executive of Bethlehem Steel told close friends that this "is the greatest betrayal of trust we have ever experienced." That event, according to one source, sealed the fate of Bethlehem Steel—and of National Steel, Chenango Steel, and Republic Steel.

Of course, the tax issue obfuscated a more complex reality:

(1) the overall declining position of domestic steel within the United States because of foreign dumping and, more generally, the problem of excess capacity in world markets;

(2) management's avoidance of capital reinvestment into their local facilities—for which management must be held accountable along with the federal government for tax policies that effectively discouraged such investments; and

(3) high labor costs, for which labor must assume responsibility, as unions pushed for what the industry could bear. The net result, no matter the explanation: Lackawanna's plants were obsolete and could no longer compete.

In 1977 Bethlehem Steel made the decision that would forever affect steelmaking in Buffalo. The company took a $750 million write-off—the biggest write-off ever taken by an American firm until that time—and closed most of two US operations, Buffalo's Lackawanna plants and those in Johnstown, Pennsylvania.

The following year, the company cut thirty-five hundred more local workers from its Buffalo-area plant rolls, leaving approximately eighty-five hundred still employed.

In 1980 the Bethlehem Steel Foundry closed.

In 1981 the twelve-inch-bar mill and its lime plant closed. Republic Steel followed suit, closing its South Park Avenue factory—twenty-five hundred jobs gone. Bethlehem's strategy was to close Lackawanna's old facilities and concentrate their activity in the new $240 million bar mill.[11] These momentous events prompted Buffalo's first industrial restructuring in one hundred years, the second ever in its history.

A longtime industrial realtor explained that the leaders "used to get excited when Bethlehem invested five million dollars in the Lackawanna plant. But they weren't doing their homework because, at the same time, other plants were getting ten times that— such as at Sparrows Point."

The loss of steel, jobs, and city income culminated in a crisis that brought about political and economic change. As the economy plunged, it pitted downtown interests against neighborhood interests, which played out at city hall, the Common Council, public agencies, and nonprofit organizations. It also energized existing tensions between the city and its suburbs.

Cascading Closures

> I . . . spent two years in the budget division—which were critical, crazy years when factories were closing by the day . . . when Mayor Makowski laid off seventeen hundred city employees (1975) . . . when eighty-eight factories closed over nine years . . . when six of the northeast railroads went bankrupt . . . and the Catholic Diocese went bankrupt. These were cascading closures. . . . And [the city was] tied down dealing with the wreckage of the industrial economy . . . while trying to attract new industries . . . and get ahead of the curve on who was closing next.
>
> —A financial and economic development official

Six of the northeast railroads went bankrupt, constituting 20 percent of the land use. None paid city taxes any longer, and neither did all the factories that closed along the rail lines or had closed earlier. City finances were not immediately affected because of the normal lag in time for tax losses to accrue. Eventually, though, losses began to hit hard. Although it was not commonly known at the time, the city came within two weeks of bankruptcy, according to a budget official. City leaders considered immediate department layoffs, but they were able to avoid them, according to one city official, through a series of financial maneuvers.[12]

Six months later, the *Buffalo Evening News*'s lead story reported, "At least 38 large manufacturing plants in the Buffalo metropolitan area have closed during the past five years, causing a loss of nearly 10,000 jobs and $125,976,830 in payroll earnings. . . . Furthermore, the exodus . . . [with] total property tax assessments in the tens of millions of dollars, has cost Erie County and its cities, towns, villages and school districts millions in lost or unpaid property taxes."[13]

According to a local economist, the city, traditionally and politically, was not geared toward hard times. Hard times undermined union workers and the entire patronage system, which, in turn, undermined the political machine and, subsequently, the party's power base. (Democrats lost the election two years later.) Systems accepted in earlier times came under fire and reconsideration.

A sense prevailed that if political attitudes did not change, the whole city might go out of business. Unlike the passivity of much of the elite leadership, and apathy among the citizenry, a sense of urgency existed among the higher echelons of the political hierarchy. City officials were on the front line and affected by the crisis in specific ways. They were faced with keeping the city government running—such as meeting payrolls, ensuring that city services continued to function, and regaining accreditation on the municipal bond markets. And they always had elections to consider.

Officials were able to cut the city's accumulated deficit by some $600,000. This made it the first time since 1970 that the city would spend less than its income in one fiscal year. The mayor told bankers that the 1976–77 budget projected further deficit reductions of more than $6 million. Most difficult, capital budgets had been crippled by the lack of bond market access. In fiscal year 1976–77, the normal rate of expenditures of about $18 million a year decreased to about $4.8 million in nine months as a result of a partial freeze.[14]

After the Fall: Labor's Cooperation

Only an economic crisis of some magnitude could have brought Buffalo's militant unions to heel. But with tens of thousands of jobs lost, they were ready to cooperate. Labor based its new strategy on the prevailing economic climate and the understanding that when labor is comparatively unproductive—where the costs of labor are too high per unit of output—the entire industry loses.

Throughout the decades, labor leaders had been part of the civic structure, but they were always "tending only to their own interests," maintains a business friend.[15] Despite acrimonious regional labor relations, the head of the AFL-CIO Labor Council sat with business leaders on the board of the Greater Buffalo Development Foundation. After the crisis, he left his mark in 1976 by founding, along with another foundation director from the management side of business, the Buffalo–Erie County Labor Management Council. The foundation provided seed funding for this project, which successfully mediated a number of strikes and brought to conclusion major grievance disputes.[16] Their long-range goals were to improve labor-management relations and facilitate industrial efficiency and competitiveness, while improving the image of regional labor-management relations to outsiders.

In terms of the power structure and industrial planning, it would be a stretch to say unions played an inside role. Instead, they acted as outside catalysts and challengers. And while they did not formulate policy, they had immense power in shaping it through their activist support of the Democratic Party and its machine. In the workplace, Buffalo's unions had as much clout as anywhere in the United States. Even a decade after the 1972 industrial study became public, the rate of union membership—27.3 percent of workers—was nearly double the national average.[17]

The council established labor-management committees at the plant and industry levels. In the first year of activity, the council established nine committees in the private sector and two in the public sector. As a mediator, the council resolved more than a dozen grievances prior to arbitration. In resolving strikes, it played a direct role in settling a strike at Buffalo Forge Company and a "tangential backstage role in resolving the Spaulding Fibre strike."[18]

A Downtown Strategy

Nine years after the consultants from Arthur D. Little had recommended writing a city plan in their "Downtown Study," the city, with the help of the Greater Buffalo Development Foundation and the state, completed the "Comprehensive Plan for Downtown Buffalo" (1971). The plan included a $20 million convention center (already in the planning stage), a $336 million rapid-transit line to connect downtown to the university campus in Amherst, and a downtown pedestrian mall. To see these through, the foundation established MET Development Corporation to work cooperatively with the city and the Niagara Frontier Transportation Authority.

About the same time, the federal government issued its first Urban Development Action Grant (UDAG) to Buffalo for an out-of-town developer to build the Hilton Hotel on the waterfront. Although, according to some, this changed perceptions about downtown, hard times lay just around the corner. The inability to market city bonds stopped many city projects in 1975.[19] Fortunately, not all projects were halted, as some funding came from other sources.

The Greater Buffalo Development Foundation put an end to another project, a $26 million covered transit mall for downtown. A foundation study (issued May 6, 1975) determined that the project was too expensive. However, this was contradicted by "Financing Buffalo's Downtown Mall," a document presented earlier at the annual meeting of the foundation board on April 18 that argued that the covered mall might, in fact, be quite workable. "The third major finding indicated that additional property taxes generated through 1995 from new development directly attributable to a

weather-protected mall are projected to be sufficient to cover operating and maintenance costs of a totally enclosed mall and annual
payments on a $3.5 million, twenty-year bond issue with a 6%
interest rate." On the other hand, "If an open mall were developed,
lower operating and maintenance costs would enable annual payments to be made on a $4.8 million [larger loan], twenty-year bond
issue with a 6% rate."[20]

With regard to rapid transit planning itself, a market research
firm (Alan Voorhees and Associates) transmitted good news that
should have given Buffalo's leaders a boost and something to
believe in. Operating figures showed that "when buses are taken off
Main Street and the efficiencies of modern rapid transit are
included, it will actually be *less* expensive to operate the proposed
rail-bus system than the current all-bus system [emphasis
added]."[21] The leadership, however, found little to champion in
rapid-transit planning.

Buffalo's dependence on government funds made urban planning difficult, given the political regime changes and the policy
shifts at the state and federal levels of government. But, obtaining
government funding without clear project plans was perhaps even
more difficult. Three city officials (including the mayor), believing
they had a good chance at succeeding, traveled to Washington to
request $8 million from HUD to prepare additional waterfront land
for private development. They were denied.[22] Housing funds, too,
from the state's Urban Development Corporation were in limbo for
additional West Side waterfront housing.[23] Things were not looking
good for Buffalo, and it seems that a special assessment by the leadership at this time would have been important.

Manufacturing's Initiative: Striving for a Role

All the while, the city's manufacturing leaders remained in the
wings. The Chamber of Commerce (a large body with thousands of
members) provided them a vehicle, yet—and despite its huge

staff—effective activity eluded them. In part, this was because of staff leadership and the fact that staff had never been hired for pro-activity. And the manufacturing members themselves confirmed that they propounded the motto, "the business of business is business." Theirs was a vision of building sound business operations, with workers' benefits and pensions, and how to make the city more business friendly as areas of concern. Then in 1976 a small group of leaders came along who wanted to do more on the industrial front.

This coterie of manufacturing and communications executives, a dynamic group of "fire-breathing industrialists," pledged to meet regularly to assess Buffalo's dire circumstances. They wanted to draw up an action plan from their unique perspective as regional industrialists to complement the plans of the Greater Buffalo Development Foundation, which presented the perspective of the bankers and other downtown interests. There was complete agreement within the group that participation needed to be restricted to manufacturing executives and colleagues—no bankers and lawyers would be invited to join.

But this was not to be. Before long one manufacturer, a loyal Greater Buffalo Development Foundation member, broke ranks with the group and invited "visitors" to meetings. Eventually, one of these visitors pressed the manufacturers to make this group part of the Greater Buffalo Development Foundation, arguing that too many groups were already working on industrial issues. Despite immediate unanimous opposition to the proposed measure, this individual eventually prevailed when several influential individuals were persuaded to change their votes, and others followed.

This sealed the manufacturers' fate. The group, now enlarged, came to be called the Area Leadership Group and was put under the aegis of the foundation, where in short time the manufacturers' agenda shifted from strategizing to listening to speeches. One participant likened these events to "putting a hot coal in the center of three pounds of wet dough." They accomplished nothing, and in 1979 the Area Leadership Group disbanded.

The Erie County Industrial Development Agency

The tension between the Chamber of Commerce and the Greater
Buffalo Development Foundation turned to "open warfare,"
according to those who were involved. Although members of the
Chamber of Commerce disassociated themselves from strategic
planning, they were incensed by the foundation's attempts to take
control. Furthermore, the foundation's "Growth Strategy" report
had challenged the chamber's orientation by suggesting strategies
that began to look at venture capital and new approaches to entre-
preneurship.[24] The Chamber of Commerce won the skirmish, and
for a brief period the Greater Buffalo Development Foundation
became relatively inactive. Publicly, "the Chamber paid lip service" to the study's recommendations, but little got done.[25]

With all that was occurring, the Erie County Legislature backed
away and cut funding to the Greater Buffalo Development Foundation. It terminated the research director's position, even though
there were many who believed that the county executive shared
foundation views. The foundation, for its part, began focusing more
narrowly on downtown projects, such as the convention center, the
waterfront hotel, and the conversion of the old post office building
for Erie Community College.

Congressman Henry Nowak, with his election in 1974 in the
post-Watergate congressional class, became a central figure in Buffalo's economic development funding and strategies. During his
tenure, he worked quietly with the Office of the Mayor and the Buffalo and Erie County Economic Development Committee. It was
Nowak, using his position on the Congressional Public Works Committee with its oversight of the Economic Development Administration, who helped Buffalo receive the nation's first Urban Development Action Grant for the development of the waterfront Hilton.

Increasingly, Buffalo became the beneficiary of federal funds
that flowed to cities in the form of Community Development Block
Grants (their use to be decided by the cities themselves), Urban

Development Action Grants (for specific economic development projects), and the Model City Program (targeting "rust belt cities" for inner-city community development projects).

State funds, too, had grown exponentially, with Buffalo receiving the lion's share because of the region's problems. State legislation in the late 1960s had encouraged the creation of Industrial Development Agencies as financing mechanisms that could be used to float taxfree industrial revenue bonds. It was this legislation that enabled the Erie County Industrial Development Agency (ECIDA) to be formed in the first place and put in the care of the Chamber of Commerce.

Despite the founding of the Erie County Industrial Development Agency and the increase in subsidies and grants, little seemed to get done. Frustrated by the inaction, a committee formed in the mid-1970s to see what could be done. Erie County Executive Edward Regan chaired the committee, with Mayor Makowski as vice chairman. Sometimes referred to as the Committee of One Hundred and Fifty, it included corporate and business leaders, bankers, the county, the city, and unions and met for a couple of years. Participants hoped regional interests would begin to work cooperatively, but there was no way to organize action. Committee cooperation fell by the wayside when internal conflict erupted over control between the Chamber of Commerce and a small group led by two business leaders—one a young but influential lawyer, the son-in-law of a politically connected attorney with strong ties to the elite banking community, and the other, the chief executive and owner of a local steel company.

Things changed when the attorney and business executive took matters into their own hands, calling together a select group of individuals known for getting jobs done to meet at the Buffalo Club. Their challenge was to determine how the already existing Erie County Industrial Development Agency might be reconfigured to do its job. At its first "open" meeting, the enlarged group created reasonable timetables and target dates for a variety of projects. The group also took the unusual step to draft legislation to expand Erie County's ability to finance industrial growth.[26]

According to a public official who was there, this "open" meeting was unique because it brought people together who did not ordinarily have contact. As a result of the coordinated effort, these business, labor, and political leaders signed a compact to promote a political concept that would unify the city and reconstitute the Erie County Industrial Development Agency. In this "unique bi-partisan proposal," the mayor of Buffalo and executive of Erie County, together with area labor, finance, and industry leaders, supported special state legislation expanding the Erie County Industrial Development Agency.[27] These procedures demonstrated what a cross-section of Buffalo's leaders could accomplish when building a determined bipartisan, public-private-nonprofit partnership. Individual interests succumbed to the group.

The compact for the Industrial Development Agency's reformulation stated that each of the signatories supported an act of the legislature to create a board representing all of them, as an integrating planning agency for economic development for the Buffalo area. Positions on its bipartisan board would be *mandated*, not appointed to suit political or personal economic agendas. The document, with its signatures, was then sent to the governor and state legislature in Albany. When a few legislators opposed the legislation, two elite leaders solicited the help of a local reporter—an investigative journalist on state politics—who, in turn, let recalcitrant legislators know that it would be in their political interest to vote for the bill.

With effort on multiple fronts, the legislation passed. As a result, the Erie County Industrial Development Agency's board was reformulated and stood independent of the Chamber of Commerce. One lingering question remained in Albany among the legislators, however: "Why do we have to pass a law to solve your local problems? Why don't you just solve them yourselves?"[28]

At the time, there was another lingering question: Why didn't the Town of Amherst work with Buffalo through the Erie County Industrial Development Agency, a county-wide entity? In part, Amherst decided to go it alone rather than wait for Buffalo's leaders to move proactively. Pro-development attitudes, in conjunction with Amherst's sizable annual marketing budget—by the late 1970s approximately ten times that of Buffalo's ($250,000 versus $25,000)—added impetus to its go-it-alone strategy. As one Amherst public official put it,

> Buffalo's leaders' reluctance to let go [of their] industrial legacy, coupled with the fact that the university decided to build its north campus in Amherst, led the people in Amherst to say, "Well, if the people downtown don't understand it, or the people in the county don't understand it, we think that the university—and in particular the schools [including the medical school] that are moving out—present us with a real opportunity to change the mix of businesses that probably bode well for our future."

There were also internal divisions in Amherst that led to the town's exclusion from the Erie County Industrial Development Agency. The story goes that in 1976, when the ECIDA was being reconstituted in Albany, the chairman of the state legislature (Dan Ward from Amherst) took a firm no-growth position on Amherst and wanted no part of economic development planning. As a result, when the legislature changed the statute defining who sat on the Erie County board being pushed by Buffalo's leaders, a position for Town of Amherst supervisor was intentionally removed from the board. As it turned out, this lack of representation on the county IDA gave great concern to another of Amherst's supervisors, Jack Sharp, who persuaded colleagues to activate its own industrial development agency. Perhaps this division could have been avoided if there had been an ongoing exchange of information and collaboration between the different local governments in the beginning. Instead, each worked in isolation from the other.

The Amherst IDA chose to make the new university in its midst (and lost to downtown Buffalo) the cornerstone of Amherst's economic development strategy, using university resources to attract and sustain industry and local development. This idea appeared in Amherst's master plan in 1972 and later in a study by the Erie and Niagara Counties Regional Planning Board, "Economic Development in the Erie-Niagara Region" (1975), which based much of its thinking on a study from the State Office of Planning titled "The Buffalo Amherst Corridor," completed in 1969. The research was loaded with projections on the nature, scale, and extent of regional growth. The goal was to stimulate a joint government development effort that would continue. The rationale was clear: "Because the Buffalo-Amherst Corridor crosses political boundaries of several municipalities, county, regional and state planning and development policies and powers must be coordinated with those of the Town of Amherst and the city of Buffalo. . . . Major public items [needing public investment] would [include] the rapid transit system and low-cost housing."[29]

The "corridor" concept demanded coordination and cooperation throughout Erie and Niagara Counties. The two campuses would be the foci of aggressive economic development planning and marketing that would tie the university—its curricula along with its business, economic, medical, and scientific resources—to the region's communities. The missing element was a joint planning effort, but this concept of joint planning proved infeasible for several reasons. For one, business and political leaders could not put aside petty rivalries and jealousies. Second, the rapid-transit system became badly hung up with delays, and those on each side of the issue, in the main, viewed it with skepticism—if not negatively. Third, from Amherst's perspective, some of Buffalo's leaders remained bitter over losing the campus to Amherst, making collaboration difficult. But there was also a fundamental difference in both need and strategy.

Buffalo's need for downtown investment meant leaders pushed development benefiting the urban core before anything else. Alternatively, Amherst's leaders' self-described strategy was market driven, where they proposed giving companies whatever they wanted, greenfield sites if necessary—and they had plenty of those—to get them into the region.

A Step toward Partnership

Prior to the 1977 election, Mayor Makowski initiated efforts to bring together the city's public officials and elite leaders, endeavors that grew after Mayor Griffin won the election. Despite these worthy activities, huge drawbacks accompanied Griffin's approach to this partnership. Nevertheless, these meetings were important because they began to break down the barriers between two ordinarily separate worlds in Buffalo's culture, the predominantly Irish Catholic political figures and the predominantly WASP establishment elites. And, at first, they used the new, reconstituted Erie County Industrial Development Agency as their vehicle for activity.

With part of the funds that Congressman Nowak had secured for the region (an amount totaling nearly $400 million), these public- and private-sector leaders had the Arthur D. Little consulting firm develop a "superplan" titled "The Buffalo Area Economic Adjustment Strategy" (prepared for the Erie County IDA in 1978). Central to the plan was the proposal to write off the steel industry, while introducing strategies to retain remaining industries. It proposed a set of actions to "trigger long-term change in the basic economic structure of the area," with the goal of creating a more self-sufficient region less dependent on federal and state assistance.

The economic focus would lie in smaller light-, medium-, and high-technology industrial sectors. It would capitalize on Buffalo's "hub" location between US and Canadian markets (a strategy recommended in the 1960s). And it would strengthen tourism as a base for service-sector jobs in the downtown area. To these ends, relations between labor and management needed to improve. The plan emphasized that the public and private sectors needed to get land, labor, and financial resources to work cooperatively on marketing and local business assistance strategies.

The "Economic Adjustment Strategy" of 1978 guided economic development for the next decade and beyond, according to one economic development professional. "We took that plan and pursued it religiously . . . especially the retention program . . . to retain existing industries."[30] Another involved party maintained that economic development was more likely to have been guided by the federal grants and funds than any plan. In fact, it seems that both are right.

The Chamber of Commerce assumed responsibility for marketing as part of the attraction strategy that the study had recommended. Everybody got behind the Chamber of Commerce, and its board hired a new director to revitalize activity.

In 1978 Mayor Griffin brought people into community development who were self-starters and proactive by nature. They worked with the Erie County Industrial Development Agency, and they created a lending corporation (the Buffalo and Erie County Regional Development Corporation) with an initial $35,000, which grew by 300 percent, and the number of companies assisted exceeded all expectations.[31] The city inaugurated a program of giving $2 million annually to the agency to assist in the formation of capital. This strategy allowed the public sector to get behind business initiatives and create, for the first time, a public-private partnership where public funds were used to invest in business and could be paid back. (Whether they were repaid is another matter.)

That same year, in October, the convention center opened, on schedule and within the $20 million construction cost. The opening was good news, but the enthusiasm had to be balanced with the fact that not enough hotel space existed to accommodate large conventions. (The waterfront Hilton would not open for another two years, and the downtown Hyatt would not open for another decade—in the late 1980s). This meant that prospective national and international business went undeveloped early on. Unfortunately, the momentum generally associated with a convention center's opening was not possible. Preceding the center's opening, the *Courier-Express* quoted its director: "Conventions are extremely important to Buffalo, but to concentrate now on bringing 5,000 to 10,000 people here without the hotels would be bad publicity." What we should concentrate on now, the director said, "is bringing in what Buffalo can handle."[32] Valuable time and money were lost.

With no major hotel within city limits, and after more than a decade since the decision for the convention center had been made, the *Courier-Express* wrote: "San Francisco developer Clement Chen's proposed waterfront hotel was described by the Griffin administration as a 'do-able project' which will improve the city's poor image in the eyes of the federal government." Further, "The local HUD office has made no secret of its feeling that the city has frittered away some $30 million in federal community development funds over the past few years on too many small, ill-conceived neighborhood projects, which failed to produce any tangible results."[33]

Mayor Griffin made no mention of the hotel's critical importance to the convention center. But having just come to office, it is clear that he wanted to move the project along. Regarding the prospects for a second hotel, the paper wrote: "Several parties in Buffalo are interested in having Hyatt Corp. build a hotel. . . . It doesn't look like Hyatt will rush into Buffalo unless [the city] gives it money to build. . . . According to one official, Hyatt might be looking for a package deal like it is getting in Baltimore. Hyatt put up $17 million for a $34 million luxury hotel. The city of Baltimore put up the other half."[34]

Still, the convention center venture proved to be a successful cooperative effort. It was financed by the county, built by the city, and managed by the nonprofit Convention Center Management Corporation. Buffalo's business community, through the Greater Buffalo Development Foundation, supported the project and raised $750,000 (in cooperation with the Bank Clearinghouse Association) toward its capital cost.

City of Buffalo in the 1950s, entrance to the Buffalo River and Ship Canal, and Outer
Harbor (*lower right*) leading to the Lackawanna Canal and Bethlehem Steel operations.
(*Courtesy of the Buffalo and Erie County Historical Society*)

Pouring hot metal into molds at Bethlehem Steel. 1950s.
(*Courtesy of the Buffalo and Erie County Historical Society*)

Top left: Seymour H. Knox Sr. (*right*), chairman of the board of the Marine Trust Company of Western New York, with Governor Nelson Rockefeller. January 1962.

Top right: Mrs. Kate Butler, president and publisher of the *Buffalo Evening News*, who assumed the position when her husband died in the 1950s, seen here receiving an award. April 1966.

(Courtesy of the Buffalo and Erie County Historical Society)

Charles R. Diebold Jr., president of Western Savings Bank. Appointed first chairman of the Niagara Frontier Transportation Authority in 1967 by Governor Rockefeller. September 1964.

(Courtesy of the Buffalo and Erie County Historical Society)

A Coast Guard cutter keeps Buffalo Harbor open for Bethlehem Steel's extensive operations, seen here in part. February 1964.
(Courtesy of the Buffalo and Erie County Historical Society)

View of the mouth of the Niagara River as it flows due north from Lake Erie and the Peace Bridge to Canada from Buffalo's west side. August 1967.
(From the Buffalo Courier-Express Collection courtesy of Buffalo State College Archives)

Ebony scholarship benefit and fashion show, sponsored by the Buffalo Chapter of Links, Inc. October 1968.
(*Courtesy of the Buffalo and Erie County Historical Society*)

Jesse E. Nash Jr. (*left*), Model City Program director and professor of sociology at Canisius College, with Mayor Sedita. The mayor's skepticism of the program is evident in the photo. December 1967.
(*From the Buffalo Courier-Express Collection courtesy of Buffalo State College Archives*)

A Block Club cleans up an off-street play area in the Ellicott District. June 1968.
(Courtesy of the Buffalo and Erie County Historical Society)

A Model City Citizens Center meeting on the city's east side. November 1969.
(Courtesy of the Buffalo and Erie County Historical Society)

Frank Sedita celebrating his triumphant re-election victory, November 4, 1969, with Democratic Party Chairman Joseph Crangle (*right*). He received the largest Democratic majority in a Buffalo mayoral race and became the first three-term (four-year) mayor. (*Courtesy of the Buffalo and Erie County Historical Society*)

Viewing a neighborhood housing model are (*left to right*) a representative from the State Urban Development Corporation, Rochester, NY; Robert Traynham Coles, a Buffalo architect; Committeeman (later city council president) George K. Arthur; and Mayor Frank Sedita. April 1970. (*Courtesy of the Buffalo and Erie County Historical Society*)

Mayor Stanley Makowski, facing huge losses in revenues because of plant closings and population out-migration, laid off 1,700 city employees in 1975 as the city teetered on the brink of bankruptcy. April 1975.

(From the Buffalo Courier-Express Collection courtesy of Buffalo State College Archives)

Arthur Eve (*right*) campaigning for mayor on the Democratic ticket, a candidacy that prompted Councilman Jimmy Griffin, a centrist Democrat, to run for mayor as a conservative independent. Griffin won four consecutive terms before retiring in 1994. July 1977.

(From the Buffalo Courier-Express Collection courtesy of Buffalo State College Archives)

Lewis Harriman Jr. (*standing*), banker and longtime proponent of a transit line to connect the university campus in suburban Amherst with downtown, at a Rapid Transit Project Hearing. May 1978. (*Courtesy of the Buffalo and Erie County Historical Society*)

Downtown development model. Congressman Henry Nowak (*left*) and Mayor Jimmy Griffin, with administration colleagues. August 1979. (*Courtesy of the Buffalo and Erie County Historical Society*)

Right:
Workers of an Italian-American business enterprise prepare their goods for shipping. 1981.
(Courtesy of the Buffalo and Erie County Historical Society)

Left:
Polish community dancers being greeted in a neighborhood parish. September 1979.
(Courtesy of the Buffalo and Erie County Historical Society)

The Bethlehem Steel mill crew at the plant's closing. 1979.
(Courtesy of the Buffalo and Erie County Historical Society)

Bethlehem Steel, after taking the biggest write-off ever by an American firm (up to that time), closed most of its Buffalo operation. 1982.
(Courtesy of the Buffalo and Erie County Historical Society)

Robert Rich Jr., president of Rich Products and a founding member of the Buffalo Eighteen, talking with Governor Cuomo. One of Buffalo's own, Rich joined forces with newcomers like Robert Wilmers to head M&T Bank and Andrew Rudnick (later, the Buffalo Niagara Partnership) to create a powerful and proactive elite leadership in the 1980s. June 1983.
(Courtesy of the Buffalo and Erie County Historical Society)

Mayor Jimmy Griffin *(second from right)* breaking ground for the Waterfront Village. March 1980.
(Courtesy of the Buffalo and Erie County Historical Society)

Buffalo's new small-boat marina in the 1980s. Today, much of the downtown side of the harbor is upscale waterfront condos and housing.
(Courtesy of the Buffalo and Erie County Historical Society)

The State University of New York at Buffalo campus in Amherst, NY, twelve miles from Buffalo's downtown. 1983. *(Courtesy of the Buffalo and Erie County Historical Society)*

Approximately 1,000 people view opening ceremonies of the transit line, then half complete. More than twenty years later, the line to link the university and the burgeoning suburban population with downtown remains uncompleted. October 1984. (*Courtesy of the Buffalo and Erie County Historical Society*)

The Light Rail Rapid Transit rises to grade level as it nears Buffalo's central business district. Originally, the downtown part of the line was to have been underground to facilitate business and commercial activity in stormy weather, but this was reversed later. November 1982. *(Courtesy of the Buffalo and Erie County Historical Society)*

"Not in Service." A rapid transit train under the weather rather than underground, with only sixteen days left for shopping. December 8, 1984. *(Courtesy of the Buffalo and Erie County Historical Society)*

City Hall, viewed down Court Street from Main. A variety of modes of transport. April 1985.
(Courtesy of the Buffalo and Erie County Historical Society)

Riders making practical use of the downtown transit line. February 1986.
(Courtesy of the Buffalo and Erie County Historical Society)

Mayor Anthony Masiello proudly shows off new housing under construction.
(Courtesy of the Office of Mayor Anthony Masiello)

Pilot Field in the 1990s, built downtown, near the waterfront in 1988. Renamed Dunn Tire Park, it is home to the Buffalo Bisons. *(Courtesy of the Buffalo and Erie County Historical Society)*

The Rapid-Transit Initiative: Part Two

In the 1970s the future of the rapid-transit system looked bright, holding out the promise of economic revitalization. A rapid-transit system would move people between the suburbs and urban core, taking them to their jobs even in severe winter storms. It would also travel miles along a corridor ripe for development. In January 1970 the federal government made a half-million-dollar grant to the Niagara Frontier Transportation Authority for a mass-transit study. This was met with a matching grant of nearly $200,000 from the New York State Department of Transportation and $65,000 from the NFTA, which included other local contributions. The transit study had two parts: an evaluation of bus transit problems and the feasibility of an exclusive right-of-way rail rapid-transit facility in the Buffalo-Amherst corridor.

That November, the NFTA board approved a consulting firm's recommendation for a steel-wheel, steel-rail rapid-transit system for the 12.7 miles between the central business district and the university. The following month, the city proposed a covered downtown shopping mall at an estimated cost of $9 million to $11 million. Not to be outdone, Buffalo's master plan, developed by the Office of Planning in the Department of Community Development in April 1971, proposed five rapid-transit lines radiating from downtown. Shortly thereafter, the New York state legislature authorized the design and construction of a rapid-transit rail line in the Buffalo-Amherst corridor, along with the creation of a regional bus transit network.

Public hearings in 1972 resulted in the reevaluation of aspects of the project, which were effectively dealt with several months later. The NFTA board passed a resolution that formally adopted the Mass Transit Project and approved three contracts for the Metropolitan Transportation Center, soil sampling, real estate appraisal, and architectural and engineering services. That next year, the authority selected its general engineering consultants for preliminary design on the transit project and its mapping consultants. Public sentiment looked good, with results from a survey showing that a majority of area residents believed the transit line was necessary. Erie and Niagara Counties Regional Planning Board reinforced this optimism when it approved NFTA's application for a $20 million final design grant.[35]

A community process began in 1973 with the announcement of ten community forums designed to bring citizens into preliminary planning for the transit line. Again, in July 1974, NFTA held formal public hearings. Local officials and the NFTA visited Washington to play up the project with the Urban Mass Transit Agency (UMTA) and transportation subcommittee members.

Problems loomed when the public became aware of tentative alignments for the transit line, on the south side of Kensington Avenue, that would sweep a row of duplex houses away. Politically disastrous, the proposed rails would pass through the living room of the president of a local community association. Members of the Area Committee for Transit tried, unsuccessfully, to dissuade the outside consultants of the so-called merits of the plan, arguing that the public relations of such a move would be disastrous. They noted also that this family, along with others in the neighborhood, had already been uprooted once. But the damage was done.

The community activist, no shrinking violet, immediately founded No Overhead Transit (NOT), which grew into a grassroots coalition of some sixty community action organizations to fight the transit plans. NOT recommended a subway directly out Main Street to the old university campus, approximately halfway to the new Amherst campus. A hospital followed suit, announcing it planned an addition (obtaining the permit shortly thereafter) that protruded into the proposed aerial routing.

Fearing delays and their costs, the Area Committee for Transit went to work and met repeatedly with the NOT coalition, hoping to come to a compromise. But committee members were at a disadvantage, since the elite leadership would not actively support them.

NOT coalition organizers recognized that the Area Committee, with its one or two elite members, did not have the backing of the business leaders' powerful organizations, the Greater Buffalo Development Foundation and the Chamber of Commerce.[36]

Events continued with a groundbreaking for the Metropolitan Transportation Center in March 1975. Then, in May, a rapid-fire succession of events occurred for the Transportation Authority and its newly formed subsidiary Niagara Frontier Transit Authority (in 1974):

- UMTA requested a "refinement" of the transit study on alternatives;
- the New York State Department of Transportation formed a coalition of Buffalo-area business and community leaders to push for federal support of the Buffalo-Amherst rapid transit line;
- the executive of Erie County and the mayor of Buffalo asked the Mass Transit Advisory Committee and Area Committee for Transit to unite in order to formalize community commitment and support for rapid transit;
- the Area Committee for Transit and the Mass Transit Advisory Committee met to map a joint strategy that would resolve differences;
- the governor's office reinforced its commitment to the project by assuring $16 million beyond its original $86 million offer in bond money for construction of the project.

But the brakes were already being applied. This time it was the result of a study underwritten by the Greater Buffalo Development Foundation concluding that an additional cost of $26 million for a covered transit mall was too expensive. The foundation wanted to study two alternative concepts. This led to the city setting aside plans for the downtown transit mall, pending the "ultimate" decision by the Urban Mass Transit Agency on the rapid-transit line after the community protests. One week later, the New York State Department of Transportation called for an immediate federal commitment to begin construction. On June 14, Congresswoman Bella Abzug voiced strong support. And, in late June, a delegation of western New York citizens, assorted business leaders, and city officials traveled to Washington to meet with the secretary of transportation to press for the project's approval.

It was at this point that the NFTA hired a new firm for "a refinement study of transit alternatives." In other words, the NFTA called for a *redesign* of the rapid-transit system, which was presented to the city.[37] With the redesign and the desire to cut costs by approximately $20 million, the NFTA and the city, along with the Greater Buffalo Development Foundation, which finally spoke up, reversed themselves. This collective group agreed that the downtown part of the transit line would be changed from an underground line to one that ran at grade. And the uptown part of the line, designed as an aboveground rail with some aerial, would go underground. Three transit stations downtown were then added to the plan, bringing the total to six stations, which also increased costs. The new plan would extend the open transit mall into the upper Main Street theater block and include a station. A majority of the funds to develop the mall were to come from both federal and state transit funds because of the integral relationship between the mall and transit system. The transit mall involved thirty-eight hundred feet at street level along Main Street for pedestrians and the light rail rapid transit.

Another surprise came when the federal transit funds arrived. Receipt of these funds was on the condition that the Niagara Frontier Transportation Authority (which had never aspired to any role in surface transportation, only air and water transport, but had been pressed into it by Rockefeller in the 1960s) be responsible and plan for all the local bus companies. These were to act as feeder lines to the rapid transit system. This did not bode well for the future, as it meant dragging a disinterested powerhouse into a key role, upon which much depended.

POLITICAL STORY

> When one considers this matter of a power structure, for Buffalo,
> it resided primarily either at City Hall, or, less importantly, at the
> county level. Buffalo's private power structure was so diffuse as
> to be virtually negligible when it came to planning for the city.
>
> —A president of the Greater Buffalo
> Development Foundation

Because elite organizations did not provide proactive leadership in
Buffalo's political and economic debates, power often resided with
the political leadership. The city was divided into thirteen city
council districts throughout the city's forty-two-square-mile jurisdiction in the early 1960s. As Buffalo lost population, these districts
were reduced to nine, with an additional five council members and
the council president elected at large. This kept the number at fifteen, despite debates to reduce council membership. (From 1960 to
1970, Buffalo's central city lost 14 percent of its population, while
the suburban ring gained 15 percent.[38] Buffalo's population was
462,768 according to the 1970 US census of populations, general
population characteristics.)

Cordial Relations, and Change

Mayors through the 1960s and most of the 1970s based their inter-
actions with the Common Council on the assumption that they
could get along with the opposition. Both Republican Chester
Kowal and Democrat Frank Sedita in the 1960s had worked this
way. At budget time, the mayor would confer with city council
members, his comptroller, and his budget director to discuss proposals and listen to the council's priorities. In this considered way,
problems could be ironed out *before* putting the final budget
together and attending the full council hearing.

Despite differences, cordial relations between the city council,
the mayor, and business leaders continued into the 1970s. Recalls

one council member, "On a regular basis, [the entire city council, the mayor, and other officials] used to sit down with the executive committee of the Chamber of Commerce and talk about what was going on in the city, what were our plans, what were their plans, how we could work together." Two presidents of the Common Council had made this partnership a priority. The first, Delmar Mitchell, an African American from Chicago with Cherokee and Irish blood, was elected in the late 1950s. Calling himself a representative of "the United Nations," this John Kennedy liberal skillfully manipulated the council, often bringing it together on divisive issues. George Arthur—also from the African American community, and who served on the council for twenty-six years (1970–1995)—likewise brought the council together. Historically a conciliator, Arthur's position "toughened" when Jimmy Griffin became mayor. A council member points out, "If Griffin saw any weakness, he would destroy you. There could be no compromise, ever." But Griffin did not take office until 1978, and much of political importance led up to his four-term tenure.

An Old-Style Mayor under Pressure

Stanley Makowski (1973–1978) completed Mayor Sedita's term and then was elected for one of his own. Mayor Makowski, from the Polish community, was a former "scooper" in the city's flour mills along the waterfront. He headed one of the unions before becoming city council member and then mayor. People describe him as an honest and simple man. Even after becoming mayor, he continued to live down in "the valley" behind a large industrial plant, and most nights he went home for dinner with his wife and many children. His education came from on-the-job training. "He was the one who was victimized by the weather," explained one Buffalonian, referencing the infamous blizzard of 1977,[39] when snowplows could not clear snow because legally parked cars lined the streets. He did not govern so much as allow those under him to govern. His vision of Buffalo was that of a "city of good neighbors," a sentiment that he thought could be translated into a pragmatic approach to politics.

Midway through Makowski's term, Buffalo's economy plummeted. The mayor faced the fallout of plant closings and jobs lost in the tens of thousands, along with a severely diminishing tax base. The crisis chipped away at the Democratic machine's hold on city government. Officials targeted city departments for the necessary cutbacks. Not surprisingly, Makowski's term faced mounting tensions between political rivals, and the public became restive. This was a time when community-based and national political organizations—the NAACP and organizations like BUILD, the Citizens Advisory Committee, and Citizens for Better Schools, to name a few—gained in strength and began to assert political and legal pressure. The mayor tackled individual problems, but he lacked the skills to resolve these larger conflicts.

The power of the Democratic Party, too, had changed. So much so that it could no longer be relied on to bring conflicting interests together. One party member said it all: "In time, people began to look elsewhere [for leadership]."[40] Buffalo needed new leadership for new times.

Restructuring Political Power

Public officials began to consider new strategies for cutting costs, such as permanently reducing the size of city departments and agencies, but this turned out to be an impossibility because of New York State regulations and labor laws. Another strategy, seriously researched, was to abolish the city and divide it into six towns, which, studies had suggested, would raise additional taxes and bring in more state aid than the current city structure. Officials rejected these strategies, however, and relied on their own "financial maneuvers" (as one who devised them referred to them) to take hold and carry the city through the toughest times.

All of the vectors were going downhill, and enough of us [at city hall and in the neighborhoods] at that point were in our early thirties, and we just decided it was time to take over. Well, entrenched power doesn't leave very easily. . . . [Some of us in city government] took that opportunity to literally organize the city into twelve planning communities and work with them to do two things: prepare the needs analyses of what was needed in terms of block grants and in terms of city services and city expenditures, and then we . . . created a citizens subcommittee under the already well-established Citizens Advisory Committee.[41]

The citizens subcommittee worked with a representative of the city budget department to create a capital budget. The objective was to consolidate city department and community requests in order to better meet all their needs through a participatory process. Everybody wanted synergy between the two. As it turned out, the committee "created an enormous constituency within the city for change in the way we did business and the way we spent money, and in appropriating city resources. . . . [It led to] a weakening base among the old guard that used to make decisions."[42]

Other roles evolved during this period as well. The *Buffalo Evening News* (soon to become the *Buffalo News* under outside ownership) became politically diminished, but with broader interests, after the deaths of its editor in chief and publisher/owner. The *Courier-Express* pushed its investigative reporting, challenging the elite as well as corrupt political leaders and disruptive union practices. The Democratic machine learned to play by new rules owing to the momentum of the grassroots participation—participation that went back as far as Mayors Kowal and Sedita, who each, respectively, established Citizens Advisory Committees.

The executive director of the Citizens Advisory Committee (an Irish American, appointed in 1971), now under Mayor Makowski, saw Nixon's Community Development Act as a way to redistribute political power. Members of the committee believed more could be done about the city's cascading decline and high unemployment through the act's mandated citizen participation if some independence from party politics could be attained. Community Development Block Grants flowing from Washington provided the funding. And the group drew from the pool of Comprehensive Employment and Training Act (CETA) workers available to the city, hiring some fifty college-trained people to work in the neighborhoods through the Little City Hall Program.

Mayor Makowski, a great believer in neighborhoods, agreed to a policy that divided the city into twelve districts and used a large portion of the federal block grant money to hire grassroots community coordinators to head each district, each reporting directly to the mayor. "Everything happening" in the districts had to go through the executive director to the mayor—and not through the district council member—effectively bypassing the "machine" altogether. In another bold step, the city hired attorneys and set up fifteen community development corporations, each given $200,000 to $600,000 of funding per year for staffing and programs. Everything was done outside of the existing structure, which "of course, violated every tenet of the party."[43] The stage was now set for the 1977 elections. But one more piece of the story, for our purposes, needs to be put in place.

Charter Revision: An Issue That Tipped the Balance

In July 1974 Common Council President Delmar Mitchell announced the formation of an eight-member committee to revise the city charter. He asserted that the time had come "to review and reform the foundation of our legislative powers."[44] In time, the issue of city charter revision became a bitter battle. The Democratic machine, representing the status quo, took on the grassroots organizers and leaders. After two difficult years of meetings, the Charter Committee made its recommendations, which were to redistribute power away from the party and elected officials to the community at large. The controversy centered on three recommendations: the ability to recall an elected official, the reduction of city council representatives by two at-large members to thirteen (which did occur in 1981); and the establishment of a citizen salary review committee. Extremely unhappy with these results, the Common Council voted all recommendations down in one fifteen-minute meeting.

This act on the part of the city council so outraged Buffalo's citizens that they took out their ire in the 1977 election, voting eleven incumbent council members out of office. This antiparty sentiment was so strong that it played a role in the mayoral election as well.[45] According to a community organizer and public official,

> 1977 was almost a fateful moment in Buffalo history. Community coordinators and activists actually ran a slate of candidates for every single council seat, every single committeeman's seat, every single Erie County legislative seat that was in the City of Buffalo. . . . We decided, basically, to challenge the entire Democratic Party in Buffalo.

An Independent's Race for Mayor

The 1977 race for city council and mayor came down to a choice between the status quo and change, despite the existence of other controversial issues. Mayor Makowski had increased the occupancy tax to raise funds for the city's solvency problems. Erie County's legislature passed an initiative that allowed legislators to raise the county sales tax. Grassroots constituencies transformed themselves and made demands that needed attention. And court-mandated integration in the schools got underway.

To make matters more exciting, Arthur Eve, Buffalo's black state assemblyman, entered the Democratic primary to defeat the party's candidate, Les Fazio, who was the former legal counsel under Makowski. Eve's candidacy prompted Councilman Jimmy Griffin, a centrist Democrat, to run for mayor as a conservative independent. In a three-way race that split the Democratic ticket, Griffin adopted an independent, populist agenda. He proposed taking the power from *both* the well-oiled Democratic machine *and* the business leadership, whom he described as having hearts as big as caraway seeds. He promised sweeping change. In his campaign, Griffin was antieverything—antibank, antiunion, anti–Democratic Party, anti–Republican Party. His appeal was to the disenfranchised white working-class worker and the unemployed who remained in the area. A political associate put it this way: These people didn't just *like* Griffin; they would have *died* for Griffin. Beyond that, many voters did not like the occupancy tax associated with Makowski.

When Jimmy Griffin became mayor, no one could have imagined that it would last sixteen years, as it did (1978–1994). Upon his first election, Griffin threw out the Democratic patronage system and replaced it with his own. He also turned his campaign pledge to not work with the business leadership on its head. He established an alliance between himself and the business leadership using vast amounts of government funding for economic development.

A tough Irishman from the South Buffalo neighborhoods near the steel mills, Griffin chose his enemies and his friends, claiming, "You're either for me or against me," and he acted out of this belief. He challenged everybody. He once punched one of his assistants in the nose in front of the new ballpark. And during blizzards, when citizens complained about the pace of snowplowing, unlike apologetic Mayor Makowski, he said, "Take your six packs of beer and shut up. Sit on your porches. We're doing everything we can!"[46] He was also heard to tell one governor bluntly what he thought, and to get what he wanted.

James D. Griffin was a political party unto himself who cared little whether a person was a registered Republican or Democrat, and he saw to it that he was not beholden to anyone. He rallied his own political club, mostly from South Buffalo, but it drew as well from the white community. Relations between Griffin and the African American community, however, worsened. A professional from the white community pointed to a fundamental problem with Griffin's approach. He was "mayor of only part of the city. He'd say, 'Well, I've appointed some black people,' and quickly name a couple. They were the only ones he knew. He by and large gave the back of his hand to the black community. And didn't depend on them for votes. And, in fact, by his actions, as much as told other people who didn't like black folks, that, yeah, he was their guy."[47]

The mayor financed economic development with community development funds, and projects got up steam. But, by the mayor's fourth term, the institutions of city government were practically immobilized because of the standoff between the mayor and city council over the use of these funds. One official who had worked with several different administrations focused on the drawbacks:

> I . . . thought Joe Crangle [Chairman of the Democratic Party] was divisive, but I hadn't really seen divisiveness until Griffin. . . . And I think Jimmy Griffin controlled more of what went on than Crangle ever did. . . . He didn't appoint people to jobs who weren't patronages to him. At least Crangle divided it up. Certificates of appointments were divided into zip codes; most of the zip codes were South Buffalo . . . a few to friends in North Buffalo or the West Side. Joe Crangle looked nonpatronage in contrast. . . . We just couldn't believe it.

The Politics of Planning, 1978 and Beyond

Differences in priorities on the use of community development funds, along with the political dispositions of the newly elected officials, led to a contentious relationship between the mayor and city council. The situation worsened considerably when the mayor created surrogate economic development agencies that would allow him to bypass the city council in the legislative and budget process. From that point on and throughout the next decade, the council "just broke down," according to a former Common Council president. Relations were such that if council members thought the mayor wanted something, or had anything to do with a proposal coming out of one of his departments, the council opposed it automatically. But problems did not end there.

Power plays and turf battles affected planning and development out in the field as well, where the politics of planning by local governments throughout the region were subject to the unspoken rules of tradition. Two short anecdotes serve as examples of problems confronting professional planners.

Anecdote Number One

Consultants for the rapid-transit project called a meeting of planning directors from Buffalo and surrounding local governments. Their objective was to gather input from local planners in different regional locations. Up to this point, a detailed vision had not been articulated for the project, and a land-use map did not exist for the proposed development area. Project consultants wanted the input of local planners upfront.

Consultants at the meeting asked the gathered planners to forecast the kind of development each of them projected for their areas over the next twenty years. According to one participant, "Immediately, we had a quiet revolt on our hands. [One of the] planning directors stated . . . 'If I ever did that, I'd have to turn in my resignation; it's the politicians who set what the land-use is going to be.'"

To get around this dilemma, two irrepressible individuals, one a political official, the other a consultant, decided to use offices in the Port Authority Building to hold periodic planning sessions to develop ideas on maps that were to remain off the record. "Everyone pledged not to . . . say what was on the map. When they were completed, these individual maps were given to the consultants to quantify. After that, [they were] to be destroyed."

Anecdote Number Two

The routine protection of political turf meant that little information sharing or cooperation occurred between regional governments and agencies. In the extreme, area professionals might have no contact whatsoever. Such was the case when planners from Buffalo and surrounding suburban towns and villages assembled to participate in a regional planning forum. When asked to elect someone to lead the planning process, one individual stood to say he couldn't nominate anyone because "the only person I know in the room is myself." The election of a leader had to be postponed to a later date, while the region's leading planning professionals introduced themselves to each other.[48]

COMMUNITY STORY

At the height of the crisis in 1975, the Greater Buffalo Development Foundation felt compelled to explain how it tried to pursue a "balanced" program between downtown and neighborhood development: "We feel, contrary to popular belief, that the interests of downtown and the neighborhoods are really quite interrelated."[49] The arrival of Griffin made whatever balancing they were or were not doing a whole lot more difficult.

Upon election, the first thing Griffin did was fire everyone associated with the community-based movement or cut their funding until their organizations were politically dead. With no neighborhood representatives on the Greater Buffalo Development Foundation board of directors, little could be done there. This left the city council as the only entity with the requisite power to speak (and fight) in these communities' behalf. Until now, black council members had tried to remain neutral or conciliatory on issues of neighborhood development and housing.

All this transpired at a time when black community organizations, which were not dependent on city funding, flourished. By 1974 the inner-city community had forty-five organizations on the East Side with recently available revenue-sharing funds from the federal government. BUILD's agitation on the issues continued in rapid-fire succession. Local chapters of the NAACP and the Urban

League provided leadership and legal initiatives, in conjunction with activist churches from among the 164 churches ministering to the community. School desegregation litigation came to the fore. Seeming irreconcilable differences between State Assemblyman Arthur Eve and BUILD became political preoccupations.

The BUILD organization came into its own when the organization's leaders sat at the table with County Executive Regan to plan how to save the old post office building. At the end of the bargaining over how to transform the historic building into a college, a *Buffalo Evening News* headline trumpeted that the BUILD organization had saved the old post office. Now BUILD, too, had the inside track in political relations with the city council. By contrast, BUILD was less successful with the business leadership. For one, BUILD's aggressive style made the WASP business leadership uncomfortable. Still, several individuals from among the business elite worked with BUILD and joined its committees. In fact, one, a nonbanker who later headed the Greater Buffalo Development Foundation, had taken the year off to lend assistance to the organization's fund-raising efforts. He made introductions between the two camps (the elite and BUILD) by taking financial executives to lunch with BUILD leaders. While the bankers were "favorably impressed that these people were trying to help themselves," no partnerships were formed to address housing or business development.[50]

Funding for nonprofit organizations proliferated in the early years with the aid of block grant and CETA funds. A young white Buffalonian, William Price Jr., having just finished his law degree and military service, was elected to the city council, where he applied community-organizing skills learned at Columbia University in New York City. He raised federal community development funds and founded the Fillmore-Leroy Community Development Corporation, known as FLARE and, within a year, had a board of directors of ten blacks and ten whites. This East Side organization leased a thirty-thousand-square-foot building from the Catholic Diocese and ran a senior-citizens center and a youth services program and, with CETA funds, hired a housing counselor, an adult coordinator, a program director, a recreation director, a public relations director, a block manager, and a maintenance man. In 1979 FLARE received $476,000 in block grant funds for the Neighborhood Strategy Area Program to prioritize neighborhood solutions to residential blight and commercial improvement. Councilman Price established a high-risk loan program for residents unable to secure loans for home improvements that banks would never consider. Councilmen from North Buffalo and South Buffalo followed and began to access funds for their own neighborhoods as well. Unfortunately for Buffalo, in 1979 President Jimmy Carter appointed him to serve on his National Commission on Neighborhoods. The city lost an important bridge between the black and white communities at a time when Buffalo could least afford it.

Power and Legalities: School Integration

In 1976 the City of Buffalo acceded to court orders to integrate its public schools. The catalyst for this event was a lawsuit the NAACP and the Citizens Council on Human Relations, with five parent-plaintiffs, brought against the commissioner and board of education, the state board of regents, the city board of education, the mayor, and the city council. The plaintiffs' brief evolved initially from a move by the Board of Education (May 1968) to construct portable classrooms at twelve predominantly white schools to provide spaces for nonwhite students, something used widely throughout US school systems.

After collecting evidence in 1972, the plaintiffs charged the defendants with intentionally segregating city schools and failing to hire minority teachers. The case went to court in 1974; the defendants were found guilty in 1976.

Said an official of the NAACP, "We were constantly dealing with the board of education, the mayor, [and] Jimmy Griffin [then councilman], who was very hostile towards us. . . . A lot of this comes down to a power relationship." For the first time, nearly half of the thirteen members of the council were black, and, along with a couple of allies, they constituted a voting majority on the city council.[51]

The plaintiffs' "Post-Trial Brief" stated:

> Councilwoman Alfreda W. Slominski moved to block this integration effort. As the testimony and other evidence revealed, this was with anti-integration motivation. She immediately introduced a resolution to prohibit the use of the portable classrooms . . . citing concern about overcrowded recreation facilities. . . . The issue was clearly racial as all recognized. [Council members] noted this . . . and confirmed this on direct and cross examination, [that is,] the fear being that it would bring in additional people from outside the neighborhood, mainly Blacks.[52]

Much of Buffalo's leadership coalesced around the need to integrate, using Boston as an example of what they hoped to avoid. The city did not remain united, however. The plaintiffs were unhappy about the use of magnet schools rather than integration across the board because magnet schools were more expensive. Integration brought a greater ethnic mix into the neighborhoods, which was not immediately welcomed in the ethnic communities. Many in the ethnic communities saw integration as disruptive to their cultural identity and daily way of life, which revolved around ethnic politics and the neighborhood parish.

Other Cases

Other civil rights initiatives were part of the community's legal strategy as well. The federal justice department brought and won a civil rights case on discriminatory hiring practices in the police and fire department. Erie County College faced an unsuccessful suit charging the college with running two sets of curricula, "the poetry of chemistry" at the city campus and real chemistry at the north campus in Amherst. Bethlehem Steel faced another unsuccessful class-action suit of placing blacks in the dirtiest, hottest, and least safe jobs in the steel mills.

Legal experts found thousands of deeds that had restrictive covenants saying no negro person or person of negro extraction could live, own, dwell, or occupy such a property unless he or she was the manservant or maidservant of the white owner. According to the US District Court (Office of Judge John Thomas Curtin), evidence showed that local banks would not grant loans to a black person wanting to move into a white area (*Arthur v. the Board of Education*). In addition, when the city began using a multiple-listing service, the head of the Greater Buffalo Realtors called black realtors together at the Park Lane. He told them that, if they wanted to sell houses under multiple listings, they could not show a black person a house in a white neighborhood. In a court case where a black realtor testified to this, the city's attorney declined to call the real estate executive to refute that statement.

This case had five individual plaintiffs, including Common Council President George Arthur, the NAACP, and the Citizens Council on Human Relations, who won their case on April 30, 1976. "When you're surrounded by that [kind of discrimination] and you're surrounded by denials by the white power structure, you can only hope to begin to develop politically . . . having been denied the opportunity to move economically."[53] So, politics it was. More precisely, black political leaders began to use the political arena to fight for a say and for funding for their projects.

Three programs resulting from these efforts were ad hoc and glacially slow. First, in 1976 Buffalo's Housing Authority and Urban Renewal Agency retained the foundation to study ways to restore the Ellicott Mall public housing complex, 590 apartments in eight high-rise buildings, with a 20 percent occupancy rate. Two years later, nothing had been done regarding the study's findings because of policy disagreements between the City of Buffalo and the US Department of Housing and Urban Development. (Again, as with Buffalo's decertification a decade earlier, Buffalo's administrative officials fell short on meeting federal obligations.) But by

1980, a development design called "Ellicott Village: A Newtown Downtown" raised the federal funds necessary to move ahead. This progressive design incorporated social principles, such as ensuring tenant safety. For example, families would be relocated to ground-floor units with private access, while adults would have exclusive use of the elevators. The Ellicott District strategy was to be enhanced by the Ellicott Mall restoration and the commercial redevelopment of Town Gardens on William Street.[54]

Second, in the Cold Spring neighborhood, a lower-income community with a large percentage of elderly minority residents, a housing program was initiated in 1975. Here, the City of Buffalo, the Buffalo Community Development Organization, and the Community Planning Assistance Center formed an informal partnership to use $12,500 to prepare a plan, an initial investment, for the rehabilitation of one hundred acres in the Cold Spring neighborhood. Two million dollars of block grant funds over two years went toward housing inspections, direct grants for low-income families, subsidies, government loans, and high-risk loans for moderate- and middle-income persons.[55]

A third example delineates how alternatives to government funding and the mainstream banking system can be utilized for projects, if accessible. In a unique move, Neighborhood Housing Services, originated by Councilman Price in 1975–76, created a cooperative business for home maintenance and energy conservation in the Kensington-Bailey neighborhood. Rather than using public funds as subsidies, it took out commercial loans from the National Consumer Cooperative Bank to underwrite the project. This, Buffalo's only such neighborhood venture, expanded beyond residential to commercial revitalization as well. HUD described Neighborhood Housing Services as a model venture and the only comprehensive commercial/residential program in the city.[56] Unfortunately for everyone, Griffin cut Neighborhood Housing Services's funding when he took office as mayor, and the organization went out of business.

The BUILD Organization

"I think we've got it right this time."
—Governor Nelson Rockefeller[57]

BUILD, the black activist organization, continued to be guided by its philosophy of promoting the control of business enterprises and other institutions in the black community that "influence the lives of the people."[58] Early in 1969, Governor Rockefeller suspended work on the university's Amherst campus and on all state building projects in response to protests concerning the lack of training and hiring of minority workers by the building trades unions.

Rockefeller designated the Minority Coalition, State Assemblyman Arthur Eve's recently formed group, to lead affirmative action efforts. Shortly thereafter, the Opportunities Development Council of the Chamber of Commerce proposed working with the coalition to develop a training program for minority workers in the building trades. Meanwhile, BUILD took exception to the designated action plan, noting that the East Side core community was divided on the issue of control. As the debate for control heated up, it seemed to some in the community that BUILD was hampering the Minority Coalition's position at the bargaining table.[59] Things regained their calm when, in February 1970, Rockefeller lifted the nine-month construction moratorium and BUILD joined the coalition in its efforts.

During his reelection campaign, in a political offering to labor, Rockefeller handed over control of the training programs to the unions, where there were no provisions ensuring a role for minority contractors to receive construction business. In late 1970, the US Department of Labor, for the second time, found the plan unacceptable on a variety of fronts. The upshot was that, for a time, BUILD controlled the project.[60] In May of that next year, after five months of negotiating over how to bring the new workers in, the unskilled worker program was "stymied."[61]

Eventually the parties came to an agreement where the State University Construction Fund would work with BUILD on this effort. BUILD was to represent the African American community in implementing the Buffalo Affirmative Action Plan for minorities, including Hispanics and Native Americans, who now constituted more than 10 percent of the area workforce. In addition, BUILD would head the local outreach program, while the State Labor Department would keep records of out-of-state union workers employed on state projects in the area.

The program lasted through three funding cycles, but increased disorganization of files at the BUILD offices led Governor Hugh Carey to cut the program in 1974. BUILD's president claimed that nearly five hundred people had been trained and approximately two hundred became employed over this period. An independent study claimed that the actual figures were much smaller, as only four or five of nineteen craft unions participated in the program, and very few trainees were ever permanently employed.[62]

The BUILD Academy

In what turned out to be a path-breaking public-nonprofit partnership, BUILD founded a school in cooperation with public school officials named the BUILD Academy. Funds were raised from Buffalo's Board of Education; the state of New York, through two state contracts; and a host of Protestant churches throughout the area. The private sector—elite organizations and business enterprises—declined to join this cooperative effort. According to one official, an element of prudence was incorporated into the planning, even as more funds came into the project, as the academy wanted an affordable program that could be easily replicated within the limits of school budgets. William Gaiter, president of BUILD, said that "the academy grew out of the 'sweat, tears, anger and relentless determination of BUILD executives, parents, and community educators.'"[63]

The academy designed its curriculum to provide a quality education for students through new programs geared to the needs and experiences of inner-city children. It opened in September 1969 for nearly four hundred youngsters in pre-kindergarten through fourth grade. The academy expanded in the second year to approximately five hundred students, with classes now through fifth grade and plans to expand through the twelfth grade. The founders established the concept of team building, a new approach to teaching that was considered innovative and systematic. Fourteen teachers and twenty-two community aides, from a variety of backgrounds, participated in a preservice training program that would bring them together in the classroom. The curriculum included African history and the contributions of blacks throughout US history. In addition, BUILD put great emphasis on parent participation in the education process, and one staff person had as her title "parent organizer." The academy involved parents in the day-to-day classroom and out-of-school activities to improve education both at school and at home. Before long, children were testing above average in reading and mathematics.

In time the school board cut funds for the teachers' aides so that even the Buffalo Teachers Federation, often at odds with BUILD, came to their defense, charging that an unexpected cut of fifteen aides would hurt the experimental school's program. Indeed, many parents reacted to the cut in funds by sending their children elsewhere. Concurrently, expansion plans of the academy into Woodlawn Jr. High on the East Side were discontinued because of fights for control of the school board, allegations of segregation (with a legal suit pending in the courts), and intransigence on the part of the Board of Education. Despite these losses, the BUILD Academy continued in a smaller form, kindergarten through third grade.

The End for BUILD

After the crisis of 1975, raising money became a distinct problem, and by 1979 the organization had folded. Some of BUILD's leaders moved into electoral politics or into higher education as instructors. The experience had schooled them in the arts of strategy and political battle. The organization's longtime president (then executive director) resigned, and a flurry of internal audits determined that years of political infighting, flagging community support, sloppy bookkeeping, and financial indebtedness had taken their toll. In the white community, by the end of the decade, there was also a sense of some anti–affirmative action sentiment, depicted by the attitude "We've given enough to blacks; it's time to cut back."[64]

Still, BUILD's work bore fruit and laid the groundwork for the NAACP's successful litigation on portable classrooms that led to school integration. It also left in its wake a model for Buffalo's nationally renowned magnet school system (and later, charter schools) with its experimental BUILD Academy. And, for a brief moment, the organization's activities complemented the style and programs of the more mainstream Model City Program.

CONCLUSION

The time was right for change—the question was, change to what? According to a city official who served for thirty years and under three mayors,

> There was a vacuum of leadership. There was very little business coming into the community. The businesses staying in western New York were moving out of Buffalo. The whole suburbanization had caught on [where] a second generation living [in the area] had never really been in the city. Conditions in the East Side had gone through the unrest of the '60s. . . . Public schools to a significant degree were segregated . . . and were threatening to people. And a lot of the leadership at the time in the community as well as in the institutions was part of the past and didn't accommodate change well.

Buffalo's leadership had a difficult time accommodating the inevitable changes. Ultimately, the political leadership and a small group of younger business leaders took matters into their own hands, forging new initiatives for economic development. By the end of the decade, a new leadership and style had coalesced.

Before 1978 the failure of leadership in Buffalo was multifaceted. It was not just a lack of proactive leadership on the part of the Greater Buffalo Development Foundation, an organization formed for the express purpose of catalyzing and leading urban development. It was also the seeming reluctance of business leaders to take *any position at all* on vital issues. More often than not, opportunities for advancement were lost, left incomplete, or passed on to others to decide.

First, the leadership failed to work in partnership with the black community. In 1972 the leadership turned its back on the "Growth Strategy for the Erie-Niagara Area" report when it declined to include "social objectives" in economic development goals. This exceptional industrial study specifically recommended "strong participation by business leaders in the Model City effort [and] the Black Development Foundation." Leaders of the Model City Program—with its jitney service development, initiatives for abandoned buildings, and neighborhood planning—and leaders of the BUILD Academy wanted nothing more than to work cooperatively with others for the benefit of the community. They articulated this desire in many ways, yet the business leadership ignored such overtures.

Second, Buffalo's entire leadership—political, economic, and community—remained obsessed with issues of power and control. Many opportunities were missed because turf battles hampered collaborative planning. The elite leadership could have set the standard with a model of cooperation between the Greater Buffalo Development Foundation and the Chamber of Commerce. In addition, the foundation, dominated by the financial industry, could have worked in equal partnership with the newly formed manufacturing group on proactive economic development strategies. The new mayor and city council could have created ways to legislate and budget for urban development that rose above their differences. Regional political rivalries (exacerbated by Republican control of county government and Democratic control of city government) could have been sidelined for the common goal of improving the region. Agencies and authorities with their political appointees (especially the NFTA) could have worked more openly on the tasks of waterfront and transportation development, along with running the ports. Finally, city leaders could have moved more effectively beyond past losses (specifically, the loss of the university to the suburbs) and worked to design a regional strategy *with* suburban Amherst based on the new reality.

Third, the leadership disregarded the city's most important proposal, the rapid-transit initiative. A poll showed that the public favored a rail system. Yet the business elite and elected officials provided no leadership for that system through the battles for more than a decade, until they disapproved of the Metropolitan Transportation Center and Transit Mall designs—at which time they overruled everyone, calling for a complete redesign with new consultants and complete control over all design plans in the future. Until the takeover, the Greater Buffalo Development Foundation offered funding for studies, but little more.

Fourth, city leaders were derelict in allowing one hotel owner to sell them a bill of goods and influence the location of the convention center, and, when the hotel became an office building, even more remiss not to make hotel development a top priority. A decade elapsed before the convention center opened in 1978. Yet it was another two years before one major hotel opened. The financial crisis of 1975 did hurt planning, but a sense of urgency should have prevailed. Without *one* major hotel, promotion and marketing efforts for the convention center had to be curtailed. And the energy and momentum that could have been generated by such an opening were lost. The net effect was to undercut the center's financial bottom line—and the city's ability to increase its revenue. Furthermore, rather than enhance the city's image, it made the city look bush league. Where were Buffalo's leaders?

Desire for a new kind of leadership brought change to Buffalo's political landscape. The Democratic Party and its machine no longer controlled city politics as a result of the 1977 election. Council members could now act independently, thus making individual politicians unaccountable to larger forces, such as a political party strategy. While political machines present certain problems, the lack of party discipline and power diffused the ability of council members to accomplish neighborhood improvements.

By the decade's end, thousands of jobs had shifted from manufacturing to the service industry. Outside investors arrived and joined with the new administration in economic development efforts. With the election of grassroots activists and the independent mayor, new political warriors held office. The mayor aligned himself with the business leadership and downtown interests. The city council majority championed neighborhood interests. Their battles played out at city hall, the Common Council, public agencies, and nonprofit organizations and energized existing tensions between the city and its suburbs. These new leaders were not risk-averse—which brings the story to the 1980s.

NOTES

1. "A Growth Strategy for the Erie-Niagara Area, No. 8: The Buffalo Area's Economic Prospects," prepared by Paul W. Dickson and Raymond W. Waxmonsky, Greater Buffalo Development Foundation, 1972.

2. "Regan Pledges County Would Be Co-ordinator of Community Effort," *Buffalo Evening News*, September 10, 1971.

3. "Growth Strategy for the Erie-Niagara Area, No. 8."

4. Interviews nos. 28, 29, and 32.

5. Interview no. 50.

6. Interview no. 31.

7. Interview no. 44.

8. "Tax Problem Proves Millstone around Bethlehem Plant's Neck," *Buffalo Courier-Express*, November 15, 1971.

9. "County's Next Hurdle on Sales-Tax Plan: Lackawanna Council," *Buffalo Evening News*, November 27, 1971.

10. Interview no. 1.

11. Interview no. 36; "Buffalo Metro Store/Office/Plant Listing: 1981, 1982, 1983, 1984, 1985, 1986, 1987," Greater Buffalo Chamber of Commerce.

12. Interview no. 50.

13. "39 Major Plants Have Left Area in Last 5 Years," *Buffalo Evening News*, January 9, 1976.

14. "Outlook Bright, Bankers Told in Mayor's Report," *Buffalo Evening News*, August 21, 1976.

15. Interview no. 44.

16. Greater Buffalo Development Foundation, "Annual Report, 1980–81: A Retrospective of 30 Years."

17. "Union Town, USA," *Buffalo News*, May 29, 2000.

18. Greater Buffalo Development Foundation, "Annual Report, 1976–77."

19. Greater Buffalo Development Foundation, "Annual Report, 1975–76."

20. Julia B. Everitt, director of government research.

21. Greater Buffalo Development Foundation, "Annual Report, 1977–78."

22. "Cities Find It Hard to Build on Reassurances," *Buffalo Courier-Express*, June 22, 1973.

23. "Buffalo Waterfront Project Kept in Flux by Planners," *Buffalo Evening News*, January 2, 1974.

24. Interview no. 32.

25. Interview no. 29.

26. "Maps Drive to Boost Economy," *Buffalo Evening News*, February 3, 1976.

27. Erie County Industrial Development Agency, "Overview Report of the Buffalo Area Economic Adjustment Strategy," October 27, 1978.

28. Interview no. 57.

29. "The Buffalo-Amherst Corridor Technical Report," Office of Planning Coordination, New York State, 1969, p. 11.

30. Interview no. 47.

31. Interview no. 50.

32. David S. Witerski, "Convention Center Already Preparing for Opening Day," *Buffalo Courier-Express*, February 27, 1978.

33. Sally Fox, "Hotel Seen as Spur to the Future," *Buffalo Courier-Express*, January 28, 1978.

34. "Regan: Hyatt May Ponder Buffalo Hotel," *Buffalo Courier-Express*, February 2, 1978.

35. Gordon Thompson, "A Chronology of Transportation Development on the Niagara Frontier, Buffalo: 1860–1975," unpublished paper, 1975.

36. Interview no. 37.

37. Thompson, "Chronology of Transportation."

38. John Meyer and José Gómez-Ibáñez, "Autos, Transit and City," a Twentieth Century Fund Report, 1981.

39. Interview no. 63.

40. Interview no. 67.

41. Interview no. 60.

42. Ibid.

43. Ibid.

44. "Panel Named to Revise City Charter," *Buffalo Evening News*, July 12, 1974.

45. Interview no. 67.

46. Interview no. 44.

47. Interview no. 63.

48. Interview no. 40.

49. Greater Buffalo Development Foundation, "Annual Report, 1975."

50. Interview no. 52.

51. Interview no. 68.

52. Plaintiffs' Post-Trial Brief: Civil Docket No. 1972-325 (excerpts), United States District Court, Western District of New York (Buffalo, January 13, 1975).

53. Interview no. 68.

54. Greater Buffalo Development Foundation, "Annual Report, 1979–80."

55. Greater Buffalo Development Foundation, "Annual Report, 1976–77"; "Annual Report, 1977–78."

56. Greater Buffalo Development Foundation, "Annual Report, 1977–78."

57. "Rocky, BUILD Agree on Program Designed to Employ More Minorities," *Buffalo Evening News.*

58. "Rev. Ford, Former BUILD President, Moving to California," *Buffalo Courier-Express*, August 20, 1972.

59. Debbie Dahlberg, "Alinsky in Buffalo: The BUILD Organization," unpublished paper, 1985, pp. 38–41.

60. BUILD Press Archives: 1964–74, p. 244.

61. Scott Nesbitt, "Building Trades Integration Session Flops," *Buffalo Courier-Express*, May 26, 1971.

62. Dahlberg, "Alinsky in Buffalo," p. 43.

63. Deborah Williams, "BUILD Academy Plans Curriculum for Specific Inner City Needs," BUILD Press Archives 1964–74, p. 227.

64. "Buffalo Blacks on the Move," *Buffalo Courier-Express*, April 1979.

Chapter Five

NEW LEADERS, OLD STRUCTURE

The 1980s

In 1983 Bethlehem Steel took the final step and closed its basic steel operation.[1] This entrained a shift in the private sector from high-paying union jobs to jobs that were relatively low in pay in the service sector, while unionized public-sector jobs remained strong. These economic events changed the city's revenue base, its neighborhoods, and the structure of political power in this period of consolidation. With each closing, people began to recognize that the shifts in the marketplace were real, that this was in fact a structural change, and that the steel mills would not be reopening. Buffalo's leadership, compelled by events, took steps toward regional cooperation and planning.

Buffalo's business elite changed. Now a younger generation of leaders, some of them sons of prominent establishment figures from earlier decades and other recently arrived investors, took over as chief executive officers of banks, food and dairy operations, high-tech ventures, Great Lakes shipping, and the city's sole surviving newspaper. These energetic business leaders, arriving from New York City or as far away as California, acted as catalysts for the city's new generation of elite leaders. These investors were not bound by Buffalo's particular socioeconomic history and culture.

They had come to invest money and to build their own prestige. They replaced the professional staff at the Greater Buffalo Development Foundation and the Chamber of Commerce, working closely and effectively with the mayor, his departments, and agencies on development initiatives for downtown.

Fulfilling larger visions of change, such as planning miles of waterfront development, remained impossible, however, because ideas of a grand scope required overcoming local fears of regional planning. Such planning remained elusive, even though a commission as far back as 1935 had recommended the formation of regional structures and processes to save money, reduce service overlap, and consolidate competing forces within the larger Buffalo area.

Massive amounts of federal and state funds, flowing into the still economically distressed and restructuring city, aggravated an already bad relationship between the mayor and the city council. The mayor (focused on revitalizing the regional economy and downtown) and the city council (focused on housing and neighborhood business development) each needed these community development funds in the form of low-interest loans and outright grants for their projects. Battles for these funds raged between the mayor and city council in a broken political process at great loss to the city. By the end of the decade, it became apparent that easy access to huge subsidies did not necessarily bring fruitful development. Some investors used these funds unwisely or in projects unrelated to any comprehensive plan. Others remained committed to the project, or Buffalo, only as long as funds lasted.

ECONOMIC STORY

Massive industrial shifts had been occurring through the 1970s and early 1980s in the region's two-county industrial base. Between 1970 and 1984, manufacturing declined by 40.6 percent, or by almost seventy thousand jobs. At the same time, the service sector gained 58.8 percent, or almost forty-one thousand jobs, largely lower-paying ones. The finance, insurance, and real estate sector (FIRE) gained by 20 percent, or a little over four thousand jobs.[2]

When Bethlehem Steel closed its basic steel operation in Lackawanna, it ended eighty years of steelmaking there.[3] Nearly all of Bethlehem's twenty factories and seventy miles of rail on fourteen hundred acres of property fell silent. A small force of approximately fifteen hundred workers remained at the bar and galvanizing mills completed in the early 1970s and at the coke facility. The economic decline of the 1970s continued, highlighted by the amount of public assistance the federal and state governments mobilized for the area in an effort to help.

Between 1980 and 1985, public funding, already high, increased by 110 percent, compared with a 30 percent increase throughout New York State during that same period.[4] The federal government alone sent more Urban Development Action Grant (UDAG) funds to Buffalo than any other municipality, save one, because its distress rate was so high. The city administration's strategy was to use these funds, primarily, to leverage private investment. "In the early 1980s . . . two federally funded hotels took shape downtown, while along Main Street, construction crews put together a $500 million light-rail line. And in City Hall, bureaucrats struggled to spend all the money arriving from Washington."[5] Combined federal and state funding in 1981 and 1982 constituted 50 percent and 52 percent of city revenues, respectively, according to the state's comptroller.[6] These numbers dropped for the remainder of the decade but stayed significant, ranging from 38 to 45 percent.

According to a university study in November 1986, Buffalo's economic development strategy had not produced the hoped for results and remained "sick." It was nearly ten years since the reconstituted Erie County Industrial Development Agency issued its $400,000 "Growth Strategy" report on economic development for the area. The report had advised using public funds for serious economic development efforts, with the hope that these funds would leverage private investment.[7] In ten years, not much leveraging had taken place.

A New Elite Leadership

> Buffalo is often described as a big small town. Our power study concurs. Talk about networking. Buffalo's powerful are a relatively small group, constantly crisscrossing. Take one . . . he's a banker—the chairman of the M&T Bank. He's a founding member of the Buffalo Eighteen, the city's self-appointed power moguls. He is chairman of the board of the Greater Buffalo Development Foundation and on the boards of the Greater Buffalo Chamber of Commerce, the Buffalo Philharmonic Orchestra and the Albright-Knox Gallery. He's everywhere. And so are the rest of the [power] people.[8]

According to one community leader, the neighborhoods won many of the fights on social issues and funding in the 1970s, "only to see the larger battle lost a few years later because the personalities changed, but the issues and structures of power didn't."[9] The business newcomers energized Buffalo's business owners and executives. One new leader, formerly part of a New York investment group, assumed the reins of M&T Bank in 1983 and turned it into a gold mine for both the city and the banks' investors. Within a short time, the bank tripled local lending and increased profits tenfold ($3.5 million to $40 million) over five years. Another newcomer, the CEO of Goldome Bank (formerly Buffalo Savings Bank), built a new headquarters. On the political front, he developed a partnership with the mayor, breaking new ground in the formation of overt political-economic relationships. The new publisher of the *Buffalo News* (bought by Warren Buffett in 1977) greatly broadened the paper's political and social perspective. The new CEO of American Steamship brought progressive ideas from California into the leadership mix. On the local side, the second-generation owner of Rich Products became integral to this group, along with two sons of one elite banker, and executives of Computer Task Group. These business leaders were joined by an equally energized group of public employees, economic freethinkers who now held community development and economic development positions with the city and county governments.

Plotting an unusual course, this new agglomeration of business executives strategized ways to wrest control from the sitting elite. Their objective was to catalyze change through a new approach to development and planning, and they figured this would necessitate a new kind of leadership. These few *conspirators* began to research how other cities approached economic development. Their findings were compelling, and they agreed that Buffalo's most pressing need was for the private sector to lead.[10] They conceded it would take more than public relations and slogans; they must assume control of the Greater Buffalo Development Foundation and the Chamber of Commerce.

They began their takeover: A few core leaders identified a group of eighteen people in the private sector they considered to be "change masters," whom they dubbed "The Buffalo Eighteen"—or "Group of Eighteen." Together they worked strategically to gain control of the targeted organizations in order to put their own people into primary positions of power. Within two years, this quasi-secret assemblage did just that, with two members of the Group of Eighteen elected the chairmen of both boards. These change masters found not only followers for their ideas but also new teachers. Once installed, the boards of directors undertook national searches for new executive directors to lead their organizations professionally. These new executive directors were expected to challenge and educate their boards of directors on the issues, drawing on their substantial professional credentials in the creation of proactive strategies. (Past executive directors were seen as facilitators and consensus builders.) Other organizations followed with transformations of their own. Roswell Park (the renowned cancer research center) and the Niagara Frontier Transportation Authority both hired new directors and personnel.

The Group of Eighteen's direct involvement in local activities paid off in political influence that they pushed statewide. They openly supported and worked with the mayor and his administration, with one banker during the 1985 mayoral campaign going so far as to write a letter to the editor in the *Buffalo News* in support of the mayor—a rare occasion in the annals of Buffalo's history. From the onset, this upstart group used Mayor Jimmy Griffin as a rallying point for economic development and its consolidation of power.

New Strategies

[It] will take an uncompromising act of political and financial will to design a new regional vehicle to undertake programs of significant regional benefit.[11]

Under Governor Mario Cuomo, the state moved into high gear. In 1982 the governor took an unprecedented step when he created a regional agency, the Western New York Economic Development Corporation, and made it a subsidiary of the state's Urban Development Corporation. The new Economic Development Corporation was empowered to plan, finance, and manage major development projects solely in the western New York region. Claimed one official, "No state administration had ever made such a major commitment to address the economic needs of the western New York area."[12] This new corporation had three priorities: (1) to establish a new business center at the state university called the Technical Enterprise Development Institute; (2) to relocate Buffalo's main port facilities to Lackawanna, where a private port operator would have some public oversight; and (3) to construct a downtown baseball stadium. Three years later, in 1985, a fourth priority came along when Bethlehem Steel sold 150 acres, including the two port areas and an industrial park, to Gateway Trade Center. This privately owned corporation had developed plans to create a foreign-trade zone in cooperation with Erie County.[13]

The Group of Eighteen pursued two strategies. The first was to develop a broad medical initiative through a collaborative approach to research and development, led by business and the state university through two centers, the Center for Advanced Technology (engineering) and the Health Instruments and Devices Institute (dentistry and pharmacy). Further, the Group of Eighteen focused on "shoring up" the leadership of the existing Roswell Park Cancer Institute, which, according to some, had become politicized. To this end, organizations that could help with planning, financing, technology assessment, and the structuring of deals became central to success. Revitalizing Roswell Park involved local leaders, the Department of Transportation for the Elm-Oak streets corridor (given Roswell Park's location, an abandoned area ripe for redevelopment having been cleared for urban renewal decades earlier), and other agencies of the federal government. An executive director's position was created to oversee the $250 million reconstruction of the medical facility. In addition, steps were taken to change the cancer institute's structure of governance by moving it from under the control of the State Department of Health to a special "quasi-public authority." The change in governance would allow much greater operating flexibility and reduce its costs, as it would be "significantly state funded."[14] Lobbying in the state capital became a large part of this plan. The medical initiative continued with the amalgamation of hospitals and the Western New York Health Sciences Consortium in the 1990s. The science consortium aimed to build a greater link between the university's medical and engineering schools to Buffalo's hospitals, creating an academic-led healthcare system, which would benefit the community and serve to attract medical industry to the area.

Despite these successful efforts, critics took the Group of Eighteen to task for not having a broader context, or vision, for its initiatives. A 1986 study prepared at the State University of New York stated flatly that "there is little regional logic to these development plans nor any understanding of which firms and industries will provide jobs, skills and income to reinforce the quality of life for the region's residents. . . . Local development agencies and officials under the present structure, respond only to the needs of the individual entrepreneur and not to the broader needs of the jurisdiction or region."[15]

The second strategy of the Group of Eighteen, devised by both public- and private-sector leaders in the group, comprised three plans for physical development: (1) a downtown "regional center" plan, focusing primarily on rezoning and calling for specific assets of the city to be directed to attracting investment; (2) a waterfront plan, still very much up in the air in 1987; and (3) the rapid-transit plan, focusing on its completion.

City officials referred to this second strategy as a master plan, but this was a misnomer. Nowhere did it include a plan for neighborhood development.

More to the point, no city government department existed at this time to plan for neighborhoods. The Division of Neighborhood and Commercial Revitalizations—whose role it was to plan for neighborhood economic and housing development—had been folded into the Home Inspections Department, clearly not a planning entity. Incredibly, neighborhood housing and business development remained outside the scope of planning for the Community Development Block Grant funds allocated annually. As one official said, "Neighborhood housing gets planned in terms of programs, not strategy, and those ad hoc programs come through the city council or the neighborhoods themselves."[16] Funds had to be fought for project by project, either through the Department of Community Development, which was focused on downtown, or through the nonprofit corporation for housing construction established by Mayor Griffin to circumvent the city council.

Business leaders, from their point of view, claimed that capital funneled into low-income neighborhoods "never comes out" to get recycled into the economic system.[17] Perhaps this was to be expected until basic issues were addressed—access to education, access to jobs, access to capital, and access to housing outside the economically depressed areas. Without remediation, for example, the black community would find upward mobility difficult. Partnerships to confront these issues *and* funds were necessary. Buffalo's white business leaders needed to introduce themselves to black community leaders and professional groups, of which the Black Development Foundation was only one, and cofound new organizations.

Although in hindsight Buffalo seems to have suffered from many lapses in planning and failures in cooperative partnerships, one economic specialist states that, at the time, Buffalo was thought to have one of the most complete economic development efforts in the country. "Good local economic development capacity: good county, and good state . . . and all working very well together." Most of the successes, of course, were the work of the public sector. And as it happened, Congressman John LaFalce's work to change the block grant formula to favor cities with older housing doubled the size of Buffalo's Community Development Block Grant.[18]

Influenced by the emergence of a growing global economy, Buffalo's economic leadership began to focus less on whether companies were owned locally and more on whether they stayed open and strong. The case of Freezer Queen is a good example where the leadership worked with all available resources to keep a local company strong and in the region. Marine Midland Bank provided a bridge loan to an investor from Dublin, Ireland, who put up substantial money to buy the company. Government assistance included a no-interest loan from the federal government, a low-interest loan from the New York Urban Development Corporation, and a combination of taxable and tax-exempt bonds from the state's Job Development Authority. Two public officials brokered the deal, one a professional at the Erie County Industrial Development Agency and the other the head of the Western New York Economic Development Corporation.

Buffalo's first UDAG provided much of the funding for the

waterfront Hilton Hotel. The developer paid a 1 to 2 percent interest rate to the Buffalo Economic Renaissance Corporation, an entity of the Erie County Industrial Development Agency. Since the city received this funding from the federal government at no cost, it was able to make money on the loan even though the interest rate was low. As activities progressed, the city loaned money to businesses and to developers at increasingly higher rates, making more money.

The community development funds fueled a network of organizations and "shell-corporations" through which these monies moved, operated by a cadre of individuals from Erie County and the city government who worked closely together. If one of these, or other, public servants had a project, he or she would make the rounds to a series of sources—each agency having evolved independently but being interlocking in the larger scheme of things. Federal loans through the various development corporations constituted no more than 25 percent of each project's total investment.

The Erie County Industrial Development Agency, structured as an authority, had the legal ability to go to a developer and offer to forgive *the city's* property taxes—something the agency considered a primary tool in its efforts. Years before this, the Chamber of Commerce had a similar ability. It would charge a fee to a company locating in Buffalo, considered a tax loophole, and the Chamber of Commerce would then forgive the company's taxes for the next thirty years. When Griffin came into office, he cried foul, and the parties came to an agreement where every municipality was given "effectively" seven years of free property taxes spread over different formulas, and no more.

Downtown

The "heady" days of downtown development began with Buffalo Savings Bank's transformation into Goldome Bank in 1982, a development project that got folded into what became known as the Main-Genesee Urban Renewal Plan. The momentum generated by this project continued through the decade and culminated in 1991. The Main-Genesee plan, for an area assuming the name Fountain Plaza in 1982, had four project elements, not including an outdoor ice-skating rink: (1) the Norstar Building, headquarters for Liberty National Bank and Trust Company; (2) the Goldome Bank Building; (3) the Pearl Street public parking ramp; and (4) the renovation of the Hyatt Regency Buffalo Hotel (with groundbreaking in 1980 and completion at the decade's end). Ten prominent firms submitted proposals to build the hotel-office complex. The Greater Buffalo Development Foundation worked with the city to make arrangements for the hotel project's complicated financing package.[19] The foundation's chairman became head of the Main-Genesee Urban Design Group, thus becoming responsible to the Buffalo Urban Renewal Agency for design objectives and criteria for the overall project and modifications, as well as monitoring construction.

The city ceded its authority along the transit mall, where the trains would stop, on lower Main Street designated "Buffalo Place." Buffalo Place incorporated as a nonprofit corporation with a board of directors that included major business owners on Main Street and public officials. The city handed over to the board all responsibility for operations, including maintenance, promotional events, and ongoing development initiatives. Buffalo Place Inc. included about one-half of downtown, all of the at-grade transit line, as well as one block north into the theater district.

With all of this development activity, the city planning board took steps to clean up pornography shops and bars on Chippewa Street, one of the side streets that intersected with Main Street. A group calling itself the Downtown Core Coalition became active in the late 1980s. "Its founder bought the Calumet Building and began its renovation, to great effect. Now both ends of Chippewa as well as this hotel did much to boost the value of the shops, restaurants, bars and offices in the middle."[20] The momentum in economic development converged with the banking boom—jobs, backroom operations, and new bank headquarters—and then the bust at the end of the decade. By 1991 Buffalo's downtown development also hit its peak.

Labor's Initiatives

Unions developed their own initiatives to facilitate development through the partial financing of projects. The Buffalo Building Trades Investment Foundation, for one, took a first mortgage position in the new Hyatt Hotel. The Building Trades Investment Foundation also made a $3 million loan to the Erie County Industrial Development Agency for the new baseball stadium. Under an agreement between the AFL-CIO and the state's comptroller, the union made economic development investments, and the New York State Pension Fund purchased the mortgages from the union. This arrangement benefited both the state and the union in that the union did the legwork on each investment, which the state was not equipped to do, and the state guaranteed the mortgage, which freed up more union pension money for other investments. Manufacturing unions also helped the regional economy by assisting in worker buyouts. When Republic Steel announced plans to close its Buffalo operations, for example, the affected unions offered to buy 51 percent of the company through an employee stock ownership plan (ESOP) in an effort to keep the plant open. In this case, however, the union effort failed, and management rejected the plan.[21]

But organized labor also made innovation difficult, according to one official close to the mayor. During the crisis, unemployment among the tens of thousands of steelworkers was a social and economic catastrophe. At one point, Mayor Griffin, a son of South Buffalo (the part of town where steelworkers and their families lived in the shadow of the steel mills), had his staff write a proposal and obtained $2 million to $3 million in federal funds. The proposal was to use laid-off steelworkers to demolish the buildings at the old, abandoned Republic Steel site to prepare it for new companies. The program would pay workers twelve dollars per hour. The steelworkers' union attacked the plan at a meeting at city hall, claiming that they had a site agreement, which meant that even if no plant existed at that site, any work there had to be done by steelworkers at the national union wage rates, currently twenty-eight dollars per hour. The union threatened to picket anyone who went into the site, whereupon the city abandoned the idea.

Behind the Scenes

Mayor Jimmy Griffin, unlike the other mayors, was beholden to no political party. He was "his own man," he worked well with those loyal to him, and he made decisions quickly. For example, a month after becoming mayor, he showed up at an introductory meeting between himself and two public officials to discuss whether to move ahead with the waterfront hotel. As an involved official tells it: "It was the second week in December. It was cold. Jimmy walked in by himself, which was totally bizarre because every time Makowski met with you, he had seven or eight people there. Griffin said, 'What do you want to do?' . . . 'Sounds great to me.' [We said,] 'Well, do you want to meet about it?' [Griffin responded,] 'No, let's do it!'"[22] Griffin hired his first community development commissioner the same way, with few deliberations or further meetings. A consensus existed among his economic development team that he wanted to get things done for the community.

Griffin's economic development officials were local and excited by the challenges. One had attended city Catholic schools and, right out of college in 1974, went to work at the Erie County IDA as one of its first employees before becoming director of economic development with the city. Another official, who had been a missionary parish priest in the city's East Side black community, worked in housing redevelopment and construction, and he later headed just about every economic development operation for the county, city, and state. Another official grew up on Buffalo's West Side; received a degree in public administration in New York;

worked as a community organizer in Harlem, Bedford Stuyvesant, Brooklyn, and on the lower East Side in New York City; returned to work at the Erie and Niagara Counties Regional Planning Board; and then worked for the city in community development and as budget director. The last, an old friend of the first, worked in the private sector before being invited over to work on the public side, which led to his becoming one of the first employees of the Buffalo development companies.

These officials shared one desire: to leverage investment for Buffalo. They did not want to "dribble" funds away. With limited resources, they needed to focus on the most effective projects. The innovations and projects enumerated earlier are a testimony of these leaders' innovations. Unfortunately, a great many block grant loans went to projects that ended up in default. To make matters worse, the city had to shoulder the burden of paying back these losses—both the principal and interest on an annual basis—with block grant entitlement funds. Thus a certain percentage of annual block grant money went directly back to HUD in repayment for bad loans rather than being used for economic development each subsequent year. A number of these same professionals admit today that the rising-water-floats-all-boats theory never reached the minority population or the moderate- and low-income communities.[23]

But the costs were not just monetary. On the savings and loan front, when Goldome and Erie County Savings Bank went into default during the banking crisis, the human loss was devastating. Four thousand people were left jobless. One retrospective view by a community development official is illuminating:

> [During the 1980s,] my opinion is . . . there wasn't a transaction that made sense [and] would not have occurred if the money had not been there. There were deals that never should have happened—that happened because government threw money at them and they subsequently failed. There are very few deals of those fun days, those exciting, those heady days, that didn't go under [or] haven't disappeared.[24]

The Horizons Waterfront Commission—
The Late 1980s

The Western New York Industrial Development Corporation proposed the construction of a downtown waterfront baseball stadium, but only if certain conditions were met.[25] Mayor Griffin and a number of business elites pushed for the downtown baseball stadium, but Governor Cuomo replied that he would wait to make a decision: "I would not now want to commit to a stadium only to find there is a more compelling need for Erie County."[26] Eventually Cuomo was satisfied, and the funding arrived. With the completion of the waterfront baseball stadium in sight, ideas for a comprehensive waterfront strategy were afoot. Five miles of land on Lake Erie (from the city border south) opened up for development with the loss of steel operations. It was the largest tract of undeveloped urban waterfront in the United States. A grand scheme such as the waterfront development entailed five critical elements: the willingness to think big and proactively, the influence and commitment of Buffalo elites to spur private-sector leadership, the desire of local jurisdictions to form partnerships, the ability of political leaders to work with their counterparts, and the legal authority to raise the money.

Agreeing with those who argued that Buffalo still had a strategic competitive advantage, Congressman Henry Nowak in Washington proposed creating a waterfront replica of New York's Battery Park. While this began as a dream, it quickly found proponents in the county and state who joined forces to move the idea ahead. The plan was to create a separate entity, an authority, that could hold both political and economic power, issue its own bonds for financing, and form its own system of patronage. Congressman Nowak nurtured a campaign to both gather and disseminate information. He obtained the assistance of a highly experienced and successful businessman who had developed New York's Battery Park and who, at one time, had been the executive director of the very powerful New York State Urban Development Corporation. For

Buffalo, he was a known quantity, someone who sat on local boards, including that of a major bank. It would have been difficult to find someone better placed for such a project.

The plan to structure the project around an authority gave the project real heft. It would become a "stand-alone" entity, relatively free of the political and economic baggage that had undermined local or regional projects in the past. Most especially, Congressman Nowak hoped the entity, through its authority status, would enable Mayor Griffin and County Executive Dennis Gorski to work together. The congressman and county executive persuaded Governor Cuomo to form the authority, and he named it the Horizons Waterfront Commission. The commission looked especially promising as it consolidated interests, establishing one center of power. Proponents reasoned that if it could work in New York City, it could work in Buffalo. But, despite efforts, the proposed waterfront commission had difficulty in rallying the necessary forces to support it. The business elite immediately turned its back on the idea, not finding it credible. The city's director of planning called it naive. The Democratic machine, still big in the county, took a strong stand against it, as the authority would become a patronage system in its own right. No doubt, too, it would have challenged the Niagara Frontier Transportation Authority as a rival and reduced NFTA's monopoly power over the port area.

Not to be deterred, the state moved ahead with the Horizons Commission and initiated a planning process on outer-harbor development. State funds provided some front-end planning money, and the state prevailed on the federal government to do the same. A former district attorney was hired to be the commission's chairman—by many accounts an incorruptible man with enough money of his own who could, and did, refuse to be pressured by political interests. The commission's work would be difficult, as "[o]ne of the toughest things in Buffalo is putting together a broad consensus in order to move forward with an initiative."[27]

The commission began work with a host of power centers: the

Erie County executive, the mayor of Buffalo, the county legislature, Buffalo's city council, the African American community, the Democratic machine—except the business community, which had "no appetite to get involved."[28] Work progressed with the hope that momentum would bring the business leaders along. The commission hired consultants to research and prepare an action plan. These professionals first reviewed earlier waterfront plans and studies for the Towns of Tonawanda, Hamburg, Evans, and Brant; the City of Lackawanna; and several others, including Buffalo's Outer Harbor Development Plan, the Harborfront Master Plan, the Draft Remedial Action Plan for the Buffalo River, the Draft Waterfront Plan, and the Buffalo Regional Center Plan. Naturally, conflicts existed both internal to the individual plans and *between* the plans. The goal of the Horizon Commission was to "lead the development of the waterfront, beginning with articulating a vision."[29]

The commission's comprehensive document laid out a detailed assortment of projects fitting an overall vision for the thirty miles of lakefront that would both be accessible and prosperous, from Grand Island and North Tonawanda south through Buffalo and Lackawanna to the Town of Evans. It included maps of each local jurisdiction, detailed plans, and the steps needed toward implementation, including zoning and road system requirements. The plan had three components: recreation and open space, development opportunities, and transportation improvements. Each component would bring further economic development to the region and improve Buffalo's quality of life, while protecting private rights. Buffalo's leaders cared about these issues; here, for the first time, was a comprehensive strategy to implement a vision that built on Buffalo's past. The action plan said it well: "Without the Horizons plan, regional growth will continue to occur predominantly on the edges of the urban area, and the underutilization of vacant land in the waterfront will continue."[30]

The effort finally failed because support was intermittent and unsustained. Monthly meetings went nowhere. Despite all levels of political involvement, including the governor, it became clear nothing would come about without the business elite's active and committed role. What had been a proactive new business leadership began to resemble a leadership bent on representing the status quo. One contributing factor may have been that a substantial number of establishment families lived, or had their summer homes, along the lakeshore.

Republican George Pataki did not like the project. When he replaced Cuomo as governor, its champion, in 1994, Pataki changed the entire structure of the commission by folding it into the state's agency on economic development, with the mandate to focus solely on the broader issue of economic development. The new governor also declined to reappoint the commission chair because politicians had decided he was not a team player. From the commission's point of view, the "usual forces" were jockeying for position in the lineup for jobs, although many of them had not supported the project in the first place.[31]

The Rapid-Transit Initiative: Part Three—End of the Line

> Had any of the elite taken sides in that three-year controversy, the delay wouldn't have happened. The business leadership sat back. [Today,] they couldn't tell you anything about it because they wouldn't remember anything about it—they don't know. There was one key man at Marine Midland; he listened, [liked what he heard], went into his board meeting the next morning, and he was strongly corrected . . . to change his mind. It was too controversial to take a stand. The only people who supported [it] were independent citizens who did not have the responsibility of running a business.
>
> —A banker and proponent of rapid transit

To recapitulate: In 1975, after years of inactivity, the Greater Buffalo Development Foundation spoke out about the rapid-transit system for the first time, challenging the professionals' design and the cost of a

$26 million covered transit mall. They charged that the design was too expensive, and they wanted two alternative concepts studies. On May 15, the city set aside plans for the transit mall pending the Urban Mass Transit Authority's decision on the transit line redesign.

The Greater Buffalo Development Foundation formed the Main-Genesee Urban Design Group. The president of the foundation chaired the group until the rapid-transit system's opening in 1986 and took over responsibility "for developing design objectives and criteria for the overall project [including the transit mall], reviewing and evaluating proposed concepts and design of the buildings and plazas, proposing necessary design modifications, recommending design proposals for approval by the Buffalo Urban Renewal Agency and monitoring construction contracts, progress and modifications." Federal UDAG funds totaling more than $16 million were used for the Main-Genesee redevelopment.[32]

The NFTA chairman reported in 1982 that the "Mall Task Group has picked four finalists in its selection of a chief architect/designer" in efforts to reduce costs through *redesign* of the transit mall. (The original architects were not on this list.) Everyone understood that the project was at a critical stage in that it needed a memorandum of understanding from the federal government that federal aid would cover a $44.3 million cost overrun.[33] The federal government did in fact cover the more than $40 million cost overrun because of delays stemming from community activist protests, total redesign of the transit system (inverting the underground and at-grade portions, respectively), and redesign of the transit mall on Main Street. Despite all the delays, the half-completed transit system and pedestrian transit mall opened in 1986. And there has been little interest since to finish the line to realize its original purpose, which was to link the university and suburbs to Buffalo's downtown.

During the redesign of the transit mall, one critical decision was not revisited: the decision to close Main Street to traffic. As one downtown planner declared incredulously, "There was never [a second internal] debate on whether Main Street should be closed [or opened] to automobile traffic."[34] In 2004 there was talk of opening the street to traffic.

POLITICAL STORY

These were warriors. All they understood was battle.
—A newspaper editor

Relations between the mayor and city council headed toward a political impasse, with serious implications for the future. Mayor Griffin had campaigned against the business elite but reversed himself once elected. Further, he created nonprofit economic development vehicles that enabled him to bypass his city council in legislating and budgeting for urban development. At the same time, he fulfilled his campaign promise to sideline the Democratic machine, replacing one system of patronage with another—his own. For city council members, the partnership between the mayor and business, in itself, was not a problem. But taking the council out of the legislative and budgeting process proved to be a lasting problem.

Mayor Griffin criticized the *Buffalo News* following its sale to Warren Buffett in 1977, the year of his election, and its importation of a new publisher. According to one of his aides, Mayor Griffin "never allowed himself to be interviewed by them in all four terms. [He] . . . felt they were a very self-important group, who were detrimental to the interests of the people of Buffalo." Beside his political concerns, he railed against the price of the paper and the price of advertising, and he disliked how it represented the Republican establishment. He was not pleased how the *Buffalo News* took him to task on his Irish hiring practices. On issues of race, he thought the paper championed every black cause for everyone except for the *News* itself: it supported school busing and the black nominee for mayor, while hiring few blacks to work at the paper.[35]

Core Issue

For sixteen years, Community Development Block Grant funds were the underlying issue between the mayor and council. Federal funds released to cities came in the form of a "block grant" (a system established in 1968 by the Community Development Act, with allocations set by formula for each city) to be divided as local officials saw fit. In Mayor Makowski's time, the city received approximately $12 million in federal funds, much of which went to the human service agencies. Through these agencies, Makowski was able to offer aid to people as they struggled over the loss of jobs and income during the worst years of the economic crisis.

By 1980 the money had increased to approximately $22 million, and Griffin was near the beginning of his tenure. "First HUD would announce how much we were going to get, then the city would have to prepare an application, and we would assign the money to various categories—human service agencies, economic development—and then that particular application would go to the Common Council. That's where the council wars started . . . initially led by a [white] council member from the university district."[36]

In the administration's early years, "a lot of horse trading" occurred between the two camps over these funds, with the mayor favoring economic and industrial development, and the city council, conversely, focused on neighborhood housing and community development. Both needed funding to jump-start private investment. The two camps' positions hardened, and deal-making became less attainable. The mayor left the planning to his staff, but he did little to breach the gap himself, claiming that no votes came out of the most vociferous council members' districts anyway. The council members likewise felt that supporting the mayor did not bolster their own support.

It was not long before the mayor made a strategic decision to change the city's basic structure for doing business. The Department of Community Development established nonprofit shell corporations to make grants and loans under the aegis of the nonprofit umbrella Buffalo Development Companies. Because the municipal structure did not allow the loaning or transfer of federal money to private interests, these nonprofit corporations were designed for several specific purposes: the Buffalo Neighborhood Revitalization Corp. handled the neighborhood housing construction funds; the Buffalo Economic Development Corp. financed industrial and smaller business projects; and Downtown Development Inc.—created years earlier to handle UDAG funds for the Hilton Hotel—prepared deals and loans for unique downtown projects. For a time, all of the above shared the same president.

For any given project, a developer might make the rounds for funds from all three nonprofit corporations. Mayor Griffin maintained control over economic development projects by appointing 49 percent of the seats on development boards. Griffin's power over these initiatives and projects persisted even after he left office in 1994 because of the ongoing tenure of his board appointees. These nonprofit corporations had in fact been created to handle federal funds and direct them wherever the mayor wanted. Nonetheless, being beyond the control of the city council, these corporations took on lives of their own. A resurrected urban renewal agency also became a "paper vehicle" for economic development that was particularly useful to the mayor.

A standoff over political control of government funds and the planning process ensued, where confrontations and delays came at a price to the city. For example, the city lost an $18 million waterfront marketplace after a series of council votes and trades with the mayor fell through in what was a complicated deal put together with UDAG funds. Near the end of negotiations when a minor technical approval was needed (an abandonment of a right-of-way, solely on paper), the council decided to use this as leverage (in effect, a quid pro quo) for the $1 million it wanted to go to a community center in the Pratt-Willert project. While the adversaries battled it out, the Marina Market Place deal unwound, with the developers saying, "Enough is enough" and walking away.[37]

By the end of the decade, the city's planning protocol was in disarray as the mayor continued to bypass his council in most decisions. A city planning official explained:

> It was too late, and the bigger moves that would have taken real coordination and buy-in from many sectors didn't happen because by the mid-1980s a very different political scene was in place. . . . The mayor was in his third term, and power after a long time is not always as responsive, and he was pretty brutal about so many things. [Also] the council was getting more and more inner city in makeup—and the council believed that he was antiblack. He may not have been, but he sure didn't do any policies to help the poor neighborhoods. He thought he did, but it was piecemeal. To make downtown revitalization work, you need all the elements to make it work: business, communities, city council, mayor . . . and this was a time of warfare. . . . The council didn't want the mayor to succeed. And the mayor wouldn't let the council succeed.

In time, the Common Council filed suit against Mayor Griffin, arguing that UDAG funds had to go through the city council. The council lost the legal case, and funds continued to flow through the Urban Renewal Agency.

COMMUNITY STORY

> These Community Development Block Grants went to downtown and to wealthy neighborhoods . . . [and] to one of the new banks that came to Buffalo in the early 1980s. This money was loaned at no interest because the bank was going to help develop downtown. After the bank received the money, it closed its downtown headquarters and moved all the support offices out to the suburbs.
>
> —Interview no. 44

While the amount of the Community Development Block Grant funds during the 1980s doubled, funds going into the neighborhoods remained at the same level. One former public official who was intimately involved suggests that this strategy, if not illegal, could have been considered immoral in that it denied the bulk of these funds to communities for whom these funds were originally designated. Others argue that the rules for the block grants in the early days were still flexible, "even though they got here on poverty so no one really challenged it at that point."[38]

City council members had supplanted Democratic Party committeemen, ministers, and grassroots organizations as the voice and *power* for communities. Blacks and whites on the Common Council united in response to the flow of nearly 98 percent of Community Development Block Grant funds to downtown development and industrial retention strategies. The council settled for two tactical, procedural strategies in confronting the mayor, since it no longer had a meaningful seat at the table. Often, as already noted, the council members took the role of "spoiler" (their own word) until they could accomplish their objectives. Sometimes council members delayed downtown projects sponsored by business executives by holding up the allocation or release of funds. Other times, council members leveraged funds for neighborhood projects by withholding votes on the mayor's bills until they succeeded in obtaining funds for neighborhood housing. When the administration wanted federal funds allocated for Goldome Bank development, the council held the project "hostage." In order for the council to sign off on the project, the administration agreed to use the bank's repayments to build the long-awaited Pratt-Willert project, a low-income housing development on the city's East Side.

While the philosophical differences between the council and the mayor were real, it was an absolute fact that Buffalo's poorest neighborhoods needed massive investment in the form of low- and no-interest loans and grants. These investments were needed to replace old public housing, to upgrade housing stock in areas devastated by urban renewal clearance, and to build highways; to facilitate businesses and the growth of capital in the black community; and to improve public education, job training, and business skills, including bookkeeping, marketing, and financial planning.

Some of the elite called the fight between downtown and the neighborhoods a "false debate."[39] Individuals espousing this view argued that 60 percent of federal funds went to the neighborhoods, implying that the poor neighborhoods received these funds. The fact is only 2.7 percent of these block grant funds went to city neighborhoods during some of Buffalo's worst years. And all special project funds (UDAGs) were used for downtown projects. The rest (97.3 percent) went to private-sector development or to projects in upper- and middle-class neighborhoods. It should be noted, too, that over $5 million of these funds, allocated for the Pratt-Willert project, had to be extracted from the mayor (through bitter battles) in return for the council's support for the Goldome Bank building project.

The Complete List of Community Development Block Grant Funds for the 1985–87 Retention Strategy

- Buffalo General Hospital, $200 million (as part of the medical strategy)
- State University of New York at Buffalo, Main Street campus, $110 million
- Niagara Mohawk Power Corporation, $7 million
- Bells Market, $5 million
- Pratt-Willert Area: housing, $4.9 million; community center, $0.8 million
- Broadway/Fillmore Area: Broadway Market, $3.3 million; Broadway and Beck Plaza, $0.7 million
- Catholic Center, $2.5 million
- Roberts Gordon Appliance Corporation, $2.4 million
- First Protection, Inc., $2 million

- Small Boat Harbor, $2 million
- Super Duper, $2 million
- Cranz Rubber and Gasket, $1.4 million
- Stratford Plaza (Main and Amherst area), $0.5 million
- Top Notch Provision, $1.7 million
- Buffalo Color Office, $1.6 million
- Bureau of Collections Headquarters, $1.5 million
- Former School 21 Site (Fay's Drugs), $1.5 million
- Allsafe, $1.2 million
- School 22 Apartments, $0.9 million
- Adamski Village, not available

Exactly $9.7 million—that is, 2.7 percent of the total allocation of $352.9 million in Community Development Block Grant funds were spent in urban neighborhoods for community development purposes.[40]

Housing

To recap events on Buffalo's East Side: The Ellicott Mall, a high-rise public housing complex built for people displaced by urban renewal twenty years earlier, was 80 percent unoccupied by the late 1970s. At this time, the Greater Buffalo Development Foundation conducted a market survey to determine tenant needs. The foundation and the Buffalo Municipal Housing Authority called for several design proposals from architects for restoration schemes. Upon review, a preference existed for a plan called "Ellicott Village: A Newtown Downtown," which planned to turn this rundown public housing project into a neighborhood setting with a pedestrian spine and side streets. The Greater Buffalo Development Foundation's "Annual Report, 1978–79" says: "BMHA can now apply to the U.S. Department of Housing and Urban Development for implementation funds."

It is therefore surprising to find the following reported in the

"Annual Report, 1984–85," six years later: The Greater Buffalo Development Foundation "provided background information to the firm of Steiglitz, Steiglitz, Tries in late 1984 as the firm was developing a plan for reusing the Ellicott Mall. . . . [The Buffalo Municipal Housing Authority] was attempting to *resecure $15,000,000 of unused federal funds* that were earmarked for renovation of the Ellicott Mall towers in 1980 but that were 'recaptured' by HUD in September 1984 because of prolonged inaction in spending the funds [emphasis added]." These two quotes, separated by five years, reveal a sorry state of affairs and a dereliction of leadership.

CONCLUSION

The 1980s saw the consolidation of a smaller manufacturing base, a new hierarchy of elite, and an independent mayor's controversial legislative and budgeting process. Changes meant new opportunities and new debates.

When Warren Buffett bought the *Buffalo Evening News*, everyone wondered what this would mean for the city. Ironically, absentee ownership, generally viewed negatively by local interests, in this instance represented an "opening" for the business leadership. Perhaps without such an opening, and the publisher's involvement in the Group of Eighteen's core group planning strategy, the takeover of elite business institutions might not have succeeded. But it was an opening in a more important way for Buffalo.

For more than a century, one family owned and operated the *Buffalo Evening News*, keeping the paper WASP, conservative, and elitist in character. This one family had enormous political, economic, and social power—a nexus of authority that represented historical continuity and, as such, was somewhat backward looking, glorying in the "old days" of commerce and burgeoning industry, when Buffalo was the first city in the nation to have electricity.

The *Buffalo Evening News* had several assets: the paper's editorial page, its television stations, its editor in chief, and its owner. Each tracked urban issues and analyzed them. A former journalist asserts that, during the early years of urban renewal, the *Buffalo Evening News* was in the Urban Renewal Office every day monitoring activities. The owner's powers of suasion could be wielded—and were—from the editorial page, in corporate and bank boardrooms, and in myriad social settings. This is not to say the *Buffalo Evening News* was Buffalo's *only* center of elite power. In fact, there were other families and individuals more influential in specific areas, such as a number of bankers and attorneys. But clearly no business leader wanted to be on the wrong side of the paper's owner, a woman highly respected, with enormous social credentials and a variegated reach. And it would have been a naive mayor or county executive indeed who'd make a political move without considering the position of the *News*. The change of ownership was both symbolic and real. Powerful, conservative links to the past were now gone, and change had begun. Outside ownership of the paper meant that the Gordian knot of almost a century of social, economic, and political power had been cut.

The *Buffalo Courier-Express*, in contrast to the *News*, represented a center of power for the ethnic communities that included Catholics, organized labor, and neighborhood interests. It often favored the Democratic perspective on the issues, but this was not a limiting factor. The *Courier-Express* challenged downtown interests, as it did politicians and union officials, through its investigative journalism. The divergent viewpoints of the two papers created a natural dialogue for the city's citizens.

For a time, the activities of the Group of Eighteen went unconstrained by the influence (or pressure) of old establishment social networks—the importance of which cannot be overstated. Eventually, however, these new leaders were either enjoined to become members of these social networks, or they themselves desired membership—which changed their perspectives to that of establishment insiders. Now it would be easier for their socioeconomic

peers in elite clubrooms to informally urge and cajole the new leadership to conform to the prevailing way of thinking. In this manner,
elite leaders had brought occasional progressive tendencies to heel
in the past.

By the decade's end, the group received mixed reviews. County
Executive Gorski said, "There are criticisms, but this is a group that
has come together to discuss public policy issues, and I think that's
positive." Mayor Griffin rated the group "about a C or D–" despite
having worked closely with it over his long tenure. By 1991 only
thirteen of the original eighteen remained.[41] But it could also be
argued that members of the Buffalo Eighteen had played their role
as catalysts so well that their work as such was complete; they had
served their purpose in transforming and consolidating a new elite
leadership. The new regional organizations they had helped create
or had rejuvenated were now the new centers of economic activity.

The Group of Eighteen did not expand minority representation
on its board of directors and working committees. It could have
begun to address the problem of racism, taking the lead in building
bridges between the different political camps and communities
through meaningful involvement. Buffalo's African Americans
needed a positive role to play in the city's power structure. For generations Catholics had likewise been excluded from the ranks of the
elite and their business organizations. Instead, as we have seen,
Catholics from the Irish, Italian, and Polish neighborhoods found
entry into the power structure through party politics and found
patronage under their elected mayors. By the decade's end, this
began to change. With reflection, the business elite and the black
community might have learned from this experience of integration.
An Irish public official put it this way:

> [The Catholic community] never reached out to the WASP busi-
> ness community, and the business community never reached out
> to us. I don't think it was fear . . . it's just that each one dismissed
> the other. At one point, a lot of businesses started to be owned by

outsiders . . . and there were emerging businesses in the suburbs which became multinationals. But through this whole thing, in terms of the power structure, there was this kind of quiet evolution . . . a revolution . . . that the Catholics who made it began to align themselves with—*and be accepted by*—the old WASPS.

Business leaders with the greatest power needed to speak out and lead in an effort to build an honest partnership with black political and professional leaders. And African American leaders needed to be open to working cooperatively. The mayor's decision to restructure the legislative and budget process was exclusionary and set a precedent with racist overtones. It would take a long time for the city to recover from the institutionalization of such divisiveness.

That Buffalo still had a "sick economy" at the end of the 1980s,[42] after massive infusions of public subsidies (at a time when aid peaked under Governor Cuomo and the state legislature passed a multiyear tax cut), should not be surprising. As Jane Jacobs pointed out in 1984, "heavy and unremitting subsidies are transactions of decline, and once adopted, the need for them grows greater with time, and the wherewithal for supplying them grows less."[43] In spite of manufacturing's decline, a regional study at the state university found that manufacturing "remain[ed] at the heart of the Buffalo economy."[44] Two of the area's largest manufacturing employers were still there at the decade's end: General Motors, with more than fourteen thousand employees, and Ford Motor Company, with nearly the same number. Indicators suggested that prospects for a new period of growth would be difficult. One reason cited was that only 14.3 percent of the larger firms (representing 10,150 workers) were computer related or industries considered to be "strong regional firms," defined nationally as high-growth, high-benefit sectors.[45]

The large amount of public funding used to leverage private investment diminished the crisis at the time—providing a burst of activity in the 1980s. During this period, the Buffalo-Erie County Development Corporation (BEDC) made more than five hundred loans to businesses helping create eleven thousand jobs. Despite these and other aggressive efforts by the Western New York Economic Development Corporation and others, the city's overall downsizing and industrial loss did not end. As transactions of decline, the subsidies took a toll of their own: private investors and public officials often made decisions that did not rise to the level of rigorous economic analysis.

Once the Home Inspections Department took over the Division of Neighborhood and Commercial Revitalizations, no city department or agency was left to plan for neighborhoods. Thus a comprehensive approach to housing and business development remained outside the scope of any planning done for Community Development Block Grant funds. Neighborhood development was planned in terms of programs, with no overarching strategy. It is no wonder that ad hoc housing programs were in such disarray and in a position to lose critical funding because of delays. With neighborhood development planning excluded from the city's comprehensive plan, and eliminated as part of a city planning strategy, council members had to fight for funds project by project. This was bad for political relations, bad for neighborhood housing, and bad for neighborhood revitalization. It made planning for comprehensive community development an impossibility.

This is not to say that a number of good projects weren't built over the decades. Quite a fuss went up, however, when an expensive housing development was planned along the waterfront. Trying to put this into perspective, the director of city planning suggested in a press interview that when discussing the city's Waterfront Village project, with town houses costing more than $100,000, it was only fair to balance that project with others in impoverished neighborhoods that had been built as well. "If you don't mention Willert Park, Emslie Park and Pratt Street Village [neighborhood housing projects], then you are providing a fragmented picture."[46] What was not mentioned was that often the funds came out of duress, seemingly the only way of getting them.

By 1990 a number of people were asking this question: How could a city that says it is serious about growth not want a fully functioning public transportation system? The rapid-transit line was to have been the first step toward a regional transportation network. Because of two redesigns and subsequent delays, the projected $239 million grew to $530 million, with a system only half built.

If the line had been completed and "the corridor" between Buffalo and Amherst developed, some economists believe it would have led to a merger between suburban Amherst and Buffalo—which, in fact, may be a critical reason why leaders in both Buffalo and Amherst declined to exert leadership on the project, fearing this would be the net result. But was that wise in the long run? Both Amherst and Buffalo lost opportunities. Buffalo could have benefited from Amherst's growth. In turn, Buffalo's downtown, with its historic architecture, could have served as a professional, cultural, entertainment, and sports center—with outdoor winter and summer activities at the parks, a harbor, and a world-class demonstration project of wind turbines in action, generating electricity and providing a glimpse of the future. Amherst could have continued to offer industrial greenfield opportunities to industries wanting to locate in the region. Competition would have ended, tax revenues would have been shared, and people from the suburbs would have become part of an exciting urban scene.

The transit system redesign compromised Buffalo in two ways. First, the costs of redesign and the lost time (three additional years) made it impossible to complete the second half of the line. Money ran out. Second, the original design, chosen after years of review, was considered the optimal choice. Design changes undermined the optimal rationale, protection from the elements along Lake Erie.

With the redesign, the city no longer had an underground transit system. And above ground, it became clear that Main Street, at one hundred feet wide, did not have enough space to accommodate both cars and rapid transit, yet it was too wide for a successful pedestrian street. Upon completion, the pedestrian street felt cavernous and lonely, making it not conducive for shopping and other activities, yet the side streets that remained open to traffic continued to be active. The critical point here is that no discussion transpired on the subject of the street's closure and the closure's impact on downtown business activity. It seems, in part, that the elimination of traffic on Main Street hinged on the Niagara Frontier Transportation Authority's requiring an exclusive right-of-way, which meant there was not enough room for both cars and the transit line. Declared a knowledgeable city official, "If only they had allowed it to be shared and a little bit wider, then we would be in good shape now."

To cover operating costs of the half-built system, Erie County imposed a mortgage recording tax and an extra 1 percent of sales tax after the transit system opened in 1986. By the decade's end, Buffalo's two congressmen wished to see the line completed, but they were in the minority. New congressional leaders elected in 1988 disagreed and refused to support the line's extension. The citizens of Amherst and the university chancellor turned against the project. Buffalo's leadership, for the most part, considered it a debacle and a dead issue. The old Area Committee for Transit (ACT), now the Citizens Rapid Transit Committee, continued whatever promotion they could in support for a continuation of the project. The NFTA did nothing to secure additional funding.

Obtaining a second round of money for completion hinged on the county's guarantee of operating expenses as a prerequisite to federal funding. The sitting county executive, at the end of the decade, refused to honor the former executive's promise to cover net operating shortfalls (saying he was not County Executive Edward Regan and was not bound by it). It seems the legislature felt the same. A news article reported that

> upon studying the details of Cuomo's budget proposals, [the executive director of NFTA] finds the money promised to be different from the aid provided in previous years. The $5.4 million proposed by the governor, for example, requires no match by Erie County. It does, however, require that the county make a commitment to a local tax for transit operations. But the executive

director said he has no reason to expect that the County Legislature will follow Albany's timetable, even if it results in a gutted transit system for Western New York.[47]

And these same attitudes continued. In the early '90s, according to a planner, millions of dollars in grants were not requested by Erie and Niagara Counties. "We are the only major metropolitan area that did not cash in on the Federal funding made available through the ISTEA [transportation] legislation during its six-year shelf-life. Following in that mode, we are the only large metropolitan area that did not gain a Congressional authorization in the TEA-21 legislation [which renewed and replaced ISTEA] . . . because this region did not ask for any money!"[48]

According to a second planner, the Niagara Frontier Transportation Authority made it clear to area officials that it would not ask for federal construction funds (to complete the line) until local dedicated funding was in place for operating and maintenance.[49] While at first it seems irresponsible to not request funds when available, it is understandable from another standpoint. Without a strong regional commitment, backed by an arsenal of initiatives, the project would be further doomed.

One last point on leadership: In the central business district of downtown, the rapid-transit line runs at grade rather than underground as originally designed. On stormy winter days when the snow blasts off Lake Erie, business employees and others standing outside waiting for the rapid transit might well reflect on the fifteen years of the system's development and the role of leadership—and, in the end, what that leadership means in real terms to a city's way of life.

NOTES

1. US Bureau of the Census, "Census of Manufacturers 1967, 1972, 1977, 1982 (Washington, DC: US Department of Commerce, Bureau of the Census).

2. US Bureau of the Census, "County Business Patterns" (Washington, DC: US Department of Commerce, Bureau of Census, 1970, 1980).

3. Buffalo Area Chamber of Commerce, "Buffalo Metro Store/Office/Plant listing," 1981–1985 (separate listings); Greater Buffalo Chamber of Commerce, "Buffalo Metro Store/Office/Plant listing," 1986–1987 (separate listings).

4. See table 5.4 in David Perry, "The Politics of Dependency in Deindustrializing America: The Case of Buffalo, New York," in *The Capitalist City*, ed. Joe Fagin and Michael Peter Smith (Oxford, UK: Basil Blackwell, 1987), p. 127.

5. "Shift in Federal, State Policies Leaves City Bleeding," *Buffalo News*, February 12, 1997.

6. Ibid.

7. David Perry, "Upstate Economy Faces Crisis and Opportunities," *Buffalo News*, November 2, 1986.

8. "100 Most Powerful People in Buffalo: Who's in Charge Here?" *Buffalo Magazine*, in the *Buffalo News*, September 27, 1987.

9. Interview no. 14.

10. Interview no. 7.

11. Perry, "The Politics of Dependency in Deindustrializing America."

12. "New Economic Development Corp. For WNY Greeted With Enthusiasm," *Buffalo News*, October 31, 1982.

13. Jeffrey A. Trachtenberg, "Warren Buffett Got There Early," *Forbes Magazine*, December 26, 1988.

14. Interview no. 39.

15. Center for Regional Studies, prepared by Robert Kraushaar, "Memo to Western New York Economic Development Corporation, Re: Analysis of Large Manufacturing Firms in Western New York" (Buffalo: State University of New York at Buffalo, March 28, 1986), p. 25.

16. Interview no. 5.

17. Interview no. 12.

18. Interview no. 60.

19. Greater Buffalo Development Foundation, "Annual Report, 1980–81: A Retrospective of 30 Years, 1951–1981."

20. Kevin Collison, "Downtown District Bids to Shake 'Sin' Tag," *Buffalo News*, November 5, 1989.

21. Interview no. 36.

22. Interview no. 57.

23. Ibid.

24. Interview no. 58.

25. "Donohue Has 3-Point Plan to Spur Area's Development," *Buffalo News*, December 9, 1984.

26. "Stadium Aid Linked to County Crisis," *Buffalo News*, October 31, 1982.

27. Interview no. 38.

28. Ibid.

29. "Horizons Waterfront Commission: Goals and Objectives for the Erie County Waterfront," prepared by Saratoga Associates, July 1990.

30. "Horizons Waterfront Commission: Action Plan," prepared by Saratoga Associates, May 15, 1991.

31. Interview no. 57.

32. Greater Buffalo Development Foundation, "Annual Report, 1980–81."

33. "NFTA Rushing Mall Work, Picks 4 Designer Finalists," *Buffalo News*, July 27, 1982.

34. Interview no. 55.

35. Interview no. 50.

36. Interview no. 58.

37. Ibid.

38. Interview no. 60.

39. Interview no. 5.

40. City of Buffalo, "Economic Trends, Buffalo," issue 5, prepared by the Division of Planning, December 1986, p. 7.

41. "Group of 18, Seeking to Promote Buffalo, Plays to Mixed Reviews," *Buffalo News*, February 10, 1991.

42. Perry, "Upstate Economy Faces Crisis."

43. Jane Jacobs, *Cities and the Wealth of Nations: Principles of Economic Life* (New York: Random House, 1984), pp. 193–94.

44. Margaret Sullivan, "Job-Loss Study Sees Irreversible Changes in WNY Economy," *Buffalo News*, March 4, 1986.

45. Sullivan, "Job-Loss Study."

46. "Planning Director Sees Bright Future On the Waterfront," *Buffalo News*, November 9, 1981.

47. "NFTA to Ready 'Disaster Plan,' Plug Transit Tax," *Buffalo News*, January 18, 1989.

48. "Memo to Diana Dillaway," January 5, 1999.

49. J.H.R., "Memo to Diana Dillaway," March 6, 1999.

Chapter 6

TOWARD REGIONALISM

RECAP

Over the course of the last one hundred years, Buffalo was transformed from a city of commerce to a center of manufacturing, and then to a city suffering huge losses in both industry and commerce. Its citizens grew less confident, less self-assured. Turning inward, Buffalo's citizens focused on community and the protection of their political and ethnocentric ways of life. Some leaders turned to historic preservation. Others sought to keep the physical environment downtown from changing—although they supported the construction of new banking headquarters for three locally based financial institutions. No state or civic leaders endeavored to build pro-growth support or coalitions, even as the city faced several major development prospects. Once again, bruising battles ensued over whether to support change in the city or maintain the status quo—in other words, whether to support growth in the city or growth in the suburbs.

The leadership chose to maintain the status quo. Led by the city's establishment newspaper, elite leaders opposed development that might significantly disrupt life downtown. Even small disruptions were unwelcome. For example, one elite opposed a project when he discovered that traffic patterns would be redirected in such a way that his evening commute would last an additional five minutes.[1] Today, Buffalo's leaders face problems that result from unsustainably low revenues to the city (and lowering property values), based both on the decrease in population, falling from 532,000 in 1960 to less than 300,000 in 2005, and on the devastating losses of industry.

Ethnic European community leaders opposed school integration and the changes it wrought because it disrupted life modeled after their old-world Italian, Polish, or Irish communities. From their point of view, school integration meant a cultural shift away from a life that revolved around the neighborhood parish and neighborhood schools. Racial prejudices reinforced these cultural attitudes. African American community leaders, by contrast, fought legal battles in the 1970s for change on several fronts: in favor of school integration, against discriminatory hiring practices (a battle that changed the composition of police and fire departments), and against restrictions dictating the neighborhoods in which African Americans could buy houses. In addition, black community leaders supported the necessary changes that would bring a university campus downtown, and they hoped to see a completed rapid-transit system.

But as the story has shown, Buffalo's leaders oversaw three development projects that could have changed the city's revenue structure and demographics: the first, an urban university campus; the second, a rapid-transit line to connect downtown with the campus thirteen miles outside of the city; the third, a more modest project but one of enormous symbolic value, a downtown football stadium. These three projects presented once-in-a-lifetime opportunities to lay a foundation for the city's revitalized future. Carrying these projects forward demanded leaders with exceptional perspicacity and a vision for turning the tide of economic decline resulting from industrial closures and corporate relocation to the sunbelt.

Perhaps Buffalo had already lost so much of its industry and population that leaders resigned themselves to regional growth on the city's periphery and to "making it" as a smaller city. If so, the story leaves little doubt that an elite few exercised power for personal agendas, while other putative leaders quietly followed. In the 1980s, a new economic and political leadership, seeking to jump-start the local economy, parlayed government funds into subsidies for private development and business retention schemes. In the process, they pushed the limits on how Community Development Block Grant funds were used. A range of projects, including new hotels and entertainment venues on Chippewa Street, generated excitement but had little lasting effect, fulfilling Jane Jacobs's assertion that subsidies are transactions of decline.

INTIMATIONS OF REGIONAL GOVERNANCE

By the early 1990s, the key public officials who had headed development corporations and agencies had moved on to other jobs. Much of the business leadership had dispersed as well, to Florida, into retirement, and elsewhere. The well-known Group of Eighteen vanished in the local nomenclature, while two leaders came to the fore: the head of M&T Bank and his protégé at the Buffalo Niagara Partnership. Both men were relatively recent arrivals to Buffalo and had participated with others in the takeover of elite business organizations, drawing these groups out of their entrenched ways.

Although governance was not discussed, Buffalo's leaders made their ideas about regional consolidation known indirectly, and they took small steps. In 1993, in a forward-looking first step, a handful of business leaders founded the Buffalo Niagara Partnership by merging the Greater Buffalo Development Foundation, the Greater Buffalo Chamber of Commerce, the International Trade Council, Leadership Buffalo, the Convention and Visitor's Bureau, and others. The intent was to consolidate business leadership into one noncompeting voice, an updated, regional chamber of commerce—

an advocate for both business and the region. These efforts were reinforced a number of years later when the partnership founded the Buffalo Niagara Enterprise to aggressively market and promote the city, using radio promotions and other advertising vehicles for the first time. The enterprise also created business development strategies for companies moving to Buffalo, making it a one-stop shop for industrial relocation and expansion in the region. Moreover, the enterprise focused on bettering its product, improving Buffalo itself. A third organization, the Buffalo Niagara Now Initiative, worked to remediate a number of issues for industry, such as high property taxes, high utility rates, and slow permitting processes.[2]

In 1999 government leaders from Erie and Niagara Counties formed the Erie-Niagara Regional Partnership (not to be confused with the Buffalo Niagara Partnership organized by private-sector leaders). This committee was co-chaired by the chairmen of the Erie and Niagara County Legislatures and included members of both legislatures as well as public- and private-sector leaders. Meetings rotated between the two counties. Many of the stated goals looked familiar. They examined transportation, economic development, job creation, and government consolidation, with the hope of developing initiatives to be passed by the respective legislatures.

Yet one flaw remained. The *structure* of power had not changed, something confirmed in a series of articles based on a six-month survey appearing in the *Buffalo News* in June 2001. The study found that bankers and lawyers alone constituted more than half of local and regional boards in the private sector. Out of 196 board members, 55 were bankers, and 54 were lawyers. The study went on to conclude, however, that the government was the dominant player throughout the region. In a reexamination of the data and the definitions, the information on this one point is accurate but misleading. Although it is true that a strong government showing existed, because of a large number of quasi-public agencies and authorities, the numbers, organized in a more comparable way, reveal that the private sector dominated. "Government," as defined in the study, included the entire public sector, while the private sector was broken down by industry. If, however, private-sector industries are combined into *one category*—titled "private sector"—then it becomes clear that private-sector leadership dominated. (This is critical, as business leaders often blamed their problems on government leadership.) The number of members on local and regional boards by the new categories are as follows:

- private sector—196 members (bankers, lawyers, real estate agents, and businesspeople in energy, investment, insurance—no manufacturing mentioned)
- public sector—135 members (elected and appointed government officials)
- nonprofit sector—90 members (educators, volunteers)
- retired and healthcare workers (any of the above)—81 members.[3]

Business leaders, led by bankers and lawyers, continued to dominate regional organizations. And, as in earlier years, manufacturers played no mentionable role (this time because of their diminished numbers); small-business entrepreneurs (Buffalo's largest group by far) remained underrepresented; and redundancy existed between the boards. The *Buffalo News* put it this way: "A *Buffalo News* study of boards of directors found certain people and certain professions—government, banking and law—dominating the Buffalo Niagara region's power structure. Conspicuously missing were big-business types and entrepreneurs. . . . [There exists] a sameness to the boards . . . from the Erie County Industrial Development Agency to the Buffalo Niagara Partnership to the Buffalo Philharmonic Orchestra."[4]

Board member redundancy concentrated power further, and the fact that greater breadth was not reached (for whatever reason) made for a "shallow pool of talent."[5] Here the numbers clearly show a concentration of government representatives on regional boards (indicating government dominance). Institutions whose employees *filled the most board seats* were:

- Erie County Government—48 seats
- City of Buffalo—39 seats
- New York State—18 seats
- M&T Bank—17 seats
- HSBC Bank—14 seats
- University of Buffalo—13 seats
- Buffalo Philharmonic—9 seats
- Blue Cross and Blue Shield WNY—7 seats
- Hodgson, Russ (law firm)—7 seats
- Phillips, Lytle (law firm)—7 seats
- Catholic Diocese (Buff.)—7 seats
- National Fuel—7 seats
- Vector Group—7 seats
- Tops Markets—6 seats
- Key Bank—6 seats.[6]

Minority representation improved somewhat, but not so much that minority leaders were meaningful partners in the structure of power. Astoundingly, at least six important boards had no minority representation whatsoever, including the Niagara Regional Transportation Council.

The minority representation on boards was as follows:

- Buffalo Economic Renaissance Corporation, 28.6%
- Erie County Democratic Executive Committee, 21.7%
- Erie County Industrial Development Corporation, 10.0%
- Niagara Frontier Transportation Authority, 9.1%
- Buffalo Niagara Partnership, 8.6%
- Erie County Republican Executive Committee, 3.7%
- Buffalo Niagara Enterprise, 2.3%
- Niagara Regional Transportation Council, 0%

- Peace Bridge Authority (American membership), 0%
- (four additional boards with no black representation).[7]

PROJECTS AND INITIATIVES

A series of Downtown Buffalo Summits in 1994 and 1995 brought hundreds of people together to discuss a vision for downtown. They focused on convenience, accessibility, education, entertainment, conventions, and a center for shopping. City leaders considered it a "work in progress" and an opportunity for citizens to become more invested in downtown.[8]

The city administration—in partnership with the City of Lackawanna—launched the South Buffalo Redevelopment Plan in 1997, in what was called the largest redevelopment plan ever offered by the city. Over a thousand acres of unused "brownfield" sites were to be linked to five hundred acres of preserved open space and parks. Remediation and infrastructure development were estimated to be in the range of $75 million to $100 million. According to plans, up to 10,500 jobs might be created in this redistribution hub for goods in transit between the United States and Canada, along with a 350-acre business campus proposed for the Republic Steel site that used existing rail corridors. Boat launches, recreational facilities, and parks would be a large part of the plan. Officials hoped to use federal and state sources, such as the state's Clean Water/Clean Air Bond Act (in the brownfields category) and proposed federal brownfields money to be allocated by the EPA and the Department of Housing and Urban Development.[9] Nothing seems to have come from this plan. Years later a public official maintained, "it's probably sitting on the shelf with all the other proposals gathering dust."[10] A statistics survey of the Buffalo–Niagara Falls metropolitan area shows that, between December 2002 and December 2003, overall nonfarm employment declined by almost half a percent. Total manufacturing jobs dropped 3.4 percent, while service employment averaged out to show no change.[11]

A Strategic Plan

In 1999 a new "Downtown Buffalo Strategic Plan" recommended building a larger convention center. Five years later, debates continued, but with the county finally deciding to renovate the old convention center. The strategic plan also called for a follow-through with developer designs for the inner harbor, including the construction of new buildings, reconstruction of historical spots, and new venues for entertainment. Much of the investment for the project was to come from cable company Adelphia: "The detailed plans that the [owners'] proposal and two other groups submitted are the strongest evidence yet that the $27 million taxpayer investment soon to begin with the Inner Harbor excavation finally has caught the attention of private developers."[12] Unfortunately, this project did not move ahead because of the legal problems of the Rigas family, the cable company's owners.

In a "Revised Strategic Plan for Downtown Buffalo" (2002), the city included office space and housing in the Theater District— ten apartments above the Irish Classical Theatre Company on Main Street and apartments of Ansonia Center near the Studio Arena Theatre.[13] The plan built on the development momentum of the 1980s on Chippewa Street, with its music and nightlife. The "Revised Strategic Plan" also acknowledged that downtown would not be "great" until its inner ring of neighborhoods were revitalized, too.[14] To this end, the Department of Community Development offered a proposal for neighborhood housing (discussed in greater detail below).

The new Buffalo Niagara Medical Campus, a hundred acres of development on Buffalo's East Side, brought together five medical institutions: the renowned Roswell Park Cancer Institute, the School of Medicine and Biomedical Sciences of the State University of New York at Buffalo, the Buffalo Medical Group, Hauptman-Woodward Medical Research Institute, and Kaleida Health (a consortium of local hospitals and special services). To create this

medical "campus," differences of turf and relocation had to be over-
come, but the project's prospects were enhanced by the state's
announcement that it had approved spending up to $100 million on
the medical campus. As a result, development in contiguous districts
improved as well. The *Buffalo News* reported that "private investment has been flowing into the Main-Washington-Ellicott streets
corridor over the last two years because those blocks border both the
Theater District and the Buffalo Niagara Medical Campus."[15]

Waterfront

In 2002 state officials spoke of introducing a bill to withdraw the
Niagara Frontier Transportation Authority's jurisdictional control
of waterfront land (formerly Buffalo's lake port) and give it to the
Empire State Development Corporation, an organization explicitly
designed for economic development. As Buffalo's commercial
harbor was no longer used, it became increasingly clear that the
NFTA had outlived its port authority mandate in this case. Two
years later, instead of withdrawing, and after decades of sitting on
the land, the NFTA took the initiative and offered to join in partnership with the City of Buffalo, Erie County, the Buffalo Niagara
Enterprise, *and* the Empire State Development Corporation to
begin a national search for qualified developers for its 120 acres of
outer-harbor land. Final approval of the master developer rests with
the NFTA Board of Commissioners, as it still maintains control of
the property.

Peace Bridge

No idea in recent years has captured Buffalonians' imagination as
much as that of a "signature" bridge on the city's West Side to
replace the Peace Bridge—which crosses the Niagara River and
links the United States and Canada at the magnificent confluence of
the river and Lake Erie. As early as 1993, the Peace Bridge

Authority (comprising Americans and Canadians) had prepared plans for a second span, a three-lane companion bridge. The project was fully permitted and bid, with construction to begin in the spring of 1999.[16] When Buffalo's citizens were presented with the completed plan, however, they rebelled and called for a more interesting approach. Soon an innovative design (created by T. Y. Lin) caught people's imagination—and, as it turned out, was the *least expensive* alternative. Project plans disclosed that it could be built faster and would be less disruptive to traffic since the old bridge could be utilized during construction.

Many elite leaders did not buy these arguments, and, led by the Buffalo Niagara Partnership, they opposed the Lin bridge. This sparked a battle royal. Senators Patrick Moynihan and Charles Schumer, among many others, weighed in on the side of the new design and argued that this was an opportunity for Buffalo to make a statement about itself. The rancorous debate became a fight without reason, filled with the symbolism of power and control. In a 1999 interview on the side of the special bridge, architect Bruno Freschi commented,

> The issue has been misunderstood. They want to say "It's *not* about aesthetics!" They're right: It's about faster, cheaper. Wake up! You're not going to get it faster and cheaper the way they're going now. . . . We'll give you a spectacular bridge, six lanes, and a new plaza in 2004. Cut the ribbon! It's all there![17]

For several years, the debate expanded to consider alternate bridge locations (narrowed down from twenty to eight in January 2003) and a variety of spots for the new plaza. One workshop drew over seven hundred people. Once again Senator Schumer entered the fray with a proposal to establish an international zone at the Canadian side of the Peace Bridge: "I believe that designating international zones will settle the sovereignty and labor management concerns that held up much of our earlier attempts at binational border management."[18] Five years after the original plans were laid, the process continued unabated between every conceivable group on both sides of the border. It is hard to know exactly what went wrong. It looked so simple: a cheaper, signature bridge could have been built—given the necessary leadership—by 2004. In late 2005, all the engaged powers finally settled on a design.

POLITICS AND NEIGHBORHOODS

In 1993 Buffalo's citizens elected Democrat Anthony Masiello mayor in the wake of Mayor Griffin's administration, with the mandate to reduce tensions between government officials. Unfortunately, relations between the administration and city council remained strained. Council president James Pitts, an African American and outspoken political leader, now led a black majority of seven to six on the Common Council, representing a community that historically had been denied political leadership. A battle was always brewing as to where limited city funds were to be spent; Pitts was not about to be a pushover. Add to this the fact that Pitts challenged Masiello, who was running for a second term, to become the Democratic nominee in the 1997 mayoral election— and lost. Despite their differences, Pitts and Masiello were both fiercely loyal to Buffalo.

Sixteen years of the Griffin administration had taken its toll on the Democratic machine. During the Griffin era, patronage revolved around Mayor Griffin and those loyal to him, not the political party. Over time, the party went into debt, divisions within its ranks emerged, and personal vendettas began to take precedence. The party no longer functioned as a disciplined and effective organizational center of political activity. While zone leaders and committeemen remained part of the structure, new political organizations formed around individuals, neighborhood clubs, and town parties countywide. Just as people flowed from the city to the suburbs, party power dispersed from the well-worn structural center to the outlying areas, leaving a more diffuse political base.

In light of the population dispersion, the question remained whether the business elite who headed the newly formed Buffalo Niagara Partnership—beginning to meet exclusively at the Buffalo Club—would draw their political and community counterparts into their new regional organizations as genuine partners. They held the power to restructure both the economic relations and the planning process. It was up to them to *lead*. In the end, one would have to answer no, as business leaders failed to forge meaningful regional alliances.

A 2002 ballot measure reduced the size of the city council from thirteen members, with an independently elected council president, to nine seats and an internally selected president. Some in the black community considered this a referendum on race. An editorial in the *Buffalo News* in December 2002 announced that 30 percent of those in the predominantly black Masten and Ellicott Districts who voted for governor neglected to cast a ballot on the measure downsizing the city council, suggesting that not everyone considered this measure a race issue. Yet race relations continued to be Buffalo's biggest social problem. A cogent commentary in the *Buffalo News* described how charter reform (a measure that did not pass) asked "the urban minority community to be first to eliminate representatives—just years after their centuries-long struggle to affect public policy finally succeeded. . . . From the black perspective, whites fled Buffalo—increasing both black population percentage and responsibility for the city's fate—and now ask minorities to reduce their voice."[19]

In 1997–98 Mayor Masiello's Department of Community Development formulated a "Consolidated Plan [on] Housing and Neighborhood Development." This initiative, devised for action, used a private-sector approach to revitalize Buffalo's housing stock. For one, in return for low-interest loans to homeowners, the city retained a "security" interest in the selected property for a minimum of five years, during which time the owner had to make it the principal place of residence. In a second approach, the home-ownership-initiative programs provided incentives to home buyers willing to own, occupy, and rehab a city home. Other innovations included a moderate-income homesteading program, home-owner-ship counseling, and the "Impediments to Fair Housing" study. City leaders continued to face the challenge posed by the city's old housing stock—with 60 percent of city homes built before 1939—by using a properties demolition plan. Public officials designed a community process that included a mayor's impact team (meeting daily) and community action teams (with monthly meetings).[20]

Under President Bill Clinton, increased federal funds directed to housing programs brought, in Buffalo's case, a critical mass of remodeling and new housing to the city's East Side.[21] The city also remodeled the old Apollo Theater, turning it into a public access television center, and began plans for a new North Jefferson Branch Library, in African motif, designed by one of the community's own leaders, a nationally known black architect.

A project initiated by M&T Bank also addressed the needs of an inner-city neighborhood. Historically, Buffalo's banks paid little attention to poor neighborhoods—although M&T Bank throughout the 1960s and 1970s had a "community representative," a banker who sat on a variety of African American nonprofit boards and interacted in the neighborhoods. More recently, the bank itself engaged on an issue, believing that "[when] the community does well, the bank does well."[22] Based on this premise and with per-mission from Buffalo's Board of Education, M&T adopted the school with the lowest test scores and the greatest challenges, School 68, renamed Westminster Community School. The new board of directors—including the banker, the school superinten-dent, and the head of the teachers' union—initiated a national search and hired a former principal from Chicago to lead the school. The bank provided $5.5 million for classroom computers, a library, building renovations, and consultants to coach the teachers. In addition, the bank responded to requests for assistance with computers, community data, and the like. The school's test scores rose enough to put it among the top 2 percent of city schools in 2002.

Over his two terms, Mayor Masiello reduced city expenses, cutting more than four hundred positions from the city workforce and civilianizing over fifty jobs in dispatch, the cell-block print shop, and other offices. He added revenues to the general fund through increased compliance with city codes, a renegotiated lease with Buffalo Civic Auto Ramps, and recovered costs from a variety of agencies and authorities (sewer, water, urban renewal, and housing). He won higher utility tax payments from telecommunications firms and traditional utilities, and he maximized lobbying for state assistance. Still, revenues fell because of the decline in population, industry, and subsequently, property values. Tax giveaways to businesses did not help add to revenues. According to the mayor, "Buffalo's decline in property values was the most precipitous decline in value recorded anywhere in New York State in at least the past 30 years."[23]

Revenues from property taxes fell nearly $19 million between 1999 and 2004. Dividing the budget pie became a nightmare, with 70 percent of the city's treasury going to pay for police, fire, and fringe benefits like health insurance. Throughout these difficult times, the city somehow managed to balance its budget. But the future financial picture looked "troubling."[24] In circumstances like these, it can help to form a state authority with the power to overrule contending local forces, both political and economic.

A Financial Control Board

In May 2003 the state comptroller announced that in all likelihood he would take control of Buffalo's finances. He argued that Buffalo and its schools would likely face a budget shortfall of $93 million to $127 million by 2006–2007, a crisis for the city, as its schools had no independent taxing authority and all school revenues came from the city. Despite cuts of approximately fourteen hundred positions in the school system over three years, the situation remained dire, with school officials considering a four-day school week. While financial aid from the state to Buffalo had more than doubled—from $51 million to $103 million in less than a decade—the state was starting to have financial problems of its own. The comptroller suggested it would be in the best interest of both the city and state to collaborate in resolving these problems. He recommended forming a board that would oversee and agree to a plan for recovery (including cuts and increased efficiencies along with the creation of additional resources), then ensure that it was implemented. Thus, the Buffalo Fiscal Stability Authority board was born.[25]

The authority was structured with many powers beyond the usual city ones. These included the ability to suspend scheduled wage increases resulting from collective bargaining agreements and an authorization requirement for any expenditure exceeding fifty dollars. Two periods of activity set the parameters for its work: first, an active period of oversight and control over the course of three balanced budgets, and a second inactive period, when the board—in its capacity as an authority—could issue bonds. The mayor participated as a member of the nine-person board. He prepared and submitted the first four-year plan with recommendations for closing budget gaps.

The plan arrived on October 16, 2003. Five days later, the fiscal stability authority responded, raising a number of issues in its "Review of Revised Four Year Financial Plan," but approving the mayor's estimates of revenues and expenses. First, the Fiscal Stability Authority Board found "the City's Revised Plan encompassing a variety of departments and agencies takes a more aggressive approach to closing revised gaps of $12 million in the current year" through "head count reduction and closure of fire companies." Second, the fiscal board ruled the school district's plan much improved and admonished the district to identify and hire a strong chief financial officer who could implement the changes and update financial operations in meeting goals. Third, the Buffalo Urban

Renewal Agency's "more developed" submission proposed eliminating fifty-one staff positions among other cost-cutting measures, and the fiscal board called on the agency to continue work with the federal Housing and Urban Development consultant. Fourth, the Buffalo Municipal Housing Authority's revised plan outlined a strategy to reduce its reliance on city subsidies, and it proposed continuing to move "units from its state to its federal portfolio, and thereby eliminate the City's $535,000 annual subsidy over the next fiscal year."[26] In this first plan lie the hopes that the groundwork for a pragmatic approach to the city's fiscal renewal is being laid.

Pending Issues

Under the Indian Gaming Regulatory Act, the Seneca Indians proposed a gaming casino to be located downtown or elsewhere. The casino agreement was strictly between the Seneca Nation and the state of New York. Governor George Pataki supported gaming in general, as reflected in his 2004 state budget, which "dramatically expand[ed] gambling ventures across the state."[27] The mayor and a handful of business leaders supported this controversial project, but Seneca leaders felt they couldn't get clear signals on a location.[28] One possibility had been to locate it downtown in the county-owned convention center, an attractive idea if the county decided to build a new, larger convention center. Finally, after years of controversy, County Executive Joel Giambra (the former city comptroller) turned down the Seneca leadership, deciding that the county would renovate rather than build a new convention center. With this final rebuff, the tribe's leadership set its sights on a Buffalo suburb, Cheektowaga. When the tribe came up with a plan to build near the Buffalo International Airport, a number of city business leaders filed a lawsuit to halt the Seneca-Cheektowaga plan, based on a 2001 memorandum of understanding between the city and tribe, claiming that the memorandum contained an agreement that the casino was to be located within city limits. From the perspective of the tribe, "the casino was the city's to lose," arguing that the mayor and county executive never advanced a concrete proposal. The tribal leader stated that dealing with city and county officials was like "hitting a stone wall." In the twelfth hour, there was a legal attempt to stop what looked inevitable, a casino on Buffalo's doorstep, drawing all the same people but with no financial benefits accruing to the city.[29] Ultimately, it was settled that Buffalo would get the casino after all. Now there is another lawsuit, this time, to keep it from opening in the city. If it ends up outside the city limits, it will be a financial loss for Buffalo: lost revenues from the casino and peripheral services and lost revenues from a convention center too small to accommodate major conventions or advance a downtown renaissance.

Another initiative that has sporadically been in the works focuses on rewriting or amending state legislation that for decades has *prohibited* Buffalo from requiring city residency for its police officers, firefighters, and sanitation workers. Every city and town in western New York can, if it chooses, have a residency requirement for its police, except Buffalo. Legislation would lift that mandate and give Buffalo this same option. As noted earlier, public employee salaries and health insurance premiums represented more than 70 percent of Buffalo's general fund appropriations in the 2004 budget. If these public employees lived within city limits, revenues would return to the city that pays such a heavy price. The resulting demand for housing would positively affect property values and, in turn, property tax revenues. And with more consumers inside city limits, enhanced sales tax revenues would accrue to the city as well.

REGIONAL CONSOLIDATION AND BUFFALO'S FUTURE

In 1960 Erie County added the position of "strong" executive to its county structure in an attempt to bring about a regional approach to governance and the delivery of services. This had been long in coming. As far back as 1935, recommendations had been made (by the Kenefick Commission) for the "Creation of [a] strong county executive, with veto power and budget control, to be elected for four years at $10,000 annually. . . . Stripping [the] board of all power, except as a legislative body."[30] More than twenty-five interesting, and relevant, recommendations were enumerated in the article, each addressing the need for regional structures and processes.

In 1968 a private-sector initiative again addressed local government inefficiencies in the delivery of services, pointing out areas where multiple levels of government had overlapping responsibilities throughout the region. The initiative proposed a regional approach in some county-wide systems, hoping, perhaps, to set some precedent in the direction of regional consolidation. This "private group," the Citizens Committee on Inter-Municipal Affairs, led the effort to consolidate local police forces county-wide. The city, the newspapers, and business organizations—the major players in Buffalo's power structure—all supported the initiative.

This initiative was put to a referendum, which, in order to form new metropolitan structures under the state constitution, needed to garner a plurality in three different classes: cities, towns, and villages. The initiative passed in the city and the towns, but lost by five thousand votes in county villages. A handful of rural villages representing 9 percent of the total population sent the regional initiative down to defeat: "The battle for a regional approach . . . was lost there." Within a year or two, the committee folded rather than take up the fight again. Several years later, the two Fortune 500 companies whose CEOs had promoted the measure left Buffalo.[31]

Effective consolidation of discrete centers of power represents the biggest juggernaut facing regions today. A study on Buffalo's "regional impulses," published in the *Journal of Urban Affairs* in 1997, found that Buffalo had two "antiregional" impulses. First, the city boundaries had remained the same for 150 years—since 1853. Second, the city and its suburban neighbors exhibited a long-standing rivalry and distrust.[32] Buffalo's leaders today must build trust between political, economic, and community power interests. Building trust necessitates shoving aside old rivalries. It means government (public) unions must come to an agreement with the city administration on a living wage that works for both the city and its workers. It means inviting leaders to join in common efforts on elite boards and in public agencies. It means becoming more transparent so that selfish interests cannot blindside the planning process.

To address these issues, the Chautauqua Institution, a not-for-profit organization, convened a four-day conference on regional governance that assembled practitioners, writers, thinkers, leaders, and citizens to explore regional thinking and models. The conference was well received by most, and the conference materials suggest this was an instructive gathering, helping to focus the debate.[33] However, a few high-ranking leaders reacted negatively or defensively. Likewise, many citizens remained skeptical of consolidation. Some city folk perceived regional consolidation to be a form of suburban *plundering* of city businesses and resources.[34] Suburban citizens saw it as a way for the city to saddle outlying areas with the city's problems and bills. Over the years, County Executives Gorski and Giambra wavered on issues of taxes and, in Giambra's case, on political restructuring. When he was city comptroller, Giambra proposed dissolving city government. He eventually "softened his position on government consolidation" before running for county executive.[35]

History points to some regional consolidation successes going back seventy years when Erie County took over most social welfare programs. Later, the county assumed responsibility for the library system, the public transportation system, cultural facilities, and, in recent years, the operation of the downtown convention center. There are plans to centralize the region's community colleges downtown, and a number of new county buildings are being built there.

In 2003, according to the *Buffalo News*, a Washington-based

consultant made clear that the time was ripe to proceed with the consolidation of government services: "The key ... is for all of Erie
County's municipalities to get behind the idea that 'big picture'
issues like land use, transportation planning, housing policy and
economic development should be handled on a regional basis."[36]

Regionalism: The Hopes and the Fears

Today, Buffalo's elite leaders, the Erie County executive, and state
legislators are all considering new regional approaches to governance and the consolidation of services. First, in the early 1990s,
Buffalo's elite leaders decided to consolidate the Greater Buffalo
Development Foundation and the Chamber of Commerce into one
organization. In so doing, they signaled an interest in new regional
approaches. The name they chose, the Buffalo Niagara Partnership,
recognized Buffalo as the key locality within the more broadly
defined Buffalo-Niagara region. Second, County Executive
Giambra has moved to have the county take control of Buffalo's
police and public works.[37] In addition, in October 2003, he allocated $100,000 from the regionalism and economic development
fund to study the feasibility of merging the records of the county
and other local governments, as well as the school and fire districts.
Third, state legislators were contacted almost daily by the Buffalo
Niagara Enterprise, the partnership, or other regional organizations
on one of any number of issues.

Taken together, the actions of these leaders outline the begin-
nings of a nascent movement. At its heart is a diminished role for
local government. Today, many experts believe regions offer "the
appropriate scale for many critical decisions related to growth and
development, including those concerning affordable housing, workforce development, jobs and housing balance, and environmental
and open space preservation."[38] Erie County's "Governance Project" informs the county leadership on the many ways cities currently approach regional issues of consolidation.[39] It turns out that

52 percent of the people in the county would approve of a merger of city and county into a single metropolitan government—in favor were 71 percent of urban voters and 44 percent of suburban voters.[40]

The hope is that the redundancy between local governments and their services can be minimized, and positive industrial and employment gains will be maximized. The effects will be positive *as long as* local governments and their constituencies have power centers of their own. For communities, the fear is that blacks, Irish, Poles, Italians, and others left in city neighborhoods will have no voice. In the past, the city councils or the Democratic machine provided them with a voice. The problem of representation in light of regional consolidation is exacerbated by Buffalo's specific circumstances: a city council reduced in size (based on a smaller population), a weak council president (a position no longer filled in the general election), a city council with less legislative authority (with the loss of oversight over services), and reduced funds (as the city meets the demands of the Fiscal Stability Authority).

Often, past regional development has concerned itself with regional economics and multiplier effects rather than issues of community development. Today, regional planning can include the full spectrum of urban issues, and for good reason. "Merging Buffalo and Erie County is not inevitable. But even without a merger, it is a virtual certainty that the structure and appearance of local government is about to dramatically change. City and suburban political boundaries have lost any relation to social and economic challenges facing localities. And those American cities that act on that reality will anchor flourishing regions."[41]

In order for economic development to work, Buffalo's political and economic leadership must incorporate minority leaders into the heart of the regional planning process. Yet it is not simply a bias toward affirmative action that makes inclusion necessary. It is important that community leaders residing in distinct geographic areas representing a variety of cultural and economic circumstances become part of an integrated regional power structure.

Another challenge will be to create a compact between local governments and agencies. According to a 2001 study by the Public Policy Institute of California, one approach would be to "authorize by statute, but not require, local governments within regions to establish regional planning compacts with state, regional, and federal agencies for the purposes of developing multipurpose regional plans. The compacts would form the legal basis for collective action to address multi-faceted, multi-jurisdictional problems in a more comprehensive way."[42] In this case, New York State could pass a broadly defined Joint Exercise of Powers Act, like that passed in Minnesota, where two or more governmental units—city, county, town, school district, or other political subdivisions, including authorities, agencies, and other governmental units— may jointly or cooperatively exercise any power common to the contracting parties, based on an agreement of purpose.[43] It may also disburse money from public funds, and a joint powers board may independently issue bonds or obligations in line with that same agreement of purpose. Activities include the joint exercise of police power, a joint powers board for housing, and the joint exercise of power for coordination and evaluation of training programs.[44]

The Joint Exercise of Powers Act could help regional efforts by providing a flexible structure through which mutually agreed-upon goals might be achieved. Local governments for their part could create joint powers authorities to provide services and propose initiatives issues where there is agreement.[45] On the other hand, they might use existing agencies or organizations for developing initiatives and implementing policies: joint powers authorities are not good at resolving long-standing conflicts between local governments and competing agencies. In Buffalo's case, these conflicts need to be resolved preliminarily, perhaps through a council of governments enabled by the state law.

Uncoordinated growth pits regional localities against one another and leads to inefficient, lopsided development. Regional approaches to all forms of services cut down on duplication and overlap of governmental services. Financial and human resources can be moved to where the money and expertise match the need, to where the need is greatest, or to where a big development effort is warranted. It allows each local entity to do what it does best without having to do everything—and without each village, town, and city having to fight each other for lucrative industries in order to pay local police and firefighters. Better to do this on a region-wide basis, letting the industries settle in areas they find desirable, sharing the revenues, reaping the benefits, and apportioning expertise throughout.

Regional collaborators need to do more than develop economic strategies and cost-effective services, however. Regional efforts must include collaborating with local political officials on investment in inner-city neighborhoods, social programs, public education, and the public infrastructure, in addition to considering environmental issues such as the preservation of open space. Moving toward such a process is daunting, with everyone giving up something but with a guarantee of shared gain.

Because companies will presumably continue to favor locating in the suburbs, urban leaders will need to stand with their suburban counterparts in designing policies for industrial growth. Suburban leaders, for their part, will need to recognize the value of revenue sharing throughout the region, including investing in Buffalo's downtown to reclaim its architectural heritage, with the goal of making Buffalo once again a center of culture, entertainment, and banking. To facilitate in a transformation of downtown, the outlying areas will have to slow housing development and growth on their fringes. At the same time, attractive housing and service businesses (food stores, cleaners, clothes shops, and restaurants) need to be developed downtown for future residents.

Change occurs in the world so rapidly today that a city and its region must quickly adapt to new norms. Flexible leadership requires a planning process and partnership that has breadth and depth, that is structurally clear. This, then, is Buffalo's challenge: to identify and implement a common ground of leadership that serves Buffalo and the region well.

NOTES

1. Interview no. 44.

2. Interview no. 75.

3. David Robinson and Jerry Zremski, "On the Board Circuit," *Buffalo News*, June 19, 2001; Zremski, "Racial, Gender Diversity, Eludes Nearly All Boards," *Buffalo News*, June 19, 2001.

4. Robinson and Zremski, "On the Board Circuit."

5. Ibid.

6. Ibid.

7. Ibid.; Zremski, "Racial, Gender Diversity, Eludes Nearly All Boards."

8. *Downtown Buffalo Summit News* (State University of New York at Buffalo) (Fall 1996).

9. Mike Vogel, "City Has Bold Plans for S. Buffalo," *Buffalo News*, March 6, 1997.

10. Interview no. 74.

11. "Non-farm Employment by Industry, New York State and Metropolitan Areas," in "Current Employment Statistics Survey" (Buffalo–Niagara Falls MSA) (Washington, DC: US Department of Labor, 2004).

12. Kevin Collison, "Poised for Private Funds," *Buffalo News*, October 31, 1998.

13. City of Buffalo, "The Revised Strategic Plan for Downtown Buffalo," *Downtown Buffalo 2002! News* 3, no. 1, special ed. (April 2002).

14. Brian Meyer, "Will There Ever Really Be a 'Neighborhood' Downtown?" *Buffalo News*, March 29, 1998.

15. Chet Bridger, "$30 Million Renovation Begins on Ex-Trico Plant," *Buffalo News*, January 21, 2002.

16. City of Buffalo, "Memorandum of Agreement between City of Buffalo and Fort Erie Public Bridge Authority," January 2003, p. 15.

17. Bruce Jackson, "I'm Talking Pragmatism Here," *Art Voice*, April 22–28, 1999.

18. "Schumer Proposes 'International Zone' to End Delays Holding Up Creation of Joint US-Canadian Peace Bridge Facility," Internet press release from Charles Schumer Web site, http://www.senate.gov/~schumer/SchumerWebsite/pressroom/press_releases/PR01638.pf.html (accessed May 13, 2003).

19. Kevin Gaughan, "United We Stand," *Buffalo News*, May 9, 1999.

20. City of Buffalo, "Housing and Neighborhood Development: Building a Better Buffalo Block by Block—The City of Buffalo's 1997/98 Consolidated Plan," final draft (City of Buffalo: Department of Community Development, 1997–98).

21. Interview no. 42.

22. Bill Atkinson, "All Banking Is Local," *Baltimore Sun*, November 17, 2002.

23. City of Buffalo, "Mayor Statement," http://www.citybuffalo.com/document_1719_178.html (accessed January 10, 2004).

24. Ibid.

25. Winnie Hu, "State Board Is Proposed for Buffalo," *Buffalo News*, May 29, 2003.

26. Buffalo Fiscal Stability Authority, "Review of Revised Four Year Financial Plan," October 1, 2003, pp. 10–11.

27. Tom Precious, "Plan Increases Taxes," http://www.buffalonews.com/editorial/20040121/1040607.asp (accessed January 21, 2004).

28. Precious, "Senecas Pick Cheektowaga," *Buffalo News*, April 10, 2004.

29. James Heaney, "Senecas OK Land Buy Near Airport, *Buffalo News*, April 11, 2004.

30. "County Court Abolition Surprise of Reform Plan," *Buffalo Evening News*, March 15, 1935.

31. Interview no. 50.

32. Kathryn A. Foster, "Regional Impulses," *Journal of Urban Affairs* 19, no. 4 (1997): 375–403.

33. Erie County Legislature, "Highlights of the Chautauqua Conference on Regional Governance, June 1–June 4, 1997; Chautauqua Institution," prepared by Tod A. Kniazuk, 1997.

34. Meyer, "Will There Ever Really Be a 'Neighborhood' Downtown?"

35. "Giambra Softens Position on Government Consolidation," *Buffalo News*, June 3, 1997.

36. Phil Fairbanks and Brian Meyer, "Is Consolidation Likely?" *Buffalo News*, February 25, 2003.

37. William Glaberson, "In Buffalo, an Upstate Mirror," *New York Times*, April 14, 1997.

38. Michael Teitz, J. Fred Silva, and Elisa Barbour, "Elements of a Framework for Collaborative Regional Decision-Making in California," occasional paper (San Francisco: Public Policy Institute of California, September 2001), p. 1.

39. Erie County, "Governance in Erie County," [The Governance Project], chap. 10.

40. Glaberson, "In Buffalo, an Upstate Mirror."

41. Gaughan, "United We Stand."

42. Teitz, Silva, and Barbour, "Elements of a Framework," p. 8.

43. Laws of Minnesota, 1999, Chapter 471 [471.59].

44. Ibid.

45. Teitz, Silva, and Barbour, "Elements of a Framework," p. 2.

ECONOMIC TABLES

Table 1
Occupational Structure: Buffalo Two-County Area, 1980

	Number of Jobs	% of Total
Managerial and Professional Specialty Occupations	**112,175**	**21.72**
Executive, Administrative, and Management Occupations	46,814	9.07
Professional Specialty Occupations	65,361	12.66
Engineer and Natural Scientists	9,592	1.86
Health: Diagnostic and Treating Occupations	15,304	2.96
Teachers, Librarians, and Counsel	26,895	5.21
Technical, Sales, and Administrative Support Occupations	**158,366**	**30.67**
Technologists and Technicians	16,010	3.10
Sales Occupations	53,077	10.28
Administrative and Clerical Occupations	89,279	17.29
Service Occupations	**72,054**	**13.95**
Farming, Forestry, and Fishing Occupations	**4,697**	**0.91**
Precision Production, Craft, and Repair Occupations	**64,465**	**12.48**
Operators, Fabricators, and Laborers	**104,588**	**20.26**
Total Employment	**516,345**	**100.00**

Source: "Census of Population: Social and Economic Characteristics, 1980"

Table 2
Establishments in Wholesale and Retail Trade:
Manufacturing Hourly Earnings

**Number of Establishments: Wholesale Trade,
Buffalo Two-County Area, 1972, 1977, 1979**

1972	1977	1979	% Change 1972–79
2,190	2,066	1,988	−9.2

**Number of Establishments: Retail Trade,
Buffalo Two-County Area, 1972, 1977, 1979**

1972	1977	1979	% Change 1972–79
10,900	9,845	6,573	−39.7

Sources: *State and Metropolitan Area Data Book*, 1979, 1982

**Manufacturing:
Average Hourly Earnings of Production Workers,
Buffalo Two-County Area**

1967	1972	% Chg	1977	% Chg	1982	% Chg
$3.47	$4.91	41.4	$7.65	55.8	$11.22	46.6

Sources: "Census of Manufacturers," 1967, 1972, 1977, 1982

Table 3
Employment in Different Sectors by Race,
Buffalo Two-County Area, 1980

	White	% of Total	Black	% of Total
Agriculture	4,361	0.92	55	0.16
Mining	293	0.06	6	0.02
Construction	17,983	3.78	736	2.15
Manufacturing	128,768	27.06	11,975	35.02
Transportation, Communications, and Other Public Utilities	33,506	7.04	2,034	5.95
Wholesale Trade	21,684	4.56	606	1.77
Retail Trade	87,051	18.30	3,063	8.96
Finance/Insurance/ Real Estate	24,862	5.23	1,564	4.57
Services	157,281	33.06	14,152	41.39
Total Employment	475,789	100	34,191	100.00

Sources: "Census of Population: Social and Economic Characteristics, 1980"

Table 4
Value of Output in Key Sectors,
Buffalo Two-County Area, 1977, 1982

	1977	1982	% Change
Manufacturing: **Value of Shipments**	$10,346,000	$11,100,000	7.3
Services, Total Receipts	$837,109	N/A	
Retail Sales	$3,856,593	$5,002,201	29.7
Wholesale	$6,946,255	$8,933,211	28.6

Sources: "Census of Manufacturers," 1977, 1982
"Census of Service Industries," 1977
"Census of Retail Trade," 1977, 1982
"Census of Wholesale Trade," 1977, 1982

Table 5
Occupational Pay Comparisons; Population
and Workplace Changes

Inter-Area Pay Comparisons for Selected Occupational Groups, 1982

Average pay level for each industry and occupational group = 100, based on the average pay levels of 262 metropolitan areas

Office Clerical			Electronic Data Processing		
All Indus	Mfg	Non-Mfg	All Indus	Mfg	Non-Mfg
94	102	86	93	94	N/A

Skilled Maintenance			Unskilled Plant	
All Indus	Mfg	All Indus	Mfg	Non-Mfg
106	108	102	112	N/A

Source: Erie County Economic Adjustment Strategy Study, Phase II Report (Table 26), December 1984, prepared by Battelle

Population and Workplace Changes, 1960–1970, Buffalo Two-County Area

% Change in Population			% Change in Jobs		
Total Area	Central City	Suburban Ring	Total Area	Central City	Suburban Ring
3.2	−14	15	4	−17	31

Absolute Change in Jobs		% Area Residents Working in Central City	
Central City	Suburban Ring	1960	1970
−43,000	61,000	56.1	44.6

Source: John Meyer and José Gómez-Ibáñez, "Autos, Transit and Cities (A Twentieth Century Fund Report)," 1981

Table 6
Change of Employment in Different Sectors,
Buffalo Two-County Area, 1960, 1970, 1980

	1960	1970	% Change	1980	% Change
Agriculture	5,575	4,520	−18.9	4,460	−1.3
Mining	311	553	77.8	302	−45.4
Construction	27,388	22,048	−19.5	18,991	−13.9
Manufacturing	181,166	170,458	−5.9	142,596	−16.3
Transportation, Communications, and Other Public Utilities	35,915	33,585	−6.5	35,873	6.8
Wholesale Trade	15,419	21,495	39.4	22,413	4.3
Retail Trade	69,628	85,334	22.6	90,855	6.5
Finance/Insurance/ Real Estate	16,849	20,621	22.4	26,570	28.8
Services	106,197	151,175	42.4	174,285	15.3
Total Employment	458,448	509,789	11.2	516,345	1.3

Sources: "Census of Populations: Social and Economic Characteristics," 1960, 1970, 1980

Table 7
Manufacturing Production Workers, and Wages, Buffalo Two-County Area, 1967–1982

Manufacturing Production Workers, Buffalo Two-County Area, 1967–1982
(thousands of workers)

1967	1972	% Change	1977	% Change	1982	% Change	Total Change
129	107.8	−16.4	102.1	−5.3	75.3	−26.2	−41.6

Manufacturing Production Worker Wages, Buffalo Two-County Area, 1967–1982
(dollars in millions)

1967	1972	% Change	1977	% Change	1982	% Change	Total Change
$905	$1,063	17.4	$1,556	46.3	$1,606	3.2	77.5

Sources: "Census of Manufacturers," 1967, 1972, 1977, 1982

Definition of *production workers*: Workers up through the level of foreman. Supervisory employees above this are excluded.

Table 8
Labor Force Characteristics: Class of Worker by Race,
Buffalo Two-County Area, 1970–1980

	1970				1980			
	White	% of Total	Black	% of Total	White	% of Total	Black	% of Total
Private wage and salary workers	403,729	79.2	26,330	79.9	372,584	78.3	24,743	72.6
Government workers	78,869	15.5	5822	17.7	79,859	16.8	8,645	25.4
Self-employed	25,611	5.0	797	2.4	21,810	4.6	667	2.0
Unpaid family workers	1,580	0.3	14	0.04	1,491	0.3	46	0.1
Total Employment	509,789	100.0	32,963	100.0	475,744	100.0	34,101	100.0

Source: "Census of Populations: Social and Economic Characteristics," 1970, 1980

BIBLIOGRAPHY

BUFFALO SPECIFIC

"Alinsky in Buffalo May 22nd, IRS Rules ESCO Tax Exempt." *East Side Community Organization Newsletter* (April–May 1966).

"Ambitious Proposal Looks to Rebirth of Shoreline." *Buffalo News*, February 15, 1987.

Annual Report, 1929. Buffalo, NY: Buffalo Chamber of Commerce, 1929.

"Arthur Campaign Trail Ends in Disappointment." *Buffalo News*, November 6, 1985.

"Assemblyman Pulls Stunning Upset as Griffin Lead Fades." *Buffalo Evening News*, September 9, 1977.

Atkinson, Bill. "All Banking Is Local." *Baltimore Sun*, November 17, 2002.

Baldwin, Richard E. "No Gains BUILD Says." *Buffalo Courier-Express*, January 16, 1969.

———. "Grass Roots Issue Snags Model City." *Buffalo Courier-Express*, in BUILD Press Archives, 1964–1974. Compiled by Robert Traynham Coles, 1974.

"Ballpark, Theater District Projects to Lead Downtown Construction." *Buffalo News*, January 25, 1987.

Besag, Frank P. *Anatomy of a Riot: Buffalo '67*. Albany: State University of New York Press, 1967.

"Bethlehem Announces 6 Demands." *Buffalo Courier-Express*, October 21, 1971.

"Bethlehem Returns to Profitability." *Buffalo Evening News*, January 26, 1978.

Black, Gary. "An Analysis of Corporate Headquarter Relocation." Master of Planning thesis, State University of New York at Buffalo, 1986.

"Black in Buffalo: A Late Century Progress Report." *Buffalo Magazine*, in the *Buffalo News*, 1996.

"Black Struggle Here Turns to Marketplace." *Buffalo News*, February 1, 1987.

Bonduki, Yamil, and Diana Dillaway. "Statistical Compendium: Buffalo and Pittsburgh." Unpublished paper, 1985.

Bridger, Chet. "Downtown Dilemma." *Buffalo News*, May 17, 1999.

————. "$30 Million Renovation Begins on Ex-Trico Plant." *Buffalo News*, January 21, 2002.

Brown, Richard, and Bob Watson. *Buffalo: Lake City in Niagara Land*. Woodland Hills, CA: Windsor Publications, 1981.

Buell, Frank. "Alinsky Plans First Moves: Finding People and Issues." *Buffalo Evening News*, October 20, 1967.

————. "Setbacks on Waterfront Dismay Renewal Unit." *Buffalo Evening News*, December 4, 1969.

Buffalo Area Chamber of Commerce. "Buffalo Metro/Store/Office/Plant Listing." Annual listings for 1981, 1982, 1983, 1984, 1985. Buffalo, NY.

"Buffalo Blacks on the Move." *Buffalo Courier-Express*, April 1979.

Buffalo Fiscal Stability Authority. "Review of Revised Four Year Financial Plan." Buffalo, NY, October 21, 2003.

"Buffalo Improving Its Negative Image." *New York Times*, December 1, 1986.

"Buffalo That Might Have Been, The." *Buffalo Magazine*, in the *Buffalo News*, February 22, 1987.

"Buffalo's Development Retarded by Political Discord," *Buffalo Evening News*, January 19, 1952.

"Buffalo Waterfront Project Kept in Flux by Planners." *Buffalo Evening News*, January 2, 1974.

"BUILD Blasts Rocky on Plan." *Buffalo Courier-Express*, January 9, 1971.

"BUILD, Buffalo State Head to Discuss 'Ghetto Academy.'" *Buffalo Courier-Express*, February 6, 1968.

"BUILD Head Endorses Jitney Plan." *Buffalo Courier-Express*, January 12, 1971.

"BUILD Names Policy Board for Woodlawn." *Buffalo Courier-Express*, August 25, 1972.

BUILD Press Archives, 1964–1974. Compiled by Robert Traynham Coles, 1974.

Center for Regional Studies. Prepared by Robert Kraushaar. "Memo to Western New York Economic Development Corporation, Re: Analysis of Large Manufacturing Firms in Western New York." State University of New York at Buffalo, March 28, 1986.

———. "Western New York and New York State Manufacturing Employment for 1977, 1980, 1982, 1983." State University of New York at Buffalo, 1986.

———. "Erie-Niagara County Trends in Manufacturing, 1983, 1984, and 1985." State University of New York at Buffalo, 1986.

Childs, John Brown. *The Political Black Minister*. Boston, MA: G. K. Hall, 1980.

Cigliano, Jan, and Sarah Bradford Landau, eds. *The Grand American Avenue, 1850–1920*. Rohnert Park, CA: Pomegranate Communications in association with the Octagon Museum, Washington, DC, 1994.

"Cities Find It Hard to Build on Reassurances." *Buffalo Courier-Express*, June 22, 1973.

City of Buffalo. "Workable Program for Slum Prevention and Elimination." Buffalo, NY: Board of Redevelopment and City Planning Commission, December 1957.

———. "A Review of Progress under the Workable Program for Community Improvement." Office of the Mayor, Chester Kowal. Submitted to the Housing and Home Finance Agency August 27, 1964. Resubmitted July 27, 1965.

———. "Buffalo Regional Center: Executive Summary." Prepared by Coombes/Kirkland/Berridge/Cooper/Eckstut Associates, 1985.

———. "Economic Trends." Issue V, Prepared by Division of Planning, Department of Community Development, 1985, 1986.

———. "Housing and Neighborhood Development: Building a Better Buffalo Block by Block—The City of Buffalo's 1997/98 Consolidated Plan." Final draft, Department of Community Development, 1997–1998.

———. "The Revised Strategic Plan for Downtown Buffalo." *Downtown Buffalo 2002! News* 3, no. 1, special edition (April 2002).

———. "Memorandum of Agreement between City of Buffalo and Fort Erie Public Bridge Authority." January 2003.

———. "Mayor Statement." http://www.citybuffalo.com/document _1719_178.html (accessed January 10, 2004).

"City Sanitation Men Have Lots of Letdowns between Their Pickups" (first of a series). *Buffalo Evening News*, May 12, 1966.

"Code to Enforce Standards for Housing Bared." *Buffalo Courier-Express*, April 24, 1965.

Coles, Sylvia. "Community versus College: Conflict in an Inner City Neighborhood." Unpublished paper, State University of New York at Buffalo, 1997.

Collison, Kevin. "Downtown District Bids to Shake 'Sin' Tag." *Buffalo News*, November 5, 1989.

———. "Poised for Private Funds." *Buffalo News*, October 31, 1998.

"Community Conference Is Solving Pittsburgh's Suburban Problems." *Buffalo Evening News*, January 26, 1951.

"Construction Fund Manager Chided." *Buffalo Courier-Express*, June 6, 1969.

"Cooperation Keeps This Bethlehem Plant in Black." *Buffalo News*, August 24, 1986.

"Council Turns Down an Invitation to Dr. Alinsky." *Buffalo Evening News*, May 5, 1967.

"County Court Abolition Surprise of Reform Plan," *Buffalo Evening News*, March 15, 1935.

Dahlberg, Debbie. "Alinsky in Buffalo: The BUILD Organization." Unpublished paper, Buffalo, NY, 1985.

D'Amico, Michael. "Urban Campus Committee Report Comment." *Spectrum* (State University of New York at Buffalo), September 7, 1966.

"Delays Cost City Renewal Program." *Buffalo Evening News*, March 24, 1965.

Department of Environmental Design and Planning. "An Analysis of Rapid Transit Investments: The Buffalo Experience." Prepared for the US Department of Transportation. State University of New York at Buffalo, 1981.

"Depression Guru," *New York Times*, August 30, 1987.

"Diocese Bars Aid to Alinsky Fund; Cites Own Efforts." *Buffalo Courier-Express*, March 4, 1965.

"Donohue Has 3-Point Plan to Spur Area's Development." *Buffalo News*, December 9, 1984.

Downtown Buffalo Summit News (State University of New York at Buffalo) (Fall 1996).

East Side Community Organization, Inc. (Buffalo, NY). Newsletter (March 1966; Winter Quarter 1967).

"East Side Group Seeks Controversial Organizer." *Buffalo Evening News*, January 23, 1965.

Economic Development Administration, US Department of Commerce. Prepared by Marcom, Inc. "An Action Development Program for the Broadway-Fillmore Section of Buffalo, New York," 1969.

"Education Must Play Vital Role in Growth of Area's Economy." *Buffalo News*, March 26, 1984.

Erie and Niagara Counties Regional Planning Board. Prepared by the Steering Committee and the Economic Consultants Organization, Inc., with assistance of the Economic Technical Advisory Committee. "Economic Development in the Erie-Niagara Region," June 1975.

Erie County. Prepared by the Governance Project. "Governance in Erie County." http://www.wnyrin.com/gove_repo/chapter_10.html (accessed May 8, 2004).

Erie County Department of Planning. Prepared by Llewelyn-Davies Associates. "The Impact of the New York State University Campus in Erie County," July 1971.

Erie County Industrial Development Agency. Prepared by Battelle. "Overview Report." Buffalo, NY, October 27, 1978.

———. "Erie County Economic Adjustment Strategy Study. Reports: Phase I and Phase II." 1984.

Erie County Legislature. Prepared by Tod A. Kniazuk. "Highlights of the Chautauqua Conference on Regional Governance, June 1–June 4, 1997; Chautauqua Institution," 1997.

"Erie G.O.P. Assemblymen Dash Hopes for Reform." *Buffalo Evening News*, April 30, 1936.

"Expanded Role Envisaged for Development Foundation." *Buffalo Evening News*, December 8, 1960.

Fairbanks, Phil, and Brian Meyer. "Is Consolidation Likely?" *Buffalo News*, February 25, 2003.

Foster, Kathryn A. "Regional Impulses." *Journal of Urban Affairs* 19, no. 4 (1997): 375–403.

Fox, Sally. "Hotel Seen as Spur to Future." *Buffalo Courier-Express*, January 28, 1978.

Garnett, Robert, and Jack Guttentag. "Help in Buffalo." *Housing Finance Review* (Washington, DC) 1, no. 4 (October 1982).

Gates, George. "Outlook Bright, Bankers Told in Mayor's Report." *Buffalo Evening News*, August 21, 1976.

Gaughan, Kevin. "United We Stand." *Buffalo News*, May 9, 1999.

"Giambra Softens Position on Government Consolidation." *Buffalo News*, June 3, 1997.

Glaberson, William. "In Buffalo, an Upstate Mirror." *New York Times*, April 14, 1997.

"GM-UAW Relations Key to the Future of Plants Here." *Buffalo News*, August 4, 1986.

Goldberg, Carey. "Boston Leading a Renewal of Old Northern Cities." *New York Times*, November 3, 1998.

Goldman, Mark. *High Hopes: The Rise and Decline of Buffalo, New York.* Albany: State University of New York Press, 1983.

———. *City on the Lake: The Challenge of Change in Buffalo, New York.* Amherst, NY: Prometheus Books, 1990.

Greater Buffalo Chamber of Commerce. "Buffalo Metro Store/Office/Plant Listing." Annual listings for 1986, 1987. Buffalo, NY.

———. Annual Report, 1986–87. Buffalo, NY.

Greater Buffalo Development Foundation. "Annual Report, 1975–76: 25th Anniversary Report"; annual reports 1976–77, 1977–78, 1978–79, 1979–80; "Annual Report, 1980–81: A Retrospective of 30 Years, 1951–1981"; annual reports 1981–82, 1982–83, 1983–84, 1984–85.

———. "Downtown Buffalo Shopping and Business Center." Prepared by the Architect's Redevelopment Collaborative. Buffalo, NY, November 8, 1962.

———. "A Growth Strategy for the Erie-Niagara Area, No. 6: Metals and

Metals Related Industries." Prepared by Paul W. Dickson and Raymond W. Waxmonsky. Buffalo, NY, 1969.

———. "Report on Metals and Related Industries," 1969.

———. "A Growth Strategy for the Erie-Niagara Area, No. 8: Buffalo Area's Economic Prospects." Prepared by Paul W. Dickson and Raymond W. Waxmonsky. Buffalo, NY, 1972.

"Griffin Intent on Solo Rule in First 30 Days." *Buffalo News*, February 2, 1986.

"Group of 18 Strives to Boost Economy." *Buffalo News*, October 12, 1986.

"Group of 18, Seeking to Promote Buffalo, Plays to Mixed Reviews." *Buffalo News*, February 10, 1991.

"Harriman Reveals HHFA Approval." *Buffalo Courier-Express*, June 27, 1965.

"Hasty Tampering with Housing Code." *Buffalo Courier-Express*, October 1, 1965.

Heaney, James. "A House Divided: The Politics of Public Housing." *Buffalo News*, July 19, 1987.

———. "Senecas OK Land Buy Near Airport." *Buffalo News*, April 11, 2004.

"High Utility Rates Are Draining Life out of Some Businesses." *Buffalo News*, March 31, 1998.

Hollins, Dennis. "Audit Reports Disclose $45,000 BUILD Liabilities." *Buffalo Evening News*, June 7, 1978.

"Horizons Waterfront Commission: Action Plan." Prepared by Saratoga Associates. May 15, 1991.

"Horizons Waterfront Commission: Goals and Objectives for the Erie County Waterfront." Prepared by the Saratoga Associates, July 1990.

Hu, Winnie. "State Board Is Proposed for Buffalo." *Buffalo News*, May 29, 2003.

"Idea for Sports Stadium Grew into Major Study of Downtown." *Buffalo Evening News*, December 8, 1960.

Jackson, Bruce. "I'm Talking Pragmatism Here." *Art Voice*, April 22–28, 1999.

Jarvis, Harold P. "Kenefick Commission to Push Reform Bill." *Buffalo Courier-Express*, March 3, 1936.

Kraus, Neil. *Race, Neighborhoods, and Community Power*. Albany: State University of New York Press, 2000.

Krone, Robert. "Light Rail Transit in Buffalo: Can It Revitalize Downtown?" Department of Transportation, University of California at Berkeley, 1984.

"Land Deal Urged to Revitalize Waterfront." *Buffalo News*, September 7, 1986.

Laws of Minnesota. "Joint Powers Act," 1999 (Chapter 471). http://www.lpa.state.mn.us/laws/joint471.html (accessed March 16, 2004).

League of Women Voters. "Government of the City of Buffalo." Document JS668.L5.

Lemann, Nicholas. "No Man's Town." *New Yorker*, June 5, 2000.

Levine, Linda. "A Waterfront University?" *Western New York Heritage Magazine* (Winter 2002).

"Locally Based Industries Are Key to Stable Economy." *Buffalo News*, March 27, 1986.

"Lutherans Remain Divided on Support for Alinsky." *Buffalo Evening News*, February 2, 1966.

"Maps Drive to Boost Economy." *Buffalo Evening News*, February 3, 1976.

Martin, William L. "A New Stadium for Metropolitan Buffalo." *Buffalo Magazine*, in the *Buffalo Evening News*, June 1967.

"Masiello: Mixed Reviews." *Buffalo News*, July 26, 1999.

McAvey, Jim. "Alinsky Says IAF against Violence." *Buffalo Courier-Express*, May 14, 1966.

McDonald, Daniel. "Waterfront vs. Amherst: A Study of the Campus Site Controversy at the SUNY at Buffalo." Unpublished paper, Department of History, State University of New York at Buffalo, December 1971.

McGovern, Stephen J. *The Politics of Downtown Development*. Lexington: University Press of Kentucky, 1998.

McKeating, Michael. "Empire State Report." Albany, NY, July 1976.

———. "The Rise of Erie County's Warring Troika: Crangle, Regan and Slominski." *Empire State Report* (July 1976).

"Mel Baker Asks Re-development." *Buffalo Evening News*, May 17, 1956.

Meyer, Brian. "Will There Ever Really be a 'Neighborhood' Downtown?" *Buffalo News*, March 29, 1998.

———. "Partnership Tallies Pluses, Minuses," *Buffalo News*, February 21, 1999.

Meyer, John, and José Gómez-Ibáñez. "Autos, Transit and City." A Twentieth Century Fund Report. New York, 1981.

Miller, Eldor. "Forced Relocation in Urban Renewal: A Sociological Analysis." PhD diss., 1970, p. 49, table III-1.

"Millonzi, Lawless Join Senate Unit." *Buffalo Courier-Express*, May 8, 1976.

Model City Conference. Transcript. Cooperative Urban Extension Center. Buffalo, NY, January 19–20, 1967.

Monaghan, Marshall Macklin, Robert Traynham Coles, and Barton Myers Associates. "The City of Buffalo Main Street Corridor Master Plan: Executive Summary." Buffalo, NY, 1985.

"Neighbor, Help Thyself: How Washington and Albany Abandoned the Cities Over Time," BUILD Press Archives, March 12, 1997.

Nesbitt, Scott. "Building Trades Integration Session Flops." *Buffalo Courier-Express*, May 26, 1971.

———. "Tax Problem Proves Millstone around Bethlehem Plant's Neck." *Buffalo Courier-Express*, November 15, 1971.

"New Economic Development Corp. for WNY Greeted with Enthusiasm." *Buffalo News*, October 31, 1982.

"New Leadership Set to Propel Foundation into Downtown Plans." *Buffalo News*, December 8, 1986.

"New Vision Needed for the Waterfront." *Buffalo News*, August 2, 1987.

"New York: The Road to Recovery." *Buffalo News*, November 2, 1986.

New York State Office of Planning Coordination. "The Buffalo-Amherst Corridor Technical Report, 1969."

"NFTA Rushing Mall Work, Picks 4 Designer Finalists." *Buffalo News*, July 27, 1982.

"NFTA to Ready 'Disaster Plan.' Plug Transit Tax." *Buffalo News*, January 18, 1989.

Niagara Falls. "History of Power." http://www.niagarafrontier.com/power.html#Sch (accessed April 21, 2004).

Niagara Frontier Transit Improvement Digest. Issued by the Citizens Rapid Transit Committee. April 27, 1999.

Niagara Frontier Transportation Authority. http://www.fta.dot.gov/library/reference/iad/NFTA.HTM (accessed May 4, 2004).

"1960 Is Proposed for First County Executive Election." *Buffalo Evening News*, May 2, 1959.

"Nouveaux Riches, The." *Buffalo Magazine*, in the *Buffalo News*, August 9, 1987.

"100 Most Powerful People in Buffalo: Who's in Charge Here?" *Buffalo Magazine*, in the *Buffalo News*, September 27, 1987.

"100 State 'Sheet Hanging' to Publicize Fire Trap." *Buffalo Courier-Express*, BUILD Press Archives, n.d.

"Panel Named to Revise City Charter." *Buffalo Evening News*, July 12, 1974.

Perry, David. "The Politics of Dependency in Deindustrializing America: The Case of Buffalo, New York." In *The Capitalist City*, edited by Joe Fagin and Michael Peter Smith. Oxford, UK: Basil Blackwell, 1987.

————. "Upstate Economy Faces Crisis and Opportunities." *Buffalo News*, November 2, 1986.

Perry, David, and staff of the Political Economy of Urban Infrastructure Project. "Ending Regional Economic Dependency: Economic Development Policy for Distressed Regions." Rev. ed. Department of Environmental Design and Planning, State University of New York at Buffalo, 1986.

Plaintiffs' Post-Trial Brief: Civil Docket No. 1972-325 (Excerpts). United States District Court, Western District of New York. Buffalo, NY, January 13, 1975.

"Planning Director Sees Bright Future on the Waterfront." *Buffalo News*, November 9, 1981.

Precious, Tom. "Plan Increases Taxes." http://www.buffalonews.com/editorial/20040121/1040607.asp (accessed January 21, 2004).

————. "Senecas Pick Cheektowaga." *Buffalo News*, April 10, 2004.

"Put Civil Service to Work at Patronage-Rich NFTA." Editorial. *Buffalo News*, July 22, 1986.

"Racial, Gender Diversity, Eludes Nearly All Boards." *Buffalo News*, June 19, 2001.

Rasmussen, George. "The Stadium in Perspective." *Buffalo Magazine*, in the *Buffalo Evening News*, February 1964.

"Regan: Hyatt May Ponder Buffalo Hotel." *Buffalo Courier-Express*, February 2, 1978.

"Regan Pledges County Would Be Co-ordinator of Community Effort." *Buffalo Evening News*, September 10, 1971.

"Regan Prefers Sales Tax Increase to Higher Property Taxes." *Buffalo Evening News*, October 17, 1971.

"Regional Salesmanship Makes Sense for WNY." *Buffalo News*, August 18, 1987.

"Rev. Ford, Former BUILD President, Moving to California." *Buffalo Courier-Express*, August 20, 1972.

Richman, David. "The University Relocation Controversy." Unpublished paper, Department of Political Science, State University of New York at Buffalo, 1975.

Ritz, Joseph P. "21 Firms Get Power from the State." *Buffalo News*, February 1, 1989.

Robinson, David. "The 1980s: Buffalo's Transitional Decade." *Buffalo News*, December 31, 1989.

Robinson, David, and Jerry Zremski. "On the Board Circuit." *Buffalo News*, June 19, 2001.

Roth, Roberta. "The Amherst Campus." Unpublished paper, Department of Political Science, State University of New York at Buffalo, December 1972.

Rust, Edgar. "Metropolitan Areas without Growth." Prepared for the National Institute for Child Health and Human Development, Washington, DC, 1974.

Ruth, Richard J. "County Has Rung Up $400,000 So Far for Outside Legal Fees in Stadium Suit." *Buffalo Courier-Express*, November 17, 1981.

"Schumer Proposes 'International Zone' to End Delays Holding up Creation of Joint US-Canadian Peace Bridge Facility." Press release. www.senate.gov/~schumer/SchumerWebsite/pressroom/press_releases/PR01638.pf.html (accessed May 13, 2003).

Schwerzler, Nancy L. "Buffalo Waterfront Project Kept in Flux by Planners." *Buffalo Evening News*, January 2, 1974.

"Search for a Campus, The." *Spectrum* (University of New York at Buffalo), October 7, 1966.

Sebastian, Pamela. "Buffalo, N.Y., Shows How Workers and Jobs Get out of Alignment." *Wall Street Journal*, September 16, 1988.

"Sedita Reports Progress in Jobs Recreation." *Challenger*, July 6, 1967.

"Shift in Federal, State Policies Leaves City Bleeding." *Buffalo News*, February 12, 1997.

Simon, Peter. "County's Next Hurdle on Sales-Tax Plan: Lackawanna Council." *Buffalo Evening News*, November 27, 1971.

"Six Proposals Advanced to Reform 115-Year-Old Erie County Government." *Buffalo Times*, March 2, 1936.

Smith, Preston. "Church Council Unit Backs Plan to Bring Alinsky Group Here." *Buffalo Evening News*, November 10, 1965.

"Stadium Aid Linked to County Crisis." *Buffalo News*, October 31, 1982.

Steinberg, Jacques. "In Buffalo, an Upstate Mirror—One Struggling City Ponders Extinguishing Itself." *New York Times*, April 14, 1997.

"Suggestions Vary as Forums Debate Industrial Decline." *Buffalo News*, June 1986.

Sullivan, Margaret. "Job-Loss Study Sees Irreversible Changes in WNY Economy." *Buffalo News*, March 4, 1986.

Summers, Robert J. "Buffalo Area's Industries Depend on Each Other, Too." *Buffalo Evening News*, August 20, 1975.

Taylor, Henry Louis, ed. *African Americans and the Rise of Buffalo's Post-Industrial City: 1940–Present*. Vol. 2. Buffalo, NY: Buffalo Urban League, 1990.

"Team to Study Buffalo Area for Redevelopment Potential." *Buffalo Evening News*, September 14, 1959.

Teitz, Michael J., Fred Silva, and Elisa Barbour. "Elements of a Framework for Collaborative Regional Decision-Making in California." Occasional paper, San Francisco: Public Policy Institute of California, September 2001.

"38 Major Plants Have Left Area in Last 5 Years." *Buffalo Evening News*, January 9, 1976.

Thompson, Gordon. "Chronology of Transportation Development on the Niagara Frontier, Buffalo: 1860–1975." Unpublished paper, Buffalo, NY, July 1975.

Trachtenberg, Jeffrey A. "Warren Buffett Got There Early." *Forbes Magazine*, December 26, 1988.

Turner, Douglas L. "For the Record." *Western New York Heritage Magazine* (Spring 2002).

"Urban Campus Committee Report." *Spectrum* (State University of New York at Buffalo), September 7, 1966.

US Bureau of the Census. "1970 Census of Population: General and Social and Economic Characteristics: New York." Washington, DC: US Department of Commerce, Bureau of the Census, 1972.

————. "Census of Manufacturers 1967, 1972, 1977, 1982." Washington, DC: US Department of Commerce, Bureau of the Census.

————. "County Business Patterns, 1970, 1982, 1984." Washington, DC: US Department of Commerce, Bureau of the Census.

US Bureau of Labor Statistics. "Employment and Earnings, 1967, 1972, 1977, 1984." Washington, DC: US Department of Labor.

————. "Non-Farm Employment by Industry, New York State and Metropolitan Areas." In "Current Employment Statistics Survey" (Buffalo–Niagara Falls MSA). Washington, DC: US Department of Labor. http://stats.bls.gov (question by e-mail, feedback@bls.gov, April 2004).

"U.S. Reluctant to Go Further until City Shows Renewal Gains." *Buffalo Evening News*, March 23, 1965.

"Vision of WNY Future Sees UB, Amherst at Hub." *Buffalo News*, September 16, 1986.

Vogel, Mike. "City Has Bold Plans for S. Buffalo." *Buffalo News*, March 6, 1997.

"Why Massachusetts Booms and New York Just Sputters Along." *Buffalo News*, June 6, 1986.

Williams, Deborah. "BUILD Academy Plans Curriculum for Specific Inner City Needs." *Buffalo Courier-Express*, in BUILD Press Archives, 1964–1974.

Williams, Fred O. "Union Town, USA." *Buffalo News*, May 29, 2000.

Witerski, David S. "Convention Center Already Preparing for Opening Day." *Buffalo Courier-Express*, February 27, 1978.

Zremski, Jerry, and David Robinson. "Who's in Charge Here? Leadership in Buffalo Niagara." *Buffalo News*, June 17, 2001.

GENERAL REFERENCE

Ács, Zoltán. *The Changing Structure of the U.S. Economy: Lessons from the Steel Industry*. New York: Praeger, 1984.

Ahlbrandt, Roger, Roger Fruehan, and Frank Giarratani. *The Renaissance of American Steel: Lessons for Managers in Competitive Industries*. Oxford: Oxford University Press, 1996.

Alinsky, Saul D. *Rules for Radicals: A Pragmatic Primer for Realistic Radicals*. New York: Vintage Books, 1971.

Bain, Donald, Jr. "The Suburban Wilderness: A Historical Approach to Metropolitan Decentralization." *South Atlantic Urban Studies* 1 (1977).

Baltzell, E. Digby. *Philadelphia Gentlemen: The Making of a National Upper Class*. Glencoe, IL: Free Press, 1958.

———. *The Protestant Establishment: Aristocracy and Caste in America*. New York: Random House, 1964.

Banfield, Edward G. *The Unheavenly City Revisited*. Boston: Little, Brown, 1970.

Bennett, Larry, Gregory D. Squires, Kathleen McCourt, and Philip Nyden. "Challenging Chicago's Growth Machine: A Preliminary Report on the Washington Administration." Unpublished paper, 1986.

Blakely, Edward. *Planning Local Economic Development: Theory and Practice*. Newbury Park, CA: Sage, 1989.

Bluestone, Barry, and Bennett Harrison. *Capital and Communities: The Causes and Consequences of Private Disinvestment*. Washington, DC: Progressive Alliance, 1980.

———. *The Deindustrialization of America*. New York: Basic Books, 1980.

Bowles, Samuel, David M. Gordon, and Thomas E. Weisskopf. *Beyond the Waste Land: A Democratic Alternative to Economic Decline*. New York: Anchor Press, 1983.

Bradbury, Katherine L., Anthony Downs, and Kenneth A. Small. *Urban Decline and the Future of American Cities*. Washington, DC: Brookings Institute, 1982.

Browning, Rufus, Dale Rogers Marshall, and David H. Tabb. "Local Control over Local Policies: Can City Politics Make a Difference for Minorities?" Paper presented at the annual meeting of the American Political Science Association, Chicago, 1983.

Bryce, Herrington. *Small Cities in Transition*. Cambridge: Ballinger, 1977.

———. *Cities and Firms*. Lexington, MA: Lexington Books, 1980.

Burchell, Robert W., and George Sternlieb. *Planning Theory in the 1980s: A Search for Future Directions*. New Brunswick, NJ: Center for Urban Policy, Rutgers University, 1978.

Burnham, Walter. *The Current Crisis in American Politics.* New York: Oxford University Press, 1982.

Burnham, Walter, and Martha Weinberg, eds. *American Politics and Public Policy.* Cambridge, MA: MIT Press, 1978.

Castells, Manuel. *The Wild City: An Interpretive Summary of Research and Analysis on the U.S. Urban Crisis.* Santa Cruz: University of California, Santa Cruz, 1975.

————. *The Urban Question.* Translated from the 1972 French edition. Cambridge, MA: MIT Press, 1977.

————. *City, Class, and Power: The Ideological and Political Factors in Urban Planning.* New York: St. Martin's Press, 1978.

————. *The City and the Grassroots: A Cross-Cultural Theory of Urban Social Movements.* Berkeley and Los Angeles: University of California Press, 1983.

Chinitz, Benjamin. *Central City Economic Development.* Cambridge, MA: ABT Books, 1979.

Clarke, Susan. "Urban America, Inc.: Corporatist Convergence of Power in American Cities?" In *Local Economics in Transition,* edited by Edward M. Bergman. Durham, NC: Duke University Press, 1986.

Clavel, Pierre. *The Progressive City: Planning and Participation, 1969–1984.* New Brunswick, NJ: Rutgers University Press, 1986.

Cohen, Stephen S., and John Zysman. *Manufacturing Matters: The Myth of the Post-Industrial Economy.* New York: Basic Books, 1987.

Corporation for Enterprise Development. *Making the Grade: The Development Report Card for the States.* Washington, DC: Corporation for Enterprise Development, 1987.

Dahl, Robert. *Who Governs? Democracy and Power in an American City.* New Haven, CT: Yale University Press, 1961.

Domhoff, G. William. *Who Really Rules in New Haven?* New Brunswick, NJ: Transaction Books, 1977.

————. *State Autonomy or Class Dominance? Case Studies on Policy Making in America.* New York: Aldine de Gruyter, 1996.

————. *Who Rules America?* 3rd ed. Mountain View, CA: Mayfield, 1998.

Dreier, Peter, Todd Swanstrom, and John Mollenkopf. *Place Matters: Metropolitics for the Twenty-First Century.* Studies in Government and Public Policy. Lawrence: University Press of Kansas, 2001.

Ewen, Lynda Ann. *Corporate Power and Urban Crisis in Detroit.* Princeton, NJ: Princeton University Press, 1978.

Fainstein, Susan, Norman Fainstein, and Richard Hall et al. *Restructuring the City: The Political Economy of Urban Redevelopment.* Rev. ed. New York: Longman, 1986.

Fainstein, Susan F., and Ann Markusen. "The Urban Policy Challenge: Integrating across Social and Economic Development Policy." In *Races, Poverty, and American Cities*, edited by John Charles Boger and Judith Welch Wegner. Chapel Hill: University of North Carolina Press, 1996.

Ferman, Barbara. *Challenging the Growth Machine: Neighborhood Politics in Chicago and Pittsburgh.* Lawrence: University Press of Kansas, 1996.

Fish, John. *Black Power, White Control.* Princeton, NJ: Princeton University Press, 1973.

Frieden, Bernard J., and Lynne B. Sagalyn. *How America Rebuilds Cities.* Cambridge, MA: MIT Press, 1989.

Friedland, Roger. *Power and Crisis in the City.* New York: Schocken Books, 1983.

Galbraith, John Kenneth. *The Anatomy of Power.* Boston: Houghton Mifflin, 1983.

Gale, Stephen, and Eric G. Moore, eds. *The Manipulated City: Perspectives on Spatial Structure and Social Issues in Urban America.* Chicago: Maaroufa, 1975.

Gans, Herbert. "American Urban Theories and Urban Areas: Some Observations on Contemporary Ecological and Marxist Paradigms." In *Cities in Recession*, by Ivan Szelanyi. Beverly Hills, CA: Sage, 1984.

Gaventa, John. *Power and Powerlessness.* Chicago: University of Illinois Press, 1980.

Gittell, Ross J. *Renewing Cities.* Princeton, NJ: Princeton University Press, 1992.

Goldsmith, William, Edward Blakely et al. "Investing Downtown vs. the Suburbs." In *Generations of Poverty: America's Underclass as an Economic and Political Dilemma.* University of California at Berkeley, Institute of Urban and Regional Development, February 1991.

Hammack, David. *Power and Society: Greater New York at the Turn of the Century*. New York: Russell Sage Foundation, 1982.

Harloe, Michael. "Notes on Comparative Urban Research." In *Urbanization and Urban Planning in Capitalist Society*, edited by Michael Dear and Allen J. Scott. New York: Methuen, 1981.

Harris, A. W. *U.S. Trade Problems in Steel: Japan, West Germany and Italy*. New York: Praeger, 1983.

Harrison, Bennett. *Metropolitan Suburbanization and Minority Economic Opportunity*. Washington, DC: Urban Institute, 1973.

Hartman, Chester. *The Transformation of San Francisco*. Totowa, NJ: Rowman & Allanheld, 1984.

Harvey, David. *Social Justice and the City*. Baltimore: Johns Hopkins University Press, 1973.

————. "The Political Economy of Urbanization in Advanced Capitalist Societies: The Case of the U.S." In *The Social Economy of Cities*, edited by Gary Gappert and Harold Rose. Beverly Hills, CA: Sage, 1975.

————. "The Urban Process under Capitalism: A Framework for Analysis." In *Urbanization and Urban Planning in Capitalist Society*, edited by Michael Dear and Allen J. Scott. New York: Methuen, 1981.

Hill, Richard Child. "Fiscal Collapse and Political Struggle in Decaying Cities." In *Marxism and the Metropolis*, edited by William Tabb and Larry Sawyers. New York: Oxford University Press, 1978.

Hogan, William Thomas. *The 1970s: Critical Years for Steel*. Lexington, MA: Lexington Books, 1972.

Hunter, Floyd. *Community Power Structure: A Study of Decision Makers*. Chapel Hill: University of North Carolina Press, 1969.

————. *Community Power Succession: Atlanta's Policymakers Revisited*. Chapel Hill: University of North Carolina Press, 1980.

Jacobs, Jane. *Cities and the Wealth of Nations: Principles of Economic Life*. New York: Random House, 1984.

Jacobson, Louis. "A Tale of Employment—Decline in Two Cities." *Industrial and Labor Relations Review* 37, no. 4 (1984).

Janowitz, Morris, ed. *Community Political Systems*. Glencoe, IL: Free Press, 1961.

Keating, Michael. *Comparative Urban Politics*. Brookfield, VT: Edward Elgar, 1991.

Kiers, Luc. *The American Steel Industry: Problems, Challenges, Perspectives*. Boulder, CO: Westview Press, 1980.

Kleniewski, Nancy. "Economic Development: The Dilemma of the Older Central Cities." Urban Studies Program, State University of New York at Geneseo. Paper presented at the 1985 meeting of the Association of Collegiate Schools of Planning, 1985.

Lake, Robert, ed. *Readings in Urban Analysis*. New Brunswick, NJ: Center for Urban Policy, Rutgers University, 1983.

Logan, John, and Harvey Molotch. *Urban Fortunes: The Political Economy of Place*. Berkeley and Los Angeles: University of California Press, 1987.

Lubove, Roy. *Twentieth-Century Pittsburgh*. New York: John Wiley and Sons, 1969.

——. *Twentieth-Century Pittsburgh*. Vol. 2: *The Post-Steel Era*. Pittsburgh: University of Pittsburgh Press, 1996.

Losch, A. *The Economics of Location*. Translated from the 2nd edition. New Haven, CT: Yale University Press, 1954.

Malizia, Emil E. "Economic Development in Smaller Cities and Rural Areas." *Journal of the American Planning Association* 52, no. 4 (Autumn 1986): 489–99.

Markusen, Ann R. *Profit Cycles, Oligopoly, and Regional Development*. Cambridge, MA: MIT Press, 1984.

Mier, Robert, Kari J. Moe, and Irene Sherr. "Strategic Planning and the Pursuit of Reform, Economic Development, and Equity." *Journal of the American Planning Association* 52, no. 3 (1986): 299–309.

Mills, C. Wright. *The Power Elite*. New York: Oxford University Press, 1956.

Mollenkopf, John. "Community and Accumulation." In *Urbanization and Urban Planning in Capitalist Society*, edited by Michael Dear and Allen J. Scott. New York: Methuen, 1981.

——. "Paths toward the Post-Industrial Service City: The Northeast and the Southwest." In *Cities under Stress*, edited by Robert W. Burchell and David Listokin. Piscataway, NJ: Center for Urban Policy, Rutgers University, 1981.

——. *The Contested City*. Los Angeles and Berkeley: University of California Press, 1983.

Myrdal, Gunnar. *The Political Element in the Development of Economic Theory*. Cambridge, MA: Harvard University Press, 1954.

———. *Against the Stream: Critical Essays on Economics*. New York: Random House, 1973.

O'Connor, James. *Fiscal Crisis of the State*. New York: St. Martin's Press, 1973.

———. *Accumulation Crisis*. New York: Basil Blackwell, 1984.

Perry, David, and A. Watkins, eds. *The Rise of the Sunbelt Cities*. Beverly Hills, CA: Sage, 1977.

Perry, David C., and Alfred J. Watkins. "Uneven Development in the USA." In *City, Class, and Capital*, edited by Michael Harloe and Elizabeth Lebas. London: Edward Arnold Publishers, 1981.

Polsby, Nelson. *Community Power and Political Theory*. New Haven, CT: Yale University Press, 1963.

Porter, Michael E. *On Competition*. Boston, MA: Harvard Business School Publishing, 1998.

Robertiello, Richard C., and Diana Hoguet. *The WASP Mystique*. New York: D. I. Fine, 1987.

Rowley, Charles K. *Steel and Public Policy*. London: McGraw Hill, 1971.

Rusk, David. *Cities without Suburbs*. 2nd ed. Washington, DC: Woodrow Wilson Center Press, 1995.

Rust, Edgar. *Metropolitan Areas without Growth*. San Francisco: Scientific Analysis, 1974.

Sawyers, Larry, and William K. Tabb. *Sunbelt, Snowbelt: Urban Development and Regional Restructuring*. New York: Oxford University Press, 1984.

Schulze, Robert. "The Bifurcation of Power in a Satellite City." In *Community Political Systems*, edited by Morris Janowitz. Glencoe, IL: Free Press, 1961.

Steel Panel Committee on Technology and International Economic and Trade Issues of the Office of the Foreign Secretary. *The Competitive Status of the U.S. Steel Industry: A Study of the Influences of Technology in Determining International Industrial Competitive Advantage*. Washington, DC: National Academy Press, 1985.

Sternlieb, George, and James Hughes, eds. *Post-Industrial America: Metropolitan Decline and Interregional Job Shifts*. New Brunswick, NJ: Center for Urban Policy, Rutgers University, 1976.

————. *Revitalizing the Northeast.* New Brunswick, NJ: Center for Urban Policy, Rutgers University, 1978.

Strohmeyer, John. *Crisis in Bethlehem.* Bethesda, MD: Adler & Adler, 1986.

Tabb, William, and Larry Sawyers, eds. *Marxism and the Metropolis: New Perspectives in Urban Political Economy.* New York: Oxford University Press, 1978.

Tassel, David van, and John Grabowski. *Cleveland—A Tradition of Reform.* Kent, OH: Kent State University Press, 1986.

Teitz, Michael B. "Planning for Local Economic Development: The Role of Small Business." *Town Planning Review* 58, no. 1 (January): 5–18.

Teitz, Michael, Fred Silva, and Elisa Barbour. "Elements of a Framework for Collaborative Regional Decision-Making in California." Occasional paper, San Francisco: Public Policy Institute of California, September 2001.

Temin, Peter. *Iron and Steel in Nineteenth-Century America: An Economic Inquiry.* Cambridge, MA: MIT Press, 1964.

Walker, Dick. "A Theory of Suburbanization: Capitalism and the Construction of Urban Space in the United States." In *Urbanization and Urban Planning in Capitalist Society*, edited by Michael Dear and Allen J. Scott. New York: Methuen, 1981.

Walton, John. *Elites and Economic Development.* Austin: Institute of Latin American Studies, University of Texas, 1977.

Waste, Robert, ed. *Community Power: Directions for Future Research.* Beverly Hills, CA: Sage, 1986.

————. *Power and Pluralism in American Cities: Researching the Urban Laboratory.* New York: Greenwood Press, 1987.

Wirt, Frederick. *Power in the City: Decision Making in San Francisco.* Berkeley and Los Angeles: University of California Press, 1974.

Wolfinger, Raymond. *The Politics of Progress.* Englewood Cliffs, NJ: Prentice-Hall, 1974.

Yates, Douglas. *The Ungovernable City: The Politics of Urban Problems and Policy Making.* Cambridge, MA: MIT Press, 1977.

INDEX

Ansonia Center, 202
antiregionalism, 212–13
Apollo Theater, 207
Architects' Redevelopment Collaborative, 61
Area Committee for an Urban University of Buffalo, 21
Area Committee for Transit, 130–31, 190
Area Leadership Group, 120
Arthur, George, 134, 146
Arthur D. Little (company), 61, 77, 118–19, 126
Arthur v. the Board of Education, 146

Baltimore, 128
Baltzell, Digby, 40
Bank Clearinghouse Association, 128
bankruptcy
  of Buffalo, 14, 106

railroads and, 115
banks and banking, 49, 53–54, 63, 171, 195
baseball stadium, 169, 172
Basic Oxygen Furnace, 32
Battery Park, 172
BEDC. *See* Buffalo-Erie County Development Corporation
Bell Aircraft, 29
Bells Market, 182
Bethlehem Steel, 28, 29, 31, 34–35, 111, 112–15, 163
  civil rights initiatives, 91, 145–46
  closing of, 33, 158, 160
Black Development Foundation, 110, 111, 152, 166
Black Rock Manufacturers Association, 72
Blue Cross and Blue Shield WNY, 200
BMHA, 183

board members
  minority representation on
    boards, 200–201
  redundancy of, 199–201
BOF. *See* Basic Oxygen Furnace
Boston, 35, 145
Brant, 174
breakwall, 27
brewing, 28
Broadway and Beck Plaza, 182
Broadway/Fillmore Area, 182
Broadway-Fillmore Merchants
  Association, 72
Broadway Market, 182
Buffalo
  bankruptcy, 14, 106
  board representation of, 200. *See
    also* Common Council; down-
    town revitalization; mayors of
    Buffalo; waterfront, Buffalo
  Charter revision, 137–38, 206
  decline of, 28–29, 30–38, 58,
    106–18, 159–61, 208
  financial control board for,
    208–209
  potential of merging with
    Amherst, 189
  and regionalism, 211–18
  residency requirements for city
    employees, 211
  strategy to abolish, 135
Buffalo Affirmative Action Plan,
  149
Buffalo-Amherst Corridor, 76,
  125, 129, 131, 189
"Buffalo Amherst Corridor, The,"
  125

Buffalo-Amherst Urban Impact
  Study, 76
Buffalo and Erie County Economic Development Com-
  mittee, 121
Buffalo and Erie County Regional
  Development Corporation,
  127
Buffalo Area Chamber of Commerce, 36, 52–53, 63, 99,
  119–20, 134, 148, 159, 162.
  See also Buffalo Niagara Partnership
  and campus location debate, 66,
    67, 72, 73
  and ECIDA, 122, 123
  and football stadium, 77–78
  marketing Buffalo area, 127
  and mass transit, 76, 131
  relationship with Greater Buf-
    falo Development Foundation,
    121, 152–53
"Buffalo Area Economic Adjustment Strategy, The," 126–27
Buffalo Board of Education, 93,
  144–45, 149–50, 207–208
  financial control board for,
    208–209
Buffalo Board of Redevelopment,
  51
Buffalo Building Trades Investment Foundation, 169
Buffalo-Canada Trade Program, 110
Buffalo Chamber of Commerce,
  20, 37, 51
Buffalo Civic Auto Ramps, Inc.,
  62, 81, 208

Buffalo Club, 42, 122, 206
Buffalo Color Office, 183
Buffalo Community Development
    Organization, 147
Buffalo Courier-Express, 20, 47
    and campus location debate, 72
    and convention center, 128
    and football stadium, 78
    Housing Property Code and fed-
        eral decertification, 83, 85
    power of, 185
    rivalry with *Buffalo News*,
        54–56, 136, 185
    and steel industry, 112, 113
    and urban renewal, 72, 73, 83, 85
Buffalo Department of Commu-
    nity Development, 37, 129,
    178–79, 202, 206
Buffalo Development Companies,
    179
Buffalo Division of Neighborhood
    and Commercial Revitaliza-
    tions, 165, 188
Buffalo Economic Development
    Corporation, 179
Buffalo Economic Renaissance
    Corporation, 167
    minority representation on
        board, 200
Buffalo Eighteen. *See* Group of
    Eighteen
Buffalo-Erie County Development
    Corporation, 187–88
Buffalo-Erie County Labor Man-
    agement Council, 117
Buffalo Evening News, 20, 50, 54,
    63, 136, 184–85

and African American commu-
    nity, 89
and campus location debate, 72
and football stadium, 78
manufacturing closures, 116
power of, 185
on redevelopment, 59, 60, 64
on saving old post office, 143
and urban renewal, 83, 85
and Walter Mahoney, 80, 81
Buffalo Fiscal Stability Authority,
    208–209, 215
Buffalo Forge, 20, 29
Buffalo General Hospital, 43, 182
Buffalo Home Inspections Depart-
    ment, 165, 188
Buffalo Housing Authority, 146
Buffalo International Airport, 210
Buffalo Junior Chamber of Com-
    merce, 72
Buffalo Magazine, 77
Buffalo Medical Group, 202
Buffalo Municipal Housing
    Authority, 183–84, 210
Buffalo Neighborhood Revitaliza-
    tion Corporation, 179
Buffalo News, 161, 163, 177, 198,
    203
    on regionalism, 213–14
    rivalry with *Buffalo Courier-
        Express*, 54–56
    on size of council, 206
    study of boards of directors,
        199–201
Buffalo Niagara Enterprise, 198
    minority representation on
        board, 200

Buffalo-Niagara Frontier Federation, 72
Buffalo Niagara Medical Campus, 202
Buffalo Niagara Now Initiative, 198
Buffalo Niagara Partnership, 20, 197–98, 199, 206, 214
  minority representation on board, 200
Buffalo Office of Planning, 37, 129
Buffalo Philharmonic Orchestra, 43, 161, 199
  board representation of, 200
Buffalo Place, 168
Buffalo Planning Department, 77
Buffalo Planning Division, 72
Buffalo Public Library, 69
Buffalo Redevelopment Committee, Inc., 59
Buffalo Redevelopment Foundation, 50–51, 60. *See also* Greater Buffalo Development Foundation
Buffalo Regional Center Plan, 174
Buffalo River, 25
Buffalo Savings Bank, 20, 161
Buffalo Seminary, 42
Buffalo State College, 21
Buffalo State University, 93
Buffalo Street Sanitation Department, 82
Buffalo Teachers Federation, 150
Buffalo Urban Renewal Agency, 146, 168, 176, 180, 185, 209–10
Buffett, Warren, 55, 161, 177, 184

BUILD, 16, 21, 71, 89–93, 94, 135, 142–43, 148–51
BUILD Academy, 93, 149–50, 151, 152
"BUILD Black Paper Number One on the Buffalo Public Schools," 91
Build United, Independence, Liberty and Dignity. *See* BUILD
Bureau of Collections Headquarters, 183
bus service, 74, 96–97, 129

Calumet Building, 168
campus location debate, 66–73
Canada and international zone, 204
Canisius College, 44, 95
Carborundum, 111
Carey, Hugh, 149
Carter, Jimmy, 144
"cash cows," 34
"casino," 80
casino, 210–11
Castells, Manuel, 19
Catholic Center, 182
Catholic Diocese, 200
Catholics in Buffalo, 41, 55, 89, 186–87
CAUSE. *See* Coalition for Action, Unity and Social Equity
Center for Advanced Technology, 164
CETA. *See* Comprehensive Employment and Training Act
Chamber of Commerce. *See* Buffalo Chamber of Commerce

Charter revision, 137–38, 206
Chase Manhattan Bank, 49
Chautauqua Institution, 213
Cheektowaga
    as site for campus, 69
    as site for casino, 210
Cheektowaga Rapid Transit Line, 76
Chen, Clement, 128
Chenango Steel, 114
Chicago, 26
Chippewa Street, 168, 197, 202
Citizens Advisory Committee to mayors, 21, 135, 136
citizen salary review committee, 138
Citizens Committee on Inter-Municipal Affairs, 212
Citizens Council on Human Relations, 144–45, 146
Citizens for Better Schools, 135
Citizens Rapid Transit Committee, 190. *See also* Area Committee for Transit
Civic Autoramps. *See* Buffalo Civic Auto Ramps, Inc.
Civil Rights Act of 1964, 91
civil rights initiatives, 91, 144–47
Clarkson Institute/Center, 21
Clean Water/Clean Air Bond Act, 201
Cleveland, 28
Clinton, Bill, 207
Clinton Street School, 93
closures, corporate, 111, 115–17
    plant closings, 135
Coalition for Action, Unity and Social Equity, 71

Cold Spring, 147
Colorado Fuel and Iron, 29
Columbus, Ohio, 29
Committee for an Urban University of Buffalo, 70–71, 73
Committee of One Hundred and Fifty. *See* Erie County Industrial Development Agency
Common Council, 20, 134, 146, 154, 178, 181, 205
    and city charter revision, 138
    conflicts with mayor, 107, 133, 140–41, 159, 177, 180
    size of, 138, 206
Community Development Act, 136
Community Development Block Grants, 121, 137, 165, 166, 171, 178, 188, 197
    downtown revitalization vs. neighborhood projects, 181–83
    list for 1985–1987, 182–83
community development funds, 140–41
community partnership, 107
Community Planning Assistance Center, 147
"Community Summaries," 75
competing realms of influence, 36–38
Comprehensive Employment and Training Act, 137, 143
"Comprehensive Plan for Downtown Buffalo," 118
Computer Task Group, 20, 162
Congressional Public Works Committee, 121

"Consolidated Plan [on] Housing and Neighborhood Development," 206

Convention and Visitor's Bureau. *See* Buffalo Niagara Partnership

convention center, 65–66, 99, 121, 127–28, 153, 202, 210

Convention Center Management Corporation, 128

corruption, 85

Council of Churches, 89

county sales tax, 81

covered transit mall. *See* transit mall

Crangle, Joe, 46, 140

Cranz Rubber and Gasket, 183

Crotty, Peter, 46, 80

Cuomo, Mario, 163, 172, 173, 187, 190

CURB. *See* Committee for an Urban University of Buffalo

Curtin, John Thomas, 146

Curtiss-Wright, 29

debutantes, 42–43

decertification, federal, 83–85, 98, 146

Delaware Lake, 80

Democratic Club House, 45

Democratic Party, 45–46, 140, 153, 173, 174, 185, 215
 Advisory Council to State Democrats, 47
 and city charter revision, 137
 control of city government, 153
 cooperation with Republicans, 81

impact of labor on, 116, 117
 lobbying efforts, 65
 loss of power, 135, 154, 177, 181, 205
 mayors of Buffalo, 15, 55, 79–80, 82–83, 133, 136, 137, 138–39
 minority representation on board, 200

Demonstration Cities Act, 93

Department of Urban Renewal, 92

Detroit, 28, 35

Diebold-Millonzi, 47

discrimination, racial, 144–46, 196

Dome Stadium, Inc., 79

Domhoff, William, 48

"Downtown Buffalo Strategic Plan," 202–203

Downtown Buffalo Summits, 201

downtown campus. *See* university campus, downtown

Downtown Core Coalition, 168

Downtown Development Inc., 179

downtown revitalization, 61, 165, 167–69, 202–203, 217
 campus location debate, 14, 66–73
 downtown mall, 87, 118–19, 129, 131. *See also* Buffalo; Main Place Mall; transit mall; waterfront, Buffalo
 and football stadium, 78
 vs. funding neighborhood projects, 181–83
 and mass transit, 75
 transit center location, 85–88

"Downtown Study" (Arthur D. Little), 118–19

Draft Remedial Action Plan for
the Buffalo River, 174
Draft Waterfront Plan, 174
Dupont, 29

East Side, 16, 43, 88, 142, 207.
See also German community;
Polish community
industrial park in, 61
East Side Community Organization, 21, 71, 89–90
ECIDA. *See* Erie County Industrial Development Agency
economic decline of Buffalo, 28–
29, 30–38, 58, 106–18, 159–61
economic development, 175, 215
"Economic Development in the
Erie-Niagara Region," 125
economic indicators, 26
employment by race, 223
employment in different sectors, 226
hourly earnings, 222
labor force characteristics by
race, 227
manufacturing production and
wages, 227
occupational pay comparisons, 225
occupational structure, 221
reduced outputs, 109
slowdown in, 28–29
value of output, 224
economic power, 47–48, 59–63
education, 144–45, 151, 207–208
and African American community, 91, 92–93, 149–50
electricity. *See* hydroelectric power
and campus location debate, 100

elite business organizations,
50–53, 184. *See also* power,
structure of
lack of leadership by, 152–53
new leadership, 59–63, 161–63
elites, 14, 49–50, 98, 143, 204
Ellicott District, 51, 59, 92–93, 206
Ellicott Mall, 146–47, 183–84
"Ellicott Village: A Newtown
Downtown," 147, 183–84
Elma as site for campus, 69
Elm-Oak Streets corridor, 164
Empire State Development Corpo-
ration, 203
employee stock ownership plan, 169
employment rate, 26
change of in different sectors, 226
by race, 223
Emslie Park, 188
EPA. *See* US Environmental Protection Agency
Erie and Niagara Counties Regional
Planning Board, 125, 130
Erie Basin Marina, 64
Erie Canal, 25, 27, 30
Erie Community College, 121
Erie County, 34, 37, 52–53, 63,
97, 163, 190, 198, 214
board representation of, 200
convention center and, 65
Executive, 122, 123, 131, 174, 211
Legislature, 78, 81, 121, 124,
138, 174, 191, 198
and regionalism, 203, 211–18
and stadiums, 78, 79, 172
study of Buffalo's economy, 108
taxes, 113, 116, 190

Erie County College, 144

Erie County Democratic Executive Committee, 200

Erie County Department of Planning, 76

Erie County Industrial Development Agency, 20, 53, 121–27, 160, 166–67, 169, 170, 199
minority representation on board, 200

Erie County Industrial Development Corporation, 37

Erie County Legislature, 78

Erie County Regional Planning Board, 76

Erie County Republican Executive Committee, 200

Erie County Savings Bank, 62, 171

Erie-Niagara Regional Partnership, 198

ESCO. *See* East Side Community Organization

ESOP. *See* employee stock ownership plan

ethnic communities in Buffalo. *See* African American community; German community; Irish community; Italian community; Jewish community; Polish community

Evans, 174

Eve, Arthur, 90, 138, 143, 148

"Existing Industry Program," 109

Fay's Drugs, 183

Fazio, Les, 138

Fillmore, Millard, 47

Fillmore-Leroy Community Development Corporation. *See* FLARE

finance, insurance, and real estate, 48, 160. *See also* real estate and realtors

"Financing Buffalo's Downtown Mall," 118

FIRE. *See* finance, insurance, and real estate

firefighters, residency requirements for, 211

First Protection, Inc., 182

FLARE, 143–44

flour mills, 27, 28, 30, 31

football stadium, 77–79, 196

Ford Assembly Plant, 29, 31, 187

foreign-trade zone, 163

Former School 21, 183

Fortune 500, 212

Fountain Plaza, 168

Freezer Queen, 20, 166

Freschi, Bruno, 204

Frick, Henry Clay, 35

Furnas, Clifford, 70

Gaiter, William, 90, 149

Garret Club, 42

Gateway Trade Center, 163

GBDF. *See* Greater Buffalo Development Foundation

General Mills, 29

General Motors, 29, 31, 187

German community, 41. *See also* German community

Giambra, Joel, 210, 213, 214

Golden Triangle, Pittsburgh, 51

Goldome Bank, 20, 161, 167, 171, 181
Goldome Bank Building, 168
Gorski, Dennis, 173, 186, 213
"Governance Project," 214
Governmental Research Institute of Western New York, 52, 63
grain port, 25, 30
Grand Island, 174
 as site for campus, 69
grassroots activities, 137
 and election of Griffin, 138
Greater Buffalo Chamber of Commerce. *See* Buffalo Area Chamber of Commerce
Greater Buffalo Development Foundation, 20, 36, 37, 82, 85, 152, 161
 Annual Reports, 183–84
 and campus location debate, 66, 67, 72, 73
 "Comprehensive Plan for Downtown Buffalo," 118
 and convention center, 128
 founding of, 50–53
 "Growth Strategy for the Erie-Niagara Area in Conjunction with the 'Profit Opportunity Series,'" 63
 and James Griffin, 142
 and mass transit, 76, 131, 132, 153, 175–76
 professional staff of, 55, 159
 relationship with Buffalo Area Chamber of Commerce, 121, 152–53, 162

"Report on Metals and Related Industries," 101, 108
 and unions, 117
 and urban renewal, 59, 62, 99, 120, 168
 See also Buffalo Niagara Partnership
Greater Buffalo Realtors, 146
Great Lakes, 25
Griffin, James "Jimmy," 20, 127, 128, 147, 167, 169, 173, 178
 and baseball stadium, 172
 and Group of Eighteen, 163, 165, 186
 leadership style, 134, 139–40, 170
 mayoral race 1977, 55, 80, 107, 126, 138–39
 power of, 144–45, 179, 205
 relations with Common Council, 177
Gross, Mason, 71–72
Group of Eighteen, 15, 161, 162–63, 164–65, 184, 185–86, 197
 and African American Community, 186–87
growth rate of Buffalo, 26
 slowdown in, 28–29
"Growth Strategy for the Erie-Niagara Area," 121, 152, 160
"Growth Strategy for the Erie-Niagara Area, No. 8 The Buffalo Area's Economic Prospects," 108–11
"Growth Strategy for the Erie-Niagara Area in Conjunction with the 'Profit Opportunity Series,'" 63

Hamburg, 174
Harborfront Master Plan, 174
Harriman Code, 85
Hauptman-Woodward Medical Research Institute, 202
Health Instruments and Devices Institute, 164
Hilton (hotel), 121, 127, 167, 179
historic preservation, 195, 217
Hodgson, Russ, Andrews, Woods and Goodyear, 47, 200
Hoguet, Diana, 42
Homestead Works, 35
Hooker Chemical, 29
Horizon Waterfront Commission, 172–74
hotels, 168
  and Buffalo waterfront, 121
  and convention center, 65–66, 99, 127, 128, 153
Houdaille, 111
housing, 59, 64, 183–84, 188, 202, 206–207
Housing Property Code and federal decertification, 83–85, 98, 146
HSBC Bank, board representation of, 200
HUD. *See* US Department of Housing and Urban Development
Hudson River, 25
Hyatt (hotel), 127, 128, 168, 169
hydroelectric power, 25, 26, 30, 41–42

ICAN. *See* Independent Catholics Act Now

ice-skating rink, 168
"Impediments to Fair Housing," 207
Independent Catholics Act Now, 71
Indian Gaming Regulatory Act, 210–11
Industrial Areas Foundation, 89
industrial development, 27
infrastructure, 14
initiatives, 18, 20
integration of schools, 144–45
Intermodal Surface Transportation Efficiency Act. *See* ISTEA
International Trade Council. *See also* Buffalo Niagara Partnership
international zone, 204
Irish Classical Theatre Company, 202
Irish community, 15, 16, 41, 46, 126, 139, 186, 196. *See also* South Buffalo
iron ore, 26
ISTEA, 191
Italian community, 15, 16, 41, 44, 46, 186, 196. *See also* West Side
  and mayors of Buffalo, 80, 82

Jacobs, Jane, 187, 197
Jewish community, 41. *See also* North Buffalo; West Side
jitney transport service, 96–97
Johnson, Lyndon, 94
Johnstown, 114
Joint Exercise of Powers Act, 216

Jones Rich Dairy Company, 92
Journal of Urban Affairs, 212

Kaleida Health, 202
Kanefick Commission, 212
Kansas City, 26
Kennedy, Robert, 93
Kensington-Bailey, 147
Key Banks, 200
"kitchen cabinet," 81, 95
Kowal, Chester, 20, 80–81, 133,
    136
  and African American commu-
    nity, 88
  and campus location debate, 72
  and urban renewal, 83

labor, 15. *See also* unions
  and decline of Buffalo, 117–18
  militancy of, 35–36
  and urban renewal, 169–70
labor force characteristics by race,
    227
Lackawanna, 163, 174, 201
  and Bethlehem Steel, 112, 113
Lackawanna plants, 35, 114, 160
Lackawanna Steel, 28
LaFalce, John, 166
Lake Erie, 25
Lake Ontario, 31
Lancaster and football stadium,
    78–79
"Lawfirm and a City, A" (Watson,
    Bob), 47
law firms, 47
  board representation of, 200
Lawless, William B., Jr., 47

layoffs, 135, 171
  by Bethlehem Steel, 33, 106, 112
  loss of manufacturing jobs, 106
leadership, 151–54, 161–63
Leadership Buffalo. *See* Buffalo
    Niagara Partnership
Lemann, Nicholas, 40
Liberty Bank, 52, 54
Liberty National Bank and Trust
    Company, 168
light-rail rapid transit, 75
Lin, T. Y., 204
"linkage" industries, 27
Little City Hall Program, 137
lumber processing, 28

magnet schools, 151
Mahoney, Walter, 50, 80, 81
Main-Genessee Urban Design
    Group, 176
Main-Genessee Urban Renewal
    Plan, 167–69
Main Place Mall, 62, 119. *See also*
    downtown revitalization
Main Street Association, 72
Main Street revitalization, 61–62,
    189–90
  closing to traffic, 176–77
Makowski, Stanley, 20, 111, 115,
    122, 126, 134–35, 136, 138,
    170, 178
Mall Task Group, 176
M&T. *See* Manufacturers and
    Traders Trust
M&T Bank Building, 61
Manufacturers and Traders Trust, 20,
    51, 53–54, 61, 63, 75, 161, 197

assistance to Buffalo Board of Education, 207–208
board representation of, 200
manufacturing, 48, 119–20
changes and wages, 227
closures, 116
earnings, 35, 222
value of output, 224
Manz, Victor, 80
Marina Market Place, 179
Marine Bank, 51, 53–54
Marine Midland Bank, 20, 63, 166, 175
Masiello, Anthony, 205, 206, 208
mass transit, 73–77, 96–97, 129–32, 175–77, 189–91
Mass Transit Advisory Committee, 131
Mass Transit Project, 129
Masten District, 206
Masten General Neighborhood Renewal Program, 83
mayors of Buffalo, 79–83. *See also* Griffin, James "Jimmy"; Kowal, Chester; Makowski, Stanley; Masiello, Anthony; Sedita, Frank
conflicts with Common Council, 107, 133, 140–41, 159, 177, 180
Mellon Bank, 21
MET Development Corporation, 118
Metropolitan Transportation Center, 129, 153
Meyerson, Martin, 68, 71, 73
Millonzi, Robert I., 47

mill port, 25, 30, 31
Minneapolis, 25, 28
Minnesota, 216
Minority Coalition, 90, 148
Mitchell, Delmar, 134, 137
Model City Program, 16, 21, 93–97, 101, 107, 122, 151, 152
Moore, Vincent, 69–70
mortgage recording tax, 190
Moynihan, Patrick, 204
multi-jurisdictions. *See* regionalism
multinational corporations, 33–35
Multiple Dwelling Law, 84

NAACP, 21, 135, 142–43, 144–45, 146, 151
National Commission on Neighborhoods, 144
National Consume Cooperative Bank, 147
National Fuel, 200
National Gypsum, 59, 63, 111
National Steel, 114
Near-East Side, 43. *See also* African American community
Neighborhood Housing Services, 147
neighborhood projects
vs. funding downtown revitalization, 181
housing projects, 202, 206–207
lack of planning for, 188
Neighborhood Strategy Area Program, 144
newspapers, 54–56

New York Battery Park, 172
New York City, 25, 28, 35
  Multiple Dwelling Law, 84
New Yorker, 40
New York State, board representa-
  tion of, 200
New York State Budget Division,
  69
New York State Department of
  Health, 164
New York State Department of
  Transportation, 74, 75, 129,
  132, 164
New York State Job Development
  Authority, 166
New York State Office of Plan-
  ning Coordination, 76
New York State Pension Fund,
  169
New York State Supreme Court,
  79
New York State Urban Develop-
  ment Corporation, 20, 37, 66,
  77–79, 97, 119, 166, 172
NFTA. *See* Niagara Frontier
  Transportation Authority
Niagara County, 34, 52–53, 198
Niagara County Regional Plan-
  ning Board, 76
Niagara Falls, 25, 26
Niagara Frontier Transit Authority,
  74, 76
Niagara Frontier Transportation
  Authority, 20, 82, 162, 173
  and campus location debate, 97
  and Main Street revitalization,
  190

minority representation on
  board, 200
rapid-transit, 49, 73–77, 129–32,
  153, 191
transit center location, 87–88
waterfront, Buffalo, 153
and waterfront development, 37,
  64–65, 203
Niagara Mohawk Power Corporation, 182
Niagara Regional Transportation
  Council, 200
Niagara River, 25, 203–204
Niagara Square, 65
Nichols School, 42
"No Man's Town," *New Yorker*,
  40
nonmanufacturing sector, 109
nonprofit organizations, 143,
  149–50, 168, 199, 213
  and federal grants, 178–79
non-WASP, 41
No Overhead Transit, 130–31
Norstar Building, 168
North Buffalo, 144. *See also*
  Jewish community
North Jefferson Branch Library,
  207
North Tonawanda, 174
NOT. *See* No Overhead Transit
Nowak, Henry, 121, 126, 172, 173

occupancy tax, 138, 139
occupational structure, 221
pay comparisons, 225
OEO. *See* US Office of Economic
  Opportunity

Office of Urban Affairs (SUNY), 75
oil crisis in 1973, 32
Omaha, 26
Opportunities Development Council, 148
Orchard Park and football stadium, 79
outer-harbor, 203
Outer Harbor Development Plan, 174

Panama Canal, 30
Pankow, Steve, 79–80
paper products, 28
Pataki, George, 175, 210
patronage jobs, 15, 16, 44, 45–46, 173, 205
Peace Bridge Authority, 201, 203–205
Pearl Street public parking, 168
Philadelphia, 40
Phillips, Lytle, 200
Pierce Arrow, 27
Pitts, James, 205
Pittsburgh, 21, 26, 28, 35, 51, 52, 60
planning, process of, 18, 20, 107
politics of planning, 140–41
police, 216
    consolidation of police forces, 212
    county control of, 214
    residency requirements for, 211
Polish community, 15, 16, 41, 46, 134, 186, 196. *See also* East Side
    and mayors of Buffalo, 79, 80

political machines, 15, 44, 46
political power, 45–46
political turf, 141–42
population of Buffalo, 44, 133
post office building, 121, 143
"Post-Trial Brief," 145
power, structure of, 18, 20, 198. *See also* elites
    and African American community, 88–93, 100–101
    change in leadership, 59–63
    economic power, 47–48, 49–50
    examples of use of power, 85–88
    leadership problems, 151–54
    political power, 45–46, 133–38
power grid, 26
Pratt Street Village, 188
Pratt-Willert project, 179, 181, 182
Price, William, Jr., 143–44, 147
private sector, 199
productivity seminars, 109–10
property taxes, 112, 113–14
    forgiving of, 167
public housing, 59, 64, 183–84
Public Policy Institute, 216
public sector, 158, 199
public works, county control of, 214

race
    employment, 223
    labor force characteristics, 227
racial discrimination. *See* discrimination, racial
railroads, 25–26, 28, 115
rail service, 74, 129

rapid-transit, 73–77, 119, 129–32, 153, 165, 175–77, 189–91, 196
  planning, 85–88, 141
real estate and realtors, 47, 85, 146. *See also* finance, insurance, and real estate
realms of influence, competing, 36–38
recall of elected officials, 138
redundant organizations, 36–38
referendums
  consolidation of police forces, 212
  on convention center, 65
  on size of council, 206
Regan, Edward, 108, 112, 122, 143, 190
regionalism, 113, 211–18
Remington-Rand, 29
"Report on Metals and Related Industries," 101, 108
Republican Party, 45–46, 50, 84, 112
  and *Buffalo Evening News*, 55, 177
  control of county government, 153, 200
  mayors of Buffalo, 73, 80–81, 88, 133
  minority representation on board, 200
Republic Steel, 29, 31, 33, 114, 169–70, 201
residency requirements for city employees, 211
restrictive covenants, 146

Retail Merchants Association, 72, 92
retail trade, 222
  value of output, 224
"Review of Revised Four Year Financial Plan," 209
"Revised Strategic Plan for Downtown Buffalo," 202–203
Rich Products, 20, 161
Rigidized Metals, 20
Robert Heller and Associates, 71–72
Robertiello, Richard, 42
Roberts Gordon Appliance Corporation, 182
Robert Traynham Coles, Architects, P.C., 20
Rockefeller, Nelson, 37, 49, 97, 113, 148
  and campus location debate, 66, 68, 71, 73, 97
  and mass transit, 74, 132
Roswell Park Medical Center, 20, 93, 162, 164, 202

St. Lawrence Seaway, 26, 31
St. Louis, 26
sales tax, 112, 138, 190
sanitation workers, residency requirements for, 211
Saturn Club, 42
Sault Ste. Marie Canal, 26
School 22 Apartments, 183
School 68, 207–208
school integration, 144–45
School of Medicine and Biomedical Sciences, 202
Schumer, Charles, 204

Sedita, Frank, 20, 62, 80, 81–83, 91, 133, 136
Seneca Indians, 210–11
service sector, 110, 158
  value of output, 224
sewer line, 27
Sharp, Jack, 124
Slominski, Alfreda, 96, 145
slumlords, 85
Small Boat Harbor, 183
South Buffalo, 43–44, 139, 144, 169. *See also* Irish community
South Buffalo Redevelopment Plan, 201
South Park plant, 33
Sparrows Point, 115
Special Technical Review Committee, 84, 85
Spencer-Kellogg, 29
stadiums
  baseball, 169, 172
  football, 77–79, 196
State University Construction Fund, 70, 149
State University of New York at Buffalo, 21, 66–73, 75, 164, 182, 202
Statler (hotel), 65
steel industry, 31–33
  loss of, 17, 26, 111–15, 159, 160
  rise of, 26, 27–28
Steiglitz, Steiglitz, Tries, 184
Stratford Plaza, 183
strikes, 117
Studio Arena Theatre, 202
subway transit line, 130, 132
Sunday newspapers, 56

SUNY. *See* State University of New York at Buffalo
Super Duper, 183

tanning, 28
taxes, 213
  mortgage recording tax, 190
  occupancy tax, 138, 139
  property taxes, 112, 113–14, 167
  sales tax, 112, 138, 190
Technical Enterprise Development Institute, 163
Thruway Industrial Park, 61, 83, 99
Tonawanda, 174
Top Notch Provision, 183
Tops Markets, 200
Town Gardens, 147
training programs for minorities, 148–49
transit center location, 85–88
transit mall, 118, 131, 132, 153, 168, 176
  redesign of, 176. *See also* downtown revitalization
transportation, 30–31
Trico Products, 29
Trinity Episcopal church, 42
Twin Coach, 29

UDAG. *See* Urban Development Action Grant
UDC. *See* New York State Urban Development Corporation
UMTA. *See* Urban Mass Transit Agency; US Urban Mass Transportation Administration

underground transit line, 130, 132, 189
Union Carbide, 29
unions, 35–36, 90, 148, 158. *See also* labor
and decline of Buffalo, 117–18
university campus, downtown, 14, 16, 69, 98, 99–100, 125, 196
University Council, 70
University of Buffalo, 66–73, 74
board representation of, 200
University of Pittsburgh, 21
Urban Development Action Grant, 118, 121–22, 160, 166–67, 176, 179, 180, 182
Urban Development Corporation. *See* New York State Urban Development Corporation
Urban Institute, 99
Urban Land Institute, 60–61, 99
Urban League, 142–43
Urban Mass Transit Agency, 130, 131
Urban Mass Transit Authority, 176
urban renewal, 16, 64–66
Ellicott District, 51, 59, 92–93
federal decertification of Buffalo, 83–85
waterfront development, 64–65, 98
US Coast Guard, 37
US Congress, Congressional Public Works Committee, 121
US Department of Housing and Urban Development, 94, 95, 119, 128, 146, 147, 171, 178, 183, 201, 210

US Department of Labor, 148
US District Court, 146
US Economic Development Administration, 121
US Environmental Protection Agency, 201
US Office of Economic Opportunity, 94
US Urban Mass Transportation Administration, 76

Vector Group, 200

wages, 222
high wages, 35–36
manufacturing, 227
occupational pay comparisons, 225
Walden-Bailey Businessmen's Association, 72
Ward, Dan, 124
War Memorial Stadium, 77
War on Poverty, 94
WASP Mystique, The (Robertiello and Hoguet), 42
WASPs, 40–43, 49, 98, 126, 143, 184
and non-WASPs, 44, 45, 46, 55, 186–87
waterfront, Buffalo, 27, 64–65, 98, 159, 165, 167, 172–74, 203. *See also* Buffalo; downtown revitalization
Waterfront School, 64
Waterfront Village, 188
Watson, Bob, 47
Welland Canal, 31

Western Electric, 111
Western New York Economic Development Corporation, 163, 166
Western New York Health Sciences Consortium, 164
Western New York Industrial Development Corporation, 172
Western Savings Bank, 47, 61
Westinghouse, 29
Westinghouse, George, 26
Westminster church, 42
Westminster Community School, 207–208
West Side, 43, 44, 45. *See also* Italian community; Jewish community

white, Anglo-Saxon, and Protestant. *See* WASPs
wholesale trade, 222
  value of output, 224
Who Rules America? Power and Politics in the Year 2000 (Domhoff), 48
Wilkinson, Samuel, 27
Willert Park, 188
Woodlawn Jr. High School, 150
"Workable Program for Community Development, A," 83
workplace changes, 225
Wulitzer, 29

Yamasaki, Minoru, 61